The Greek Text of Judges

—HARVARD SEMITIC MUSEUM—

HARVARD SEMITIC MONOGRAPHS

edited by
Frank Moore Cross, Jr.

Number 23
THE GREEK TEXT OF JUDGES
Recensional Developments
by
Walter Ray Bodine

Walter Ray Bodine
THE GREEK TEXT
OF JUDGES
Recensional Developments

Scholars Press

Distributed by
Scholars Press
101 Salem Street
Chico, California 95926

THE GREEK TEXT OF JUDGES
Recensional Developments
Walter Ray Bodine

Library of Congress Cataloging in Publication Data

Bodine, Walter Ray.
     The Greek text of Judges

     (Harvard semitic monographs ; no. 23 ISSN 0073-
0637)
     Revision of the author's thesis, Harvard
1973.
     Bibliography: p.
     Includes index.
     1. Bible. O.T. Judges—Criticism, Textual. 2. Bible
etc. 2. Bible. O.T. Judges. Greek—Versions. I. Title II.
Series
BS1305.2.B62   1980   222'.32048   80-12578
ISBN 0-89130-400-2

Printed in the United States of America
1   2   3   4   5
Edwards Brothers, Inc.
Ann Arbor, Michigan 48106

To Betty

PREFACE

This study is a revised form of my 1973 doctoral dissertation. The first three chapters have received only slight revision. Chapter four, however, has been considerably expanded by the addition of the commentary on the tabulated readings and most of the material regarding the Hexapla.

It is a pleasure to express thanks, first of all, to Professor Frank Moore Cross, Jr. During my student days, his instruction in ancient Near Eastern lore was stimulating. I especially value the generous portions of his time and the incisive guidance which he gave throughout the preparation of the thesis and its subsequent revision.

In the thesis stage of my study, I benefited from several suggestions made by Professor John Strugnell. Frequent interaction with fellow students, especially Dr. Eugene Ulrich, whose thesis has already appeared in this series, and Dr. Leonard Greenspoon, was also beneficial.

Several have assisted technically in the production of both the thesis and the study in its present form. A first draft of the thesis was typed by Betty Sterling; and the final draft by Joan Kendrick, with assistance from Carol Cross. The present manuscript was typed throughout, when he was quite busy already, by Wayne J. Buchanan. Help has come in matters of form from suggestions of Barbara Lindsey and Dr. John Witmer and in form and content from those of Dr. Eugene Ulrich.

My children, Ray, Don, Ken, and Jon have made allowances and have offered a great deal of support in their individual ways. My appreciation goes to each of them. I am deeply grateful to Betty. In the face of frequent adjustments due to this project, her enthusiasm and devotion have encouraged me and refreshed our family. Finally, I wish to recognize with gratitude the help of Him whose Word is studied here.

C O N T E N T S

ABBREVIATIONS AND SIGLA xi

INTRODUCTION 1

I. THE IDENTIFICATION OF THE VATICANUS FAMILY OF
JUDGES WITH THE ΚΑΙΓΕ RECENSION 11

II. NEW ΚΑΙΓΕ CHARACTERISTICS FROM THE VATICANUS
FAMILY OF JUDGES 47

III. CHARACTERISTICS PECULIAR TO THE VATICANUS
FAMILY OF JUDGES 67

IV. OTHER RECENSIONAL DEVELOPMENTS IN THE GREEK
TEXT OF JUDGES 93

        Table of Readings
        Commentary
        The Survival of the Old Greek
            Lucian
            The Old Latin
        The Hexapla with Special Reference to the
            Fifth and Sixth Columns
            The Fifth Column
            The Sixth Column
        The Nature of the Remaining Text Groups
            The Alexandrinus Family
            The K Family

CONCLUSION 185

APPENDIX: OTHER FEATURES OF THE ΚΑΙΓΕ TEXT
OF JUDGES 187

BIBLIOGRAPHY OF WORKS CITED 191

INDEX OF MODERN AUTHORS 197

INDEX OF GENERAL SUBJECTS AND ANCIENT AUTHORS . 201

ABBREVIATIONS AND SIGLA

A	Alexandrinus
AJSL	American Journal of Semitic Languages and Literatures
α´	Aquila
B	Vaticanus
BA	Biblical Archaeologist
ByZ	Byzantinische Zeitschrift
B-M	A. E. Brooke and N. McLean, with H. St. J. Thackeray for vols. II and III, eds., *The Old Testament in Greek*, vols. I-III (London, 1906-40).
CBQ	Catholic Biblical Quarterly
CRDK	*Chronology and Recensional Development in the Greek Text of Kings*, J. D. Shenkel (Cambridge, Mass., 1968).
DA	*Les Devanciers d'Aquila*, Dominique Barthélemy (Leiden, 1963).
ε´	Quinta
Field	F. Field, ed., *Origenis Hexaplorum quae supersunt*, 2 vols. (Oxford, 1875).
H-P	R. H. Holmes and J. Parsons, eds., *Vetus Testamentum graecum cum variis lectionibus*, 5 vols. in 4 (Oxford, 1798-1827).
H-R	E. Hatch and H. A. Redpath, *A Concordance to the Septuagint*, 3 vols. in 2 (Graz, Austria, 1954).
HTR	Harvard Theological Review
IEJ	Israel Exploration Journal
JBL	Journal of Biblical Literature
JQR	Jewish Quarterly Review
JTS	Journal of Theological Studies
K	Koine family (MNhyb$_2$)
L	Lucianic text
$\cancel{L}$	Old Latin

LAB	Pseudo-Philo's *Liber Antiquitatum Biblicarum*
L-S	H. G. Liddell and R. Scott, *A Greek-English Lexicon*, 9th rev. ed. by H. S. Jones (New York, 1940).
Lug	*Heptateuchi partis posterioris versio latina antiquissima e codice Lugdunensi*, ed. Ulysse Robert (Lyon, 1900).
MT	Masoretic Text
OG	Old Greek
QTSJ	*The Qumran Text of Samuel and Josephus*, E. C. Ulrich, Jr. Missoula, 1978.
R	D. Barthélemy's Minor Prophets scroll from Naḥal Ḥeber
RB	Revue Biblique
R-T	J. Reider, *An Index to Aquila*, completed and revised by N. Turner (Leiden, 1966).
σ´	Symmachus
𝔖	Syro-hexapla
Sab	P. Sabatier, ed., *Bibliorum sacrorum latinae versiones antiquae* (Paris, 1751).
SJW	*The Septuagint and Jewish Worship*, H. St. J. Thackeray (London, 1921).
ϑ´	Theodotion
The Three	α´, σ´, and ϑ´
THGG	*Text History of the Greek Genesis*, J. W. Wevers (Göttingen, 1974).
ThLZ	Theologische Literaturzeitung
TRE	*The Theodotionic Revision of the Book of Exodus*, K. G. O'Connell (Cambridge, Mass., 1972).
Vg	*Biblia Sacra iuxta latinam vulgatam versionem ad codicum fidem iussu Pii PP. XI cura et studio Monachorum Abbatiae Pontificiae S. Hieronymi in urbe ordinis S. Benedicti edita*, vol. IV (Rome, 1939).
VT	Vetus Testamentum
ZAW	Zeitschrift für die alttestamentliche Wissenschaft

Ziegler   J. Ziegler, ed., *Septuaginta: Vetus Testamentum Graecum*, vols. XIII-XVI (Göttingen, 1939-57).

Other abbreviations and sigla follow those of the Cambridge Larger Septuagint.

INTRODUCTION

Past Study of the Greek Text of Judges

The study of the Greek text of Judges has been traced
back to at least as early as 1625. Several surveys have been
written which trace this study from that point, or soon thereafter, into the present century.[1]

Past study has been engaged primarily with the question
of the relationship of the A and B texts of Judges to one
another. The problem has been the extensive divergence of the
two text types throughout the book.[2] It has been debated as
to whether one represents a revision of the other, or whether
both are independent translations. The question of the respective ages of the two texts has also been involved, and
whether one or the other represents the earliest recoverable
form of the Greek translation of Judges.

Varied answers to these questions have been given; and,
since the surveys noted above are available, the details of
past study will not be repeated here. Rather, this review
will begin at the point where these surveys have left off.
This calls, first of all, for mention of the work containing
the most detailed survey of the history, for it represents one
of the three most substantial investigations of the text of
Judges published since 1950.

The work of I. Soisalon-Soininen constitutes a comparative study of the major Greek text groups of Judges in an
effort to identify their place in the historical development.[3]
He regards them all as having a common translation base and as
being either Origenic, or under such influence from Origen's
fifth column as to be Origenic for all practical purposes. In
either case, all text groups are, for him, post-Origenic. He
rejects Pretzl's view of the group MNhyb$_2$ as being pre-Origenic
and locates this group as a successor of both the A and B
groups.

Mention should be made of the work of Joseph Schreiner,
for it is also a full-length treatment of the text of Judges.[4]
It is not so pertinent to the present study, however. Whereas

1

much valuable data is included, the purpose is only to compare
the various Greek text groups with the Hebrew; and it is
basically carried no further than that. Generalizations are
not drawn, and conclusions are not broached regarding the
nature of the Greek families.

The third significant treatment of the Greek text of
Judges is to be found in relevant portions of a book which is
concerned with broader issues and which constitutes the point
of departure for the present study. It is Dominique Barthélemy's *Les Devanciers d'Aquila*.[5] This work consists of three
main parts, in which the author presents an extensive characterization of an ancient Greek recension which he identifies
as καιγε;[6] a discussion of the relation of the recension in
Samuel-Kings to the "ancient Septuagint," of its origin, and
of some of its constituents; and an analysis of the Minor
Prophets scroll from Naḥal Ḥeber, which he identifies as a
member of the newly defined καιγε recension. It is
Barthélemy's assertion that the B text of Judges and its
congeners constitute a part of this recension which ultimately
gives rise to the present study.[7]

Foundations of the Present Study
Manuscript Groupings

Coming in the wake of previous investigations of the
Greek text of Judges, this study builds on foundations already
laid. In the case of the grouping of Greek manuscripts into
families, the results of past work have been employed. Apart
from minor refinements, the division of manuscripts into related groups in Judges has basically been accomplished and is
quite adequate for the purposes of the present investigation.

The groupings of Field[8] and Moore[9] were carefully worked
out, but in many cases concern manuscripts different from those
collated by Brooke and McLean, whose text has been employed in
the present study.[10] Therefore, these groupings will not be
listed here.

Pretzl's assignment of manuscripts represents the consensus of scholars in the main, but has since been refined.[11] It
is generally agreed that the Greek text of Judges displays
four major families; and these are identified by Pretzl with

the following groups: the Alexandrinus family with A and its
congeners Gabckx, the Lucianic family with KZdglnoptvw, a third
group with MNhyb$_2$, and the Vaticanus family with B and its congeners (d)efij(o)qrsuza$_2$.

Billen's groupings are in the same major divisions, but
are more selective.[12] He assigns groups as follows: Aabcx;
KZglnow, dpt; MNyb$_2$; and Befjqsz. He has made the contribution
of separating out the Lucianic subgroup dpt(v) from the major
group KZglnow.[13]

The groupings of Soisalon-Soininen are closer to those
of Pretzl, especially in the case of the B text.[14] They are
as follows: AGabckx; KZgln(o)w, (d)ptv; MNhyb$_2$; and
B(d)efjm(o)qsz, imrua$_2$. His particular contribution is the
separation of the B family into two subgroups, with imrua$_2$
being considered the weaker witness to the B text. He also
notes that weaker witness to the A family is found in k, and
to the group MNyb$_2$ in h. This alignment of manuscripts is the
one most closely followed in the present study.

Barthélemy has suggested that in the Vaticanus family
the subgroup irua$_2$, while being the weaker witness to the family, is the stronger witness to the καιγε recension.[15] He
cites as witness to this recension in Judges the two groups
irua$_2$ and Befsz. While the precise relationship of these two
groups of manuscripts to B varies, all are agreed that these
subgroups, together with B, constitute a major family in the
Greek text of Judges. The identification of this family in
the recensional development of that text will constitute the
primary concern of the following discussion. Before that
discussion proper can commence, however, more must be said
about its foundations, for the way has already been prepared
by others.

Textual Theory

Barthélemy's description of the καιγε recension was built
upon the work of Thackeray in the text of Samuel-Kings.[16]
Thackeray had already distinguished the portions labeled by him
as βγ and γδ[17] as being the work of one translator and as

having certain distinctive characteristics.

Barthélemy developed that distinction into an extensive delineation and characterization of a Greek recension which appears at various points throughout most, if not all, of the Old Testament.[18] In this he has made a major contribution to Old Testament textual study, especially of the Greek text; and this contribution has provided the theoretical context in which the present investigation has been developed.

In the early part of this century, Professor George F. Moore expressed a caution against the "hasty labelling" of recensions in the study of the Greek text of the Old Testament, calling rather for the careful process of determining characteristics and relationships and, thereby, discerning recensions.[19] This caution is much in order. The same words were quoted by Charles M. Cooper in presenting the first published results of his research in the Greek text of Judges.[20] His purpose was to present eventually a "complete description and characterization of the A and B texts of Judges."[21] Unfortunately, nothing further from this undertaking has yet appeared.[22]

Since this research, however, and even later than the work of Soisalon-Soininen and of Schreiner, the background for the study of the Greek text of Judges has radically changed. With the appearance of Barthélemy's work, two major advances have been made. One is the description of the καιγε recension already discussed above. With this recension so clearly introduced, students of the Greek Old Testament now have before them another distinct possibility to consider in their efforts to describe certain portions of text in their historical development.[23]

The second advance to be credited to Barthélemy is his proposal that the Vaticanus family of Judges constitutes a member of that recension.[24] While he has gathered significant evidence for this identification, it is not sufficient to be considered positive proof.[25] Furthermore, since Barthélemy's writing, further research has been carried on in certain portions of the καιγε recension, producing a much more extensive characterization of the recension and, thereby, many more characteristics to be used in testing the potential identification of other members. Therefore, the time seems ripe for a new investigation of the Vaticanus text of Judges along these lines.

The Plan of the Present Study

This study will consist, first of all, of an application of the new data just mentioned to the Vaticanus family of Judges. The purpose will be to test its identity as a part of the καιγε recension. In the second and third chapters, those new characteristics thus far discovered in the B family of Judges will be presented, first those which appear elsewhere in the καιγε recension and then those which are peculiar to the B family of Judges. These three chapters will constitute the central portion of the study. A fourth chapter will consist of a discussion of the remaining Greek families and some other witnesses. Finally, an appendix will present several additional features of the Judges B family.

INTRODUCTION

1. The most thorough survey of this history, to the writer's knowledge, is that of I. Soisalon-Soininen in his work, *Die Textformen der Septuaginta-Übersetzung des Richter-buches* (Helsinki, 1951), pp. 7-15 (to which should be added several pertinent discussions by Alfred Rahlfs which have been pointed out by Katz [Walters] in his review of Soisalon-Soininen's work [*ThLZ* 77(1952), 156]). Other useful surveys include Joseph Schreiner, *Septuaginta-Massora des Buches der Richter* (Rome, 1957), pp. 1-4; and Charles M. Cooper, "Theodotion's Influence on the Alexandrian Text of Judges," *JBL* 67 (1948), 63-64.

2. This divergence is so great that Lagarde (Paul Anton de Lagarde, *Septuaginta Studien I* [Göttingen, 1891], pp. 3-72) and Rahlfs (Alfred Rahlfs, *Septuaginta: Id est vetus Testamentum graece iuxta LXX interpretes I* [Stuttgart, n.d.]) both printed the two texts separately on adjacent pages, and B-M indicated all divergences of the A text in Clarendon type in the apparatus of their edition.

3. Cf. Soisalon-Soininen, pp. 110-17, where his conclusions are stated, and *passim*.

4. Cf. the reference in note 1.

5. Dominique Barthélemy, *Les Devanciers d'Aquila* (Leiden, 1963), p. 47 (hereafter DA).

6. Throughout this study accents, breathings, and *iota* subscripts will be omitted from all Greek entries. Vowel points will be included with Hebrew entries only when they indicate necessary distinctions.

7. Although Boling's commentary on Judges does not concern the text as such, he does deal with this aspect of the book in more depth than most commentators (Robert G. Boling, *Judges: Introduction, Translation, and Notes*, The Anchor Bible [Garden City, 1975]). His primary effort, however, is to recover the original text; and this is not the concern of the present study.

8. Frederick Field, *Origenis Hexaplorum quae supersunt...Fragmenta* (Oxford, 1875), I, 399.

9. George Foote Moore, *A Critical and Exegetical Commentary on Judges*, The International Critical Commentary (New York, 1895), pp. xliii-xlvii.

10. In addition to Judges, the Greek text of B-M has been followed for all books for which it has been prepared. For other portions of the Old Testament (and for Genesis,

Deuteronomy having appeared after the greater part of this
study as it now stands was completed), the Göttingen series,
edited by Hanhart, Kappler, Rahlfs, Wevers, and Ziegler, has
been followed. For those sections not included in either of
these editions, the three-volume edition of Swete has been employed (Henry Barclay Swete, ed., *The Old Testament in Greek*,
vols. I-III [Cambridge, 1877]). For the Hebrew text of Judges
the new edition (R. Meyer, ed., *Josua et Judices*, vol. IV:
Biblia Hebraica Stuttgartensia, ed. K. Elliger et W. Rudolph
[Stuttgart, 1972]) has been followed. Elsewhere the prior
edition of Kittel has been used (R. Kittel, ed., *Biblia Hebraica* [Stuttgart, n.d.]; both will be referred to hereafter as
MT). The Syro-Hexapla has been cited from Lagarde's edition
for those sections covered therein (Paul de Lagarde, *Bibliothecae Syriacae a Paulo de Lagarde collectae*, ed. Alfred Rahlfs
[Göttingen, 1892]) and from Ceriani for other sections which
his edition includes (Antonio Maria Ceriani, ed., *Codex Syro-
Hexaplaris Ambrosianus*, vol. VII of *Monumenta sacra et profana*
[Milan, 1874]), and has been compared with the editions of B-M,
Ziegler, and Field when it is quoted in these. The citations
from versions in general will follow the apparatuses of B-M
and the Göttingen volumes.

11. Otto Pretzl, "Septuagintaprobleme im Buch der Richter," *Biblica* 7 (1926), 233.

12. A. V. Billen, "The Hexaplaric Element in the LXX
Version of Judges," *JTS* 43 (1942), 12-13.

13. Probably Billen intended that v also be included in
this subgroup, although it is not listed, since he has it in
the Lucianic group as a whole, but not in the divisions (ibid.,
p. 13).

14. Soisalon-Soininen, pp. 20-21.

15. DA, pp. 34, 47.

16. H. St. J. Thackeray, "The Greek Translators of the
Four Books of Kings," *JTS* 8 (1906-07), 262-78.

17. The references are 2 Samuel 11:2--1 Kings 2:11 (βγ)
and 1 Kings 22:1--2 Kings (γδ), "The Greek Translators," p. 263.

18. Many books are represented, according to Barthélemy's work, only by the sixth column of Origen's Hexapla (cf.
DA, p. 47). Those specific members he has identified are the
standard Greek translations of Lamentations, Canticles, and
Ruth; the B family of Judges, as mentioned above; the Theodotion text in Daniel and in the additions to Job; the anonymous
additions to Jeremiah; the Quinta of Psalms; and the Nahal
Heber scroll of the Minor Prophets (which Barthélemy lables R).

19. "The Antiochian Recension of the Septuagint," *AJSL*
29 (1912-13), 46.

20. "Theodotion's Influence," p. 64, n. 10.

21. Ibid., p. 64.

22.   Even Cooper's dissertation, which contains much more material than he presented in his article, was reported missing by the library at Dropsie College in the spring of 1973 and so has been inaccessible to the present writer.

23.   For a convenient introduction to the study of the Old Testament text and specifically to the study of the Greek recensions, see the introductory guide by Klein (Ralph W. Klein, *Textual Criticism of the Old Testament* [Philadelphia, 1974], especially pp. 1-26 and 62-84).

24.   This proposal is original with Barthélemy only to the extent that his full description of the καιγε recension is original.   The relation of the Judges Greek text to that of 2 Samuel-2 Kings was proposed already by Redpath in 1905-06 (H. A. Redpath, "A Contribution Towards Settling the Dates of the Translation of the Various Books of the Septuagint," *JTS* 7 [1905-06], 606).   In 1906-07 Thackeray more specifically raised the question of the relationship of the Vaticanus text of Judges to βδ in Samuel-Kings (his βγ and γδ, H. St. J. Thackeray, p. 278).   In 1961, following Barthélemy's initial article on the Naḥal Ḥeber scroll ("Redécouverte d'un chaînon manquant de l'histoire de la Septante," RB, 60 [1953], 18-29), Schreiner, in a study of the B text of Judges, chapter five, suggested the identification of the Judges B text with the kind of recension evidenced by the newly found scroll ("Zum B-Text des griechischen Canticum Deborae," *Biblica*, 42 [1961], 358).

25.   Cf. Frank Moore Cross, Jr., "The History of the Biblical Text in the Light of Discoveries in the Judaean Desert," *HTR* 57 (1964), p. 283, n. 10 and Emanuel Tov, "The Textual History of the Song of Deborah in the A Text of the LXX," *VT* 28 (1978), 224.

CHAPTER I

THE IDENTIFICATION OF THE VATICANUS FAMILY OF JUDGES
WITH THE ΚΑΙΓΕ RECENSION

The purpose of this first chapter is to demonstrate that
Barthélemy's identification of the B family in the Greek text
of Judges with the καιγε recension elsewhere is, in fact,
valid. In his own work, Barthélemy marshaled significant
evidence to support the identification.[1] His data will be
reviewed for the sake of a full presentation of the argument
and in order to make several refinements. Then the καιγε
characteristics which have been published since Barthélemy's
work will likewise be applied to Judges. When the B family of
Judges is tested by this collection of criteria, which is now
quite extensive, the identification can be shown to be established on a sound basis.

Criteria from Barthélemy

This analysis will begin with a reexamination of the
καιγε characteristics presented by Barthélemy because it was
he who clearly delineated this recension and, at the same time,
located the B family of Judges within it. His criteria will
be presented and applied in the order in which they appear in
his work.[2]

1. גם/וגם = καιγε

This translation by the Greek recension in question has
been used by Barthélemy to name the recension itself. It
stands in contrast to the usual OG rendering by a simple και.[3]
The Hebrew particle appears 28 times in the MT of Judges.
Of these the B family of Judges shows the expected καιγε revision 4 times against all other groups.[4] The revision appears
9 times in contrast to some other groups or significant witnesses.[5] The καιγε reading is shared by all groups 3 times,
although in 2 of these 𝔏 omits.[6]
In 2 instances the B family stands over against the καιγε

11

reading elsewhere.[7] There are 8 cases in which the revision does not appear in any of the Greek families.[8] In 2 cases the reading of the B family must remain unclear due to omission.[9]

Thus, the B family shows the καιγε reading in contrast to some or all other witnesses a total of 13 times; whereas it fails to show the reading when it appears elsewhere only 2 times. The remaining 13 instances are indecisive, so that the evidence of this characteristic favors the identification of the B family with the καιγε recension.[10]

2. אׁיש (each one) = ανηρ

This rendering illustrates well the general καιγε tendency to conform to Hebrew usage even when the result is not desirable Greek.[11] The typical OG rendering is εκαστος.[12]

The word אׁיש appears with this meaning in the text of Judges 21 times.[13] In all 21 instances, the B family has the καιγε rendering. Whereas K and ϱ also have it in 17 of these, they do show the OG 4 times; and, whereas the A family has the καιγε rendering in 16, it shows the OG 5 times. More significant still are the 9 instances in which the OG reading appears in L and the 10 in which it appears in Ƚ, 5 of these being different from those of L.[14]

In terms of the B family, this criterion yields the following results. The καιγε revision is seen there exclusively 3 times.[15] It appears in the B family and elsewhere, but with the OG also appearing elsewhere, 9 times.[16] It stands 9 times with no certain revision.[17]

This criterion demonstrates the basic importance of Ƚ as a primary avenue to the OG, as has been suggested above.[18] It yields, in this case, the fullest preservation of the OG of all the Greek witnesses (and the clearest, vis-à-vis the frequently conflate nature of L).[19]

3. מעל = επανωθεν (απανωθεν)

This καιγε rendering is in contrast to the translation of the OG by simple απο or επανω.[20]

The Hebrew preposition stands 11 times in Judges. Of these, 7 yield no evidence of καιγε revision,[21] and 1 has the καιγε reading everywhere but in Bck.[22] In the remaining 3 cases, the B family shows the expected revision against all others, except for K in 2 cases and Ƶ in 1.[23]

This, then, is a case in which the revision in Judges is only partial; nevertheless, it does clearly appear. This phenomenon has already been seen in the treatment of וגם/גם, and it will be seen frequently. If a characteristic rendering appears for each instance of a given Hebrew word, so much the better. If not, this does not rule out the recognition of a characteristic. Each case must be examined individually.[24]

4. נצב/יצב = στηλόω

According to Barthélemy, this translation arose as an extension of the rendering of מצבה by στήλη; and the use of the verb form in reference to people is an innovation in Greek lexicography. It is said to be a departure from the OG usage of ἵστημι and derivatives.[25]

A reexamination of the evidence for this characteristic has raised doubt about its validity as a mark of the καιγε recension. It should be said first that it does not hold in Judges; the evidence is directly contrary. Of the 5 occurrences of the verb, its translation by στηλόω appears only 2 times; and both of these are in non-καιγε material.[26]

Several positive examples do appear in καιγε material elsewhere. They are, as Barthélemy has indicated, 1 Samuel 17:16 (θ´); 2 Samuel 18:30; 23:12; and Lamentations 3:12. These are all significant, since they all have to do with people. Those instances in which καιγε material shows the root, but which do not refer to people, should be noted as well.[27] The usage of the root by Aquila could also be cited as evidence, although he is not consistent, as noted previously.[28]

In opposition to this rendering being a true καιγε characteristic are the passages in καιγε material in which the revision does not appear, both those which have to do with people[29] and those which do not.[30] There are several other instances in which the expected reading does appear, but not in καιγε material; these are 2 Samuel 8:14b;[31] 18:18a;[32] and in σ´ and Ƶ of Lamentations 2:4.[33]

This reevaluation of evidence would seem to indicate,

14

at least, that the rendering is not consistent in any of the
καιγε material and possibly that it is not a true characteristic at all. In any case, the inconsistency in Judges is
paralleled elsewhere and, therefore, is less weighty in opposition to the identification of the B family in Judges with the
καιγε recension. Notice, however, will be taken of all potentially contrary evidence in the conclusion of the chapter.

5. שופר = κερατινη

This translation is one of the most clearly demarcated
features of the καιγε recension. It stands in contrast to the
OG usage of σαλπιγξ for both שופר and חצצרה, καιγε using
σαλπιγξ only for the latter.[34]

In Judges the translation of שופר by the B family is
thoroughly consistent with the καιγε recension elsewhere. All
10 occurrences are rendered by κερατινη.[35] In 8 of the 10
cases, L retains the OG reading.[36] In 7 of these 8, Ŀ agrees
with L.[37] Contrary to the general tendency in Judges, the A
family, K, and Ș all side with the καιγε recension in this
reading.[38]

6. The Elimination of the Historical Present

This characteristic is presented by Barthélemy, but not
applied to the book of Judges.[39] In the entire book, only 1
case appears. Here the evidence is contrary to the present
argument, for the present tense stands in the B family and K;
whereas an aorist is employed by the A family and L and is followed by Ș and Ŀ.[40] It should be noted that this characteristic is of limited appearance in the καιγε recension generally
due to the seeming rarity of the historical present in the
OG,[41] although it is frequent in Samuel-Kings.[42] The 1 instance in Judges will be noted with other potentially negative
evidence in the conclusion to this chapter.

7. אין = ουκ εστιν (in a context of aorists)

According to Barthélemy, the atemporal character of this
negative particle was emphasized by the καιγε recension with
the translation ουκ εστιν in the midst of a series of aorist
verbs.[43]

The evidence of the B family in Judges is less thoroughgoing than in the case of other criteria. Of the total of 18
uses of the Hebrew particle in Judges, the revision appears in
the B family exclusively 4 times[44] and 1 time is shared with
the A family, K, and Ʂ.[45]

It appears in the A family apart from the B family 4
times.[46] In 1 further instance it appears in Ʂbx alone.[47] As
Barthélemy has pointed out, L consistently resists the revision
in Judges, as does ꞁ.[48]

Thus, the B family is mixed with regard to this characteristic, sometimes showing the καιγε revision and sometimes
not, even when it does appear elsewhere.

While the matter must be left at that, it can be pointed
out that this characteristic is not thoroughgoing elsewhere in
the καιγε material either. Contrary instances not pointed out
by Barthélemy include 5 cases in which καιγε elsewhere does
not revise,[49] and 1 instance of the expected καιγε reading in
non-καιγε material.[50] On 3 occasions, at least, in addition
to those mentioned by Barthélemy in the course of his discussion, there has been a revision from the future to the
present of ειμι in non-καιγε material.[51]

It should be said that a thorough reexamination of all
of the presently identified καιγε material does seem to confirm Barthélemy's demarcation of this reading as a genuine
characteristic. In addition to his findings, Job 7:8 and 35:
15;[52] Daniel (θ´) 10:21; and Lamentations 1:21 support the
conclusion. However, this reexamination has also shown that
the characteristic appears only partially elsewhere; thus, its
mixed appearance in Judges is rendered less significant as
evidence against the present argument.

8. אנכי = εγω ειμι

This form of the first singular personal pronoun was
distinguished from the shorter form, אני, by the καιγε recension through the use of the two words εγω ειμι, in contrast
to the OG use of εγω for both pronouns. Furthermore, the two
words were treated as a unit and could serve as the subject of
a finite verb.[53]

The B family of Judges clearly joins the καιγε recension

in this characteristic. Of the total of 17 occurrences of
אנכי, the B family alone shows the revision 5 times.[54] In 3
instances the revision appears in the B family and elsewhere,
but with exceptions.[55] In 3 cases the revised translation is
common to all.[56]

In the remaining 6 instances, the revision does not
appear at all.[57] Thus, the B family is solidly καιγε, although the revision does not appear in each case.

The following criterion discussed by Barthélemy, the
rendering of Hebrew לקראת, will be deferred until chapter
three because it belongs there in the present analysis.

The above completes the major characteristics which
Barthélemy presents. He has a further group which he proposes
as καιγε characteristics which were further developed by
Aquila.[58] From these only those which pertain to the book of
Judges will be discussed, i.e., those whose Hebrew counter-
parts appear in the MT of Judges.

9. נגד = forms of εναντι

The OG rendering of this preposition is varied and is
made consistent in the καιγε recension by the use of forms of
εναντι.[59]

Only 2 instances appear in Judges.[60] In both of these,
εξ εναντιας is employed by all Greek families. Whether this
is the OG in need of no καιγε revision, or καιγε revision
throughout, it is neutral evidence for the present argument.

10. לפני = ενωπιον

This equivalence was detected by Barthélemy primarily in
Judges and Samuel-Kings.[61]

Of the 22 occurrences of the preposition in Judges, the
B family shows the expected revision 10 times. In 5 of these
the revision is exclusive,[62] and in 5 it is shared with other
groups.[63] In 7 cases the καιγε reading is shared by all with
no revision being demonstrable.[64]

In 1 case the B family stands against all others and the
expected καιγε reading.[65] In the remaining 4 instances, the
καιγε reading does not appear at all.[66] Taken as a whole, the
evidence of this reading again identifies the B family of

Judges as a part of the καιγε recension.

11. על כן = δια τουτο

Whereas in the OG ενεκεν τουτο often appears for this
conjunction and for על זאת (which does not appear in Judges),
δια τουτο is employed for both by καιγε.[67]

There are 3 occurrences of על כן in Judges. In the first
it appears only in ℊ (with ※) and bcx of the A family. In the
other 2, all groups read δια τουτο.[68] The addition of ℊ
('al hādê) could stand for either δια τουτο or επι τουτω (the
reading of bcx, επι τουτο in b). It is, in either case, an
addition of Origen himself, as evidenced by the asterisk. It
simply confirms what has been clear from most of the characteristics already discussed, i.e., that καιγε revision was not
thoroughly consistent. The latter 2 readings probably represent such revision; but this cannot be said assuredly, since
no evidence of a different OG reading exists.

12. לעולם = εις τον αιωνα

Whereas the OG sometimes renders this phrase imprecisely,
the καιγε recension reestablishes precision by a more exact
rendering.[69]

The expression occurs only once in Judges; and there the
reading is the literal one of the καιγε recension, shared by
all Greek witnesses again in this case.[70]

13. אסף = συναγω

In those cases in which this verb is translated by the
OG as εκλειπω, in καιγε it is revised to συναγω.[71]

Of the 12 instances of the verb in Judges, 8 show the
literal rendering of συναγω in Greek, but with no demonstrable
revision.[72] In 3 cases it seems that the B family has revised
to the καιγε reading, although not from εκλειπω. In 2 of
these the revision is exclusive,[73] and in 1 it is shared by
K.[74]

In 1 instance the καιγε reading does not appear at all.[75]
Perhaps Barthélemy's criterion should be enlarged to include
καιγε revision to συναγω from varied OG renderings. In Judges

προστιθημι,[76] προσαγω,[77] and εξερχομαι[78] all appear with
strong support.

14. מהר = ταχυνω

This rendering is in contrast to the OG use of σπευδω.
Since this characteristic was noted already by Barthélemy,[79]
it is presented here, rather than with the new characteristics
discovered by Shenkel, who also discusses it.[80]

Of the 2 uses of the verbal root in finite form in
Judges, only 1 is rendered by a finite verb in Greek. That 1
rendering conforms to the καιγε recension elsewhere, although
no revision is certain.[81] The other Hebrew finite verbal
form[82] and the 3 adverbial uses of the root in Judges[83] are
all translated by an adverbial form of the same Greek root.
Thus, the evidence here is in harmony with the B family being
καιγε in Judges, although, as with other cases in which no revision is certain, it cannot be adduced as positive proof.

Criteria from Thackeray

Preceding the work of Barthélemy, Thackeray had already
identified the distinctive nature of two sections of the books
of Samuel-Kings. These were 2 Samuel 11:2--1 Kings 2:11 and
1 Kings 22:1--2 Kings, labeled by him as βγ and γδ respectively.[84] The first of these two sections has been shown by
Shenkel to begin rather at 2 Samuel 10:1,[85] and this expansion is followed in the present study. In his own research,
Thackeray isolated 10 characteristic renderings in this
material. Since 6 of them were further developed by Barthélemy, they have been considered among his criteria. Two
involve Hebrew words not present in Judges; thus, only the
other 2 will be considered here.[86]

15. יען אשר = ανθ ων οσα

The related characteristic, ανθ ων οτι, does not appear
in Judges and seems tenuous anyway, because it is given with
no certain Hebrew equivalent. However, its companion, ανθ ων
οσα, does occur once; and there it serves as the translation
of the same Hebrew phrase that Thackeray studied in Samuel-

Kings, יען אשר.[87]

Although all major groups agree with this rendering, the
Lucianic witness 1 and subgroup dptv read, rather, ανϑ ων and
are supported by Lug. with *propter quod*. That this Ⱡ testimony
is in agreement with 1, dptv and not the majority reading is
confirmed by Sab. which reads *propter quod tanta*, the exact
equivalent of ανϑ ων οσα. Therefore, an OG reading seems likely
to be preserved in 1 and dptv; and a καιγε revision is evidenced in the B family and other groups. Since, however, καιγε
revision is not certain and since this is the only instance of
the characteristic in Judges, it will be regarded as neutral
evidence in the present argument.[88]

16. Misc. = ηνικα

This preposition appears in Judges 9 times, but with no
consistency. On 4 occasions it is common to all groups.[89] On
4 it appears in the A family and other groups, but not in the
B family.[90] On only 1 occasion does it appear in the B family
against the others.[91] Thus, if the criterion were reliable, it
would militate against the argument of this chapter.

However, question must be raised about the reliability
of the criterion on two grounds. In the first place, it stands
as the translation of no exact Hebrew equivalent. This is not
in keeping with the nature of the καιγε recension, which is
that of establishing uniform Greek equivalents for certain
specific Hebrew expressions.[92] In the second place, while
the Greek conjunction does occur in βγ and γδ, but not elsewhere in Samuel-Kings,[93] it appears throughout the Heptateuch
(concertedly in Genesis and Exodus),[94] frequently in Proverbs[95]
and Isaiah,[96] and elsewhere as well. In other words, it is not
a characteristic καιγε word at all. At best it could only be
seen as a characteristic of βδ, and this seems doubtful.

A Criterion from Smith

17. הורה = φωτιζω

A single criterion for distinguishing the καιγε recension
has been published by Michael Smith.[97] It is the translation
of the *hiphil* of ירה by the verb φωτιζω. Smith's research has
proven sound upon reexamination, and the data would seem to

20

firmly establish the translation as a καιγε characteristic.[98]

In Judges there is only 1 occurrence of the Hebrew verb.[99]
It appears in the Greek traditions contrary to the present
argument. The B family[100] uses the verb συμβιβαζω, one of the
typical OG translations, whereas all other witnesses show the
καιγε reading.[101]

Since this is the only instance in Judges, its significance is limited. In many of the preceding and following καιγε
characteristics, there are occasional inconsistencies, but a
clear pattern. Had several more cases of the Hebrew verb been
present in Judges, the Greek picture could have entirely
changed.

Also, several explanations are possible for the inconsistency. The reading in the non-καιγε witnesses could be the
result of revision later than καιγε, e.g., Hexaplaric, which
could have generally influenced the others.[102] The reading of
the B family could be due to later influence as well, such as
a restoration of the OG.[103] On the other hand, the καιγε
reviser(s) of Judges may have deliberately avoided the use of
the verb φωτιζω.[104] These and other explanations are possible.
Whatever the true explanation may be, evidence based on 1 reading cannot be given much weight over against the cumulative
force of so many other characteristics which appear in multi-
ple instances. Nevertheless, this, together with all other
negative evidence, will be given due consideration in the conclusion of the present chapter.

Criteria from Shenkel

The new καιγε characteristics discovered by Shenkel in
the course of his work in Samuel-Kings will now be considered
in relationship to the Greek text of Judges. One of these
(לא [אבה] = θελω) will be deferred until chapter three, where it
should appear in the present argument due to its peculiar
outworking in Judges.

18. בעיני = εν οφθαλμοις

This is perhaps the most striking of all of the new
καιγε renderings uncovered by Shenkel. It exhibits at once
the avoidance of anthropomorphism found in the OG[105] and the

more literal[106] (consequently, often more anthropomorphic) and
more consistent rendering of the καιγε recension. The OG is
said to have avoided the literal translation of this preposition when the object was יהוה and to have used it only rarely
when the object was a suffix equivalent to יהוה. It employed
ενωπιον or εναντιον instead. On the other hand, when the
object was a suffix or a noun referring to someone other than
יהוה, the literal translation was often utilized. In contrast
to this, the καιγε recension renders the preposition literally
regardless of the object.[107]

Of the 15 occurrences of the preposition in Judges, 8
show a typical OG reading with no revision at all.[108] In each
case the object is יהוה explicitly. In 2 cases, both with an
object other than יהוה, the literal rendering appears in all
witnesses.[109] In 2 of the remaining, the B family shows
exclusive revision to the καιγε rendering. The first of these
has a suffixed object referring to יהוה; the second has an
object other than יהוה.[110] The 3 other instances show some
preservation of the OG nonliteral rendering, and the B family
has the καιγε rendering in each case. In the first, the object
is a suffix equivalent to יהוה; in the others, the objects are
suffixes not equivalent to יהוה.[111]

Thus, the same revision appears in the B family of Judges
as in the καιγε sections of Samuel-Kings, though in modified
form. There will be cause to note this difference in the argument of chapter three below.

19. זבח = θυσιαζω

The OG equivalent for this verb, θυω, was altered by the
καιγε revision to θυσιαζω.[112]

The Hebrew verb occurs twice in Judges.[113] In both of
these the A family, L, K, and presumably 8[114] have the OG form.
In the first, the B family alone has the normal καιγε revision.
In the second, there is no clear revision; but the καιγε reading may possibly have stood in B and does appear in a and q.[115]

It may be noteworthy also that in the latter of these
passages, the noun זבח is used as a cognate accusative of the
verb just mentioned. Whereas it is translated by θυσια in all

other Greek witnesses, B translates it by θυσιασμα, a longer
form, as with the characteristic καιγε verb. This is simply
mentioned here, rather than in chapter two as a καιγε characteristic in itself, because it does not seem to present a clear
pattern elsewhere and occurs in Judges only in this reference.

The following characteristics isolated by Shenkel form
an appendix to his work and will be discussed in the order in
which they appear there,[116] with the exception already
mentioned.[117]

20. רדף = διωκω

This is a revision from the common OG rendering of
καταδιωκω.

Of the 11 occurrences of the verb in MT, 5 are insignificant, 3 showing the καιγε reading, but with no variants,[118]
and 2 the OG with no variants.[119] In 3 cases, however, the B
family shows exclusive revision to the καιγε reading;[120] and
in 2 it shares that revision with other groups.[121] The 1
remaining instance has not been listed as a καιγε revision
because it does not have the verb identified by Shenkel as
καιγε.[122] Nevertheless, it may represent καιγε revision, as
the OG word appears in the A family (abcx), L (gnw), 𝔖,[123] and
𝔏 (persecuti sunt). In the entire B family, A, and K, the verb
κατατρεχω is used.

21. שר (ה)צבא = αρχων της δυναμεως

This is a revision from the common OG form αρχιστρατηγος.
The 2 occurrences of the Hebrew phrase in Judges are
both translated by the καιγε phrase with no variants.[124]

22. חכם = σοφ-

This root is used by καιγε in place of a form of the
root φρον- in the OG.
The 1 occurrence of the Hebrew root in Judges[125] shows
the καιγε reading in all of the Greek witnesses.[126] The L
text, however, is conflate in the rendering of this entire
verse and the following; and the Hebrew root in question is

translated by φρονησις in the second of these renderings.
That the latter set of variants represents the OG in this case
is confirmed by the agreement of Ƚ (Lug.).[127] Therefore, καιγε
revision is likely here, having spread to all of the Greek
families, the OG being preserved only in the second member of
the conflate reading of L and in Ƚ.

23. חרש = κωφευω/חשה = σιωπαω

Whereas the OG seems to have used σιωπαω for both of
these, καιγε, according to Shenkel, made a distinction.

The evidence of Judges is in keeping with this picture,
but does not furnish primary support for the identity of the B
family with the καιγε recension. In the 2 instances of חרש,
the καιγε verb is used both times, but without variation.[128]
The verb חשה is used once.[129] There the A family, L, and ᵹ
all have the expected OG reading, σιωπαω; but the B family and
K have ησυχαζω. Since this latter verb does not appear to be
a καιγε rendering of חשה elsewhere, it cannot be used as
evidence of καιγε revision here, although it may represent
such.

24. הרה = εν γαστρι εχω/λαμβανω

The OG equivalent of this verb is said to be συλλαμβανω.

If the criterion is valid, the results in Judges might
seem to be negative for the present argument. There are 3
instances in Judges. In 2 all witnesses agree in having a form
of the phrase εν γαστρι εχω, showing differences in tense
only.[130] The other occurrence shows the same (purportedly
καιγε) reading in all groups but the B family, which has the
purportedly OG reading.[131]

An examination of every occurrence of the Hebrew verb in
the Old Testament seems to support the validity of this characteristic. It is consistent in all 5 instances of the verb in
βγ and γδ of Samuel-Kings, and 3 of these stand against L.[132]
Also, in all 4 preserved readings of Theodotion, the καιγε word
occurs.[133]

However, in all of the rest of the material thus far
identified as καιγε, except for Judges and 1 reference in Can-

ticles, the verb does not occur. The 1 reference in Canticles shows, rather, the OG reading.[134] Furthermore, the proposed καιγε reading occurs not infrequently in the OG, a total of some 17 times in a wide range of material.[135] Thus, it must at least be said that, even if the phrase εν γαστρι εχω/λαμβανω is a characteristic rendering in καιγε material, it is frequent in the OG as well. Also, in 1 καιγε reference outside of Judges, the verb συλλαμβανω is used.

One further general observation should be made. It concerns an apparent distinction within the OG itself. Apparently, whereas the verb συλλαμβανω was the most frequent reading, this verb is used most often for the Hebrew imperfect.[136] When another form is used (perfect, participle, or adjective),[137] the phrase εν γαστρι εχω/λαμβανω is normally used. There are 20 such instances outside of Judges, and in 12 of these the latter phrase is used.[138] This, as well as καιγε revision, could account for the use of the phrase in all 3 instances in Judges, for, in every case, the Hebrew verb is either a perfect or a participle/adjective.

The only remaining factor left unexplained is why in Judges 13:3 the B family should employ the most common OG verb, when all other groups have what is in Samuel-Kings and ϑ´ the καιγε reading. Since the B family reading is also the reading of Canticles 3:4 (for a participle), it may not be an inconsistency at all, but simply a difference within the καιγε recension as a whole, i.e., συλλαμβανω could have been the preferred καιγε reading in this case.[139]

Still another explanation is possible. The manuscripts Bejqsz could preserve the OG reading. These manuscripts alone omit a translation of the following Hebrew verb וילדת. In this case, the group irua₂, which also reads συλλημψη, but which adds και τεξη (with all other Greek families, ϐ, and 𝕃), would represent καιγε revision to the Hebrew which did not, however, alter the verb συλλημψη; and the change to εν γαστρι εξεις would be a later revision, possibly incorporated into the fifth column of Origin's Hexapla and then spread from there to the other traditions.

The first of these alternatives may be the more likely in light of the general distinction between the OG translation

of the imperfect of הרה and its other forms. However, the
evidence in Judges does not seem adequate to warrant a firm
conclusion. Whichever translation of הרה in Judges 13:3 may,
in fact, represent the OG, the καιγε nature of the B family is
not excluded. Furthermore, it will be apparent when the evidence of this entire chapter is summarized that, even if this
characteristic were interpreted as contrary, it would not alter
the final conclusion to be drawn.

The criterion published by Grindel[140] will not be discussed, as the Hebrew word does not occur in Judges.

Criteria from O'Connell

The final selection of characteristics is drawn from the
study of the sixth column material of Exodus by Kevin G.
O'Connell.[141] His conclusion in this study is that the Theodotionic revision of Exodus forms an integral part of the recension labeled καιγε by Barthélemy.[142] In light of this, these
characteristics may be used to confirm the identification of
καιγε material elsewhere.[143]

25. בין = ανα μεσον

O'Connell suggests that Theodotion in Exodus apparently
differs from both the OG and Aquila in translating this preposition and that his rendering may have been the above each
time, though some instances are uncertain due to difficulty in
retranslating from Syriac.

The Hebrew preposition occurs 19 times in Judges. Of
these, 18 show no significant variation.[144] The other does,
in that the A family and 𝔖 read μεταξυ, 𝔏 has sub, and the
group dptv has εν μεσω. This could be a preservation of the
OG, either in the A family and 𝔖, or in 𝔏, and, thus, a καιγε
revision in the B family.[145] However, it seems best, in this
case, to regard the evidence as neutral.

26. בקרב = εν μεσω

Here again, Theodotion differs in Exodus from the OG and
also from Aquila, though the latter difference is difficult to

26

identify.

Of the 7 occurrences of the preposition in the MT of
Judges, 6 show εν μεσω in the Greek without significant variation.[146] In the other,[147] the A family, L, K, 𝔖, and 𝔏 have
εν, apparently the OG in this case; but the B family shows εν
μεσω, in accord with the revision identified by O'Connell in the
ϑ´ material of Exodus.

27. חזק (piel) = ενισχυω

O'Connell sees this rendering (shared by ϑ´ and α´) as
possibly part of a concerted move toward reinterpretation.[148]

Of the 3 instances of the Hebrew verb in Judges, all are
translated by this same Greek verb in the B family. There is
no variation among the other groups in 2 of these.[149] In the
other, the A family, L, and 𝔖 translate by a form of κατισχυω,
likely the OG being preserved;[150] but the B family again
employs ενισχυω.

28. חרב = ρομφαια

The OG equivalent of this noun varies. The Theodotionic
rendering is common in the OG, as is μαχαιρα and others. In
Exodus, α´ and σ´ use μαχαιρα.

This characteristic is especially useful in Judges
because the Hebrew noun occurs 23 times. Of these, 11 have
ρομφαια with no variation;[151] and 3 have μαχαιρα with no variation.[152] The remaining 9 show the B family with ρομφαια and
other witnesses with μαχαιρα, either individual manuscripts of
no apparent significance (6 times),[153] or the A family and L
(3 times, K joining in 2 of these).[154] In contrast to the
usual situation in Judges, 𝔖 sides here with the B family in
all of these latter readings.[155]

29. חָתָן = νυμφιος/חֹתֵן = γαμβρος

The OG employs γαμβρος for both of these. Thus, the
Theodotionic material in Exodus makes a distinction between the
two Hebrew nouns.

In Judges this distinction is also maintained in the B
family. חָתָן occurs on 2 occasions; and for both the B family

has νυμφιος against the A family, L, and K (in the first instance).[156] $ seems to comport with the B family in these
cases.[157] חָתָן occurs 5 times. In each case the B family has
γαμβρος;[158] in 4 of the 5 the A family, K, and $ do as well.[159]

Elsewhere in the OT the scheme is not quite so neat,
though sufficient data for a clear picture is lacking. There
is no other usage of חָתָן in known καιγε material, apart from
Exodus and Judges, except for θ´ of 1 Samuel 18:18, which
translates, contrary to the above pattern, γαμβρος. Yet in all
4 of his preserved readings, Aquila translates by νυμφιος, once
revising from the OG γαμβρος.[160] In all 5 of his preserved
readings, Symmachus also employs the purportedly καιγε word.
If Symmachus based his work on a καιγε text, this would be
significant.[161] The characteristic seems to stand. Though the
OG used γαμβρος for both חָתָן and חֹתֵן, καιγε revision seems to
have been carried out in the case of the former from γαμβρος to
νυμφιος, thus establishing a distinction. This distinction is
clearly made by the B family of Judges.

30. עבד = δουλ-

In Exodus O'Connell found that Theodotion uses only
forms from the Greek root δουλ- for Hebrew forms from the root
עבד. Whereas the same rendering occurs in the OG, many variations also occur.

A check of this usage for the verb form throughout the
presently identified καιγε material seems to verify the
criterion, though it is not everywhere consistent. Neither the
verb nor any related noun occurs in the Minor Prophets fragments
published by Barthélemy. The rendering of the verb where it
does appear in καιγε material is as follows.

In βγ it occurs 5 times and is rendered 4 times by
δουλευω[162] and 1 time by λατρευω.[163] In γδ it occurs 19 times
and is rendered 13 times by δουλευω[164] and 6 by λατρευω.[165]
Of these readings 2 appear to be contrary to the proposed
characteristic, for in the last 2 references boc₂e₂ employ
δουλευω.[166] It should be observed, however, that the pre-
ponderant καιγε reading is δουλευω and that these 2 exceptions
occur in the same verse.

No καιγε material appears in the Psalms, and only 1

asterisked reading appears in Job. It shows δουλευω in both ϑ′
(with ※) and σ′.[167] The references in Jeremiah, however, are
numerous and clearly in favor of the proposed characteristic.
There are 9 instances of asterisked additions to the Greek text.
Of these, 8 show the verb δουλευω;[168] and 1 shows λατρευω.[169]
The word normally used in the καιγε recension was δουλευω.

In the 1 contrary instance in Jeremiah, Aquila revises
to δουλευω; and according to R-T he uses this word without exception for the verb עבד in the simple *qal* stem. For the
hiphil, he uses the related verb δουλοω, the Greek causative of
the same root. He apparently has taken a characteristic of the
καιγε recension and carried it through to full consistency.
This is a further confirmation of the criterion.

In reference to Judges, the B family again joins the
καιγε recension elsewhere. The verb עבד occurs 17 times. Of
these, 5 appear in Greek as λατρευω;[170] 7 appear as δουλευω;[171]
and 1 appears as δουλος,[172] all without variation. The remaining 4 all appear as λατρευω in the A family, L, K (3 times),
and ß; in the B family, however, they appear as δουλευω.[173]

In the OG of Judges, the pattern seems to be that δουλευω is used when the object is human and λατρευω when it is
divine.[174] In the 4 instances of apparent καιγε revision on
the part of the B family, the object is divine, thus the OG
reading λατρευω, and thus a further confirmation of the καιγε
character of the B family in Judges. Revision has been made to
secure greater consistency with the Hebrew text, consistency of
a word-to-word sort, at the expense of a nuanced distinction in
Greek usage.[175]

Of the Hebrew nouns related to the verb עבד, only the
basal noun עבד occurs in Judges. Its rendering in Greek does
not furnish evidence in favor of the present argument; and it
could be seen as contrary, but not necessarily so. The word
occurs 6 times, and only 1 of these shows any variation. Of
the 6 occurrences, 4 appear in Greek as δουλος,[176] and 1 as
παις,[177] all without variation. The remaining instance appears
as δουλος in the A family, K, and presumably ß.[178] L shows the
noun παις; and, of the B family, Befjqsza₂ show a form of
παιδιον. This would seem to be contrary evidence, but two factors minimize its significance, in addition to the fact that

there is only 1 such occurrence. One is the variation between
L (with παις) and B and related minuscules (with παιδιον).
Since L has already been seen as a primary avenue to the OG of
Judges,[179] and if it represents such here, then B and these related minuscules could represent a later alteration, e.g., by
Hesychius.[180] More importantly, the three most consistent
representatives of the καιγε recension in Judges, iru, together
with m,[181] agree here with those groups that read δουλος. This
represents evidence that the characteristic καιγε reading stood
here in its proper place and that, in the other manuscripts of
the B family, it was further revised, or has been obscured
through some irrecoverable process.

Conclusion

Although other aspects of the present question could be
considered, as, for example, other kinds of characteristic
features of the B family of Judges over against other groups
(such as its relationship to the Hexaplaric asterisk and obelus,
transliteration, etc.), it becomes more difficult to use these
as evidence upon which to build a conclusion. Such features
will be pointed out and discussed at appropriate places in the
following chapters and some specifically in the appendix. The
criteria used in this chapter have been those καιγε characteristics already identified by others on the basis of material
outside of Judges.[182] These constitute, at present, the most
objective basis upon which to identify καιγε revision in any
section of the Greek Old Testament. It now remains to summa-
rize the results of the preceding study and to state the conclusion of the chapter on the basis of this evidence.[183]

A total of 30 characteristics of the καιγε recension,
or of significant parts of it, outside of Judges have been
applied to the Greek text of Judges itself. The purpose has
been to test the identification proposed by Barthélemy of the
B family of Judges with the καιγε recension elsewhere. The
identification stands and is soundly confirmed by the application of this body of criteria.

The evidence may be summarized as follows. Of the 30
characteristics, 16 positively favor the identification; and 12
of these rest on a broad base of at least 3 and normally many

more instances.[184]

Those that definitely oppose the identification amount
to 4 at the most.[185] Question has been raised in the above
discussion about the validity of 2 of these,[186] and it has
been shown that neither is consistent elsewhere and that the
former may not be valid at all. However, even if all 4 were
valid and consistent elsewhere, 3 appear in only 1 instance;
and the other in only 2 in Judges.[187] In other words, they are
insignificant, since a broader base could easily have reversed
the picture and since they stand against a clear majority of
characteristics, most of which rest on a broad base.

One characteristic produced a mixed picture in the B
family of Judges.[188] It was pointed out that the same is true
for this characteristic in other καιγε material thus far identified.

Of the remaining 9 criteria, 8 must be listed as neutral,
since they all show the expected καιγε reading, but in each
case without certain revision.[189]

The final criterion was judged to be definitely invalid
and, therefore, is ruled out as evidence of any sort.[190]

Mention should also be made of the 2 published characteristics which have been deferred until chapter three.[191] They
both reveal the divergence of the B family in Judges from the
other groups, but in ways peculiar to Judges itself, and
should, therefore, be regarded as neutral evidence for the
argument of this chapter.

Granting all benefit of the doubt to the possibility of
a negative conclusion, the result is still positive. The B
family of Judges clearly constitutes a part of the Greek
recension known as καιγε.

NOTES

CHAPTER I

1. DA, pp. 34-35, 47-80, and *passim* 81-88.

2. Several observations about the following presentation of data should be made. The criteria will be numbered
consecutively throughout the chapter so that a final synthesis
of the evidence may conveniently be made. Verse notation will
follow the MT unless otherwise indicated, e.g., on those occasions when the statistics are drawn directly from H-R. In
listings of data, all totals will be indicated by Arabic numer-
als in order to facilitate comparison and evaluation. In the
presentation of evidence, manuscript groups will be separated
by punctuation, but not individual manuscripts, except for
purposes of clarity.
    One abbreviation calls for an explanation, since it
anticipates a conclusion of chapter four. It is the use of K
to stand for the text group $MNhyb_2$. This group was regarded
by Pretzl as a koine of pre-Origenic provenience (Otto Pretzl,
"Septuagintaprobleme im Buch der Richter," *Biblica* 7 [1926],
353-61). Whereas the pre-Origenic date has been shown to be
wrong, and this conclusion is confirmed by the present study,
the text group does appear to be mixed. Thus, Koine has been
deemed an apt title; and this will be indicated by K. The
Lucianic group will be indicated by L and Jerome's Vulgate by
Vg. Abbreviations for other texts and versions will follow
those of B-M.

3. DA, pp. 31-47.

4. 2:10a, 21; 3:31; 17:2. In 3:31 the A family and K
omit; whereas L, 𝕾, and 𝕷 have καɩ. In 17:2 the characteristic
appears only in irua₂.
    Attention will be given in this work to the historical
development of the Greek text groups of Judges, especially the
B family. Therefore, these will be the points of comparison in
the following presentation of evidence. In addition, 𝕾 will be
quoted consistently, as will 𝕷 when it shows significant variation, because of their immediate relevance to the Greek textual
development. Other versions will be noted occasionally, e.g.,
when a reading has only weak support from Greek witnesses, but
does appear in one or more of the other versions. When Greek
manuscripts, 𝕾, or 𝕷 are not noted explicitly, they may be
assumed, as in B-M, to agree with the reading of the B text.
    The appearance of the καɩγε reading in 5:4a in bcx of
the A family and in 𝕾 following an asterisk signals a phenomenon of frequent occurrence in the Greek Judges. Whereas the B
family clearly has the preponderance of καɩγε readings, these
readings are so frequent and widespread in the other text
groups that the very preservation of the OG is often called
into question.
    The explanation of this extensive καɩγε influence in the
non-καɩγε texts of Judges is likely to be found in the work of

Origen. In chapter four, it will be demonstrated that Origen
employed a καιγε type text in the revision of his base text and
that the other major Greek families all show Hexaplaric influence, though in varying degrees. The family showing the least
influence of Origen's revision, i.e., the L text, is also the
one with the fullest preservation of the OG, especially when it
stands in agreement with 𝓛. (Cf. chapter four, pp. 134-36.)

As for the recognition of the OG, the research of others
has been followed in those characteristics already published.
The only exceptions in these cases are those criteria which
have been reexamined (cf. the discussions to follow). In chapters two and three, the OG has been sought through the usage of
the majority Greek text in all sections except those in which
the majority text is καιγε. Generally the concordance of H-R
has been followed for these statistics, unless there was reason
to check each reference individually. This has been done in
those cases in which the statistics are not cited from H-R.

A complicating factor in the discernment of the OG of
Judges in those cases in which the καιγε reading appears in
non-καιγε texts is the following practice. Often the OG rendering of a Hebrew term varied among several possibilities. In
many of these instances, it appears that one of these possible
OG translations was selected as the καιγε rendering. Whenever
this is the case, and when the term selected by καιγε appears
in a non-καιγε text, it is ambiguous as to whether it is the OG
preserved or καιγε revision spread to that text. Individual
study of each of these instances would be required for a firm
resolution of the ambiguity. This is not the purpose of the
present work, but such observations as can be made from the
writer's study thus far will be presented below. In general,
instances of this sort will be considered as neutral evidence
for the present argument; and only those readings in which
καιγε revision can be clearly affirmed will serve as the basis
of the conclusion to be drawn in the present chapter.

5. As stated in note four, the Old Latin will be noted
in this and the following two chapters in addition to the major
families of Greek manuscripts when it shows significant variation. In introducing his edition of the *Book of Rules of Tychonius*, Burkitt makes the observation that that Old Latin text
"may preserve genuine readings independent of all our Greek MSS"
(F. C. Burkitt, *The Book of Rules of Tychonius*, vol. III of
Texts and Studies, ed. J. Armitage Robinson [Cambridge, 1895],
p. cvii). Billen has pursued this possibility in Judges and
has found it to be true (A. V. Billen, "The Old Latin Version
of Judges," *JTS* 43[1942], 140-49). The present study supports
his conclusion. The 𝓛 in Judges is often the surest guide to
the earliest form of the OG. (This point will be discussed in
chapter four.)

The 9 instances referred to in the text are as follows:
1:3 (irua$_2$, A fam., K, 𝕾 against L, B befoqsz); 2:10b (B fam.,
K against A fam., L, 𝕾, 𝓛); 3:22 (B fam., etc. against 𝕾 and L
[lw Thdt. (και), gn omit]); 5:4a; 8:31 (B fam., glw [καιγε και],
etc. against 𝕬, 𝕭, 𝓛, kn [all with και]); 9:19 (B fam., L
against A and K [omitting], and A fam., 𝕾, 𝓛 [και]), 49a (B
fam., A fam., K, 𝕾 [⁎ γε] against A, L, 𝓛), 49b (B fam., K, 𝕾
[⁎ γε] against A fam., L, 𝓛 [all omitting]); 11:17 (B fam.,
A fam., K, 𝕾, L [και γε και] against B kq 𝕬 𝓛).

6.   1:22 (∅ and 𝕃 omit); 2:17; 19:19a (𝕃 omits; 𝔸 and ∅
have και).

7.   5:4b (καιγε in A only); 19:19c (καιγε in A fam., L,
𝕊). In cases such as these, in which the καιγε reading appears
apart from the καιγε text, several explanations are possible.
The OG reading could have been restored later in the καιγε text
at points at which revision had already been made. Another, and
perhaps a more likely, possibility is that καιγε type revision
could have been carried out after the basic καιγε text was complete; and then that revision could have spread to the other
traditions through its incorporation into Origen's fifth column.
For precisely this latter possibility in the Judges Greek traditions, see the discussion of Origen's work in chapter four
below. However these instances may be explained, they are minimal in the context of all of the characteristics to be discussed in this chapter and do not affect the final conclusion
regarding the B family.

8.   2:3; 7:18 (the omission of και in B oq, 𝔸 could
easily have been due to haplography in the Greek text, there
being 3 words in succession beginning with *kappa*, assuming the
earlier presence of και); 8:9 (omission by all), 22a-c (α΄ has
καιγε in all 3 cases); 19:19b; 20:48.

9.   6:35; 10:9. The καιγε reading appears in these instances only in minuscule 128 at 6:35.

10.   In the following discussion of each characteristic,
the same general pattern will be followed. The B family has
been the primary point of comparison in the writer's analysis.
Statistics will be presented for each characteristic which
indicate the number of times the B family has the καιγε word(ε)
exclusive of any other Greek group, 𝕊, or 𝕃 and the number of
times the B family has the characteristic in common with some
of these other witnesses, with those differing being noted as
well. The instances in which the καιγε reading is common to
all or is absent from all will be enumerated, as will those in
which the καιγε reading appears apart from the B family.   On
the basis of this data, a conclusion will be drawn regarding
the alignment of the B family in the case of each characteristic. At the close of the chapter, the evidence will be summarized; and a general conclusion will be presented on that
basis.

11.   Cf. DA, pp. 102-9.

12.   DA, pp. 48-54.

13.   This count includes 4:20a, which, although it does
not have the precise force of *each*, but rather of *anyone*, does
reveal the same revision, in this case from τις.

14.   Both L and 𝕃 show 1 omission in addition to these
(L in 7:8 and 𝕃 in 7:7).

15.   2:6 (B alone); 4:20a; 7:21.

16. 7:8 (versus 𝕃, L omits); 8:24 (vs. 𝕃), 25 (vs. 𝕃);
9:49 (with L [conflate]), 55 (vs. 𝕃); 10:18 (vs. 𝕃); 20:8b (vs.
𝕃); 21:21 (vs. L), 22 (vs. L).

17. This is not to say that in these cases there has
been no revision; only that it cannot be proven. The references are 6:29; 7:7, 22; 16:5; 17:6; 20:8a; 21:24a-b, and 25. In
17:6 and 21:25, L is conflate.

18. Cf. note 5.

19. Barthélemy also lists 3:29 as an example of the revision (DA, p. 54, n. 2). It should be noted, however, that in
3:29 only n lacks ανηρ; the other witnesses Barthélemy cites
are conflate. Cf. regarding the characteristic conflation of
the Lucianic text, Bruce M. Metzger, *Chapters in the History of
New Testament Textual Criticism* (Grand Rapids, 1963), p. 25.

20. DA, pp. 54-59.

21. 1:14; 3:19, 20; 8:3; 15:14; 16:12, 19.

22. 13:20. The anomalous ανωθεν of c may be an error,
as may be the reading of Bk. In any case, the B family, apart
from Vaticanus, shares the καιγε reading.

23. 3:21; 4:15; 16:12, 19. In 3:21 and 4:15, K may show a
rather sophisticated type of conflation. In 4:15, 𝕃 seems to
side with the καιγε/MT reading. In 16:20 both καιγε translations appear in the B family, but the family is united in being
καιγε.

24. Cf. Shenkel's comment on this phenomenon in the
καιγε text of 2 Kings (CRDK, p. 15) and Albert Pietersma,
"The Greek Psalter," *VT* 26 (1976), 68.

25. DA, pp. 59-60.

26. 18:16 (A fam., L, K), 17 (A fam., K). These 2 passages are listed by Barthélemy among his positive examples of
καιγε revision and are, thus, potentially misleading (DA, p.
60). The other 3 appearances of the Hebrew root in Judges are
3:22; 9:6; and 20:2. In 9:6, Aquila does have στηλωμα, but he
is not at all consistent in following this proposed characteristic. Elsewhere he renders יצב by παριστημι; נצב by ιστημι,
στερεοω, and στηλοω; נציב by στηλοω and υποστημα; מצב by στασις
and υποστασις; מצבה by στηλωμα; מצבה by στηλη; and מצבה by στη-
λωσις (according to R-T).

27. 2 Sam. 18:17, 18b-e; 2 Kings 3:2; 10:27; 17:10a-b;
18:4; 23:14; Ps. 74:17 (θ´, α´); Ezek. 26:11 (θ´); Hos. 3:4
(οι λ, 𝔰).

28. Cf. note 26. The instances are, in addition to
those already cited, 1 Kings 22:48; Ps. 39:6; and 45:10.

29. Ruth 2:5, 6; 2 Sam. 13:31; 18:13; 21:5; 23:14.

30. Josh. 4:3 (οι λ, 𝕲 [with ⁂]); 1 Sam. 13:3 (ϑ΄);
14:1 (ϑ΄, cf. Field); Ps.̥ 5:6 (ϑ΄, cf. the apparatus of Field);
Nah. 2:8 (R). The purported characteristic could be employed
in these cases, as well as in those referring to people.

31. In Abcj (mg., with ⁂) oxz (mg.) c₂e₂, Thdt.

32. In r.

33. This is especially significant, since it refers to
a person's hand. Cf. DA, pp. 261-65 on the relationship of σ΄
to καιγε in the Minor Prophets. Yet in Lamentations the majority text is supposed to be καιγε. (2 Kings 10:26 was not
mentioned in this group of readings because the καιγε reading
στολη may be an error for στηλη, which appears in many other
minuscules. The reading could stand as it is, however.)

34. DA, pp. 60-63.

35. 3:27; 6:34; 7:8, 16, 18a-b, 19, 20a-b, 22.

36. In all but 3:27 and 6:34. In each case, L is represented by glnw.

37. In all but 7:8. In Codex Lugdunensis (Lug.),
κερατινη is rendered by *tuba cornea* and σαλπιγξ by *tuba*. In
the 𝓛 of Sabatier (Sab.), only 6:34 is preserved. There the
reading is *cornea*.

38. In 𝕲 *qarnâ* represents κερατινη in these cases, for
σαλπιγξ is consistently rendered by *šᵊpûrâ* elsewhere in Judges.

39. DA, pp. 63-65.

40. 1:7. The group efsz does, however, have the same
past tense as the A family, L, 𝕲, and 𝓛.

41. The rarity of the historical present in the OG is
observed by O'Connell for Exodus (TRE, p. 280) and by Greenspoon for Joshua (Leonard Jay Greenspoon, "Studies in the Textual Tradition of the Book of Joshua," Ph.D. dissertation,
Harvard University, 1977, p. 365). The same may be true for
the Minor Prophets (cf. DA, p. 200).

42. DA, pp. 63-65.

43. DA, pp. 65-68.

44. 3:25; 12:3 (only B); 18:7a-b. Barthélemy omits 3:25
and 12:3, perhaps because they are both suffixed forms. Neither did he note that 18:7b shows the verb εχω instead of
ειμι; however, καιγε revision is still likely in this case.

45. 18:28b

46. With K and 𝕲 in 18:28a and 19:15, and with K in
11:34 (and ϑ΄) and 21:9.

47. 7:12.

48. Those instances not yet mentioned are 6:5; 13:9; 14:6; 17:6 (here c has the revision); 18:1; 19:1, 28; 21:25.

49. 1 Kings 22:1; 2 Kings 4:31a-b; Job 32:12 (ϑ´ [with ✶]); Lam. 1:21.

50. Num. 22:26 (h).
Attention might also be called to Genesis 37:29, although a different Hebrew *Vorlage* could be involved in this case. The Greek has the present of οραω. The past of οραω stands in 𝔅 and in the text of 𝔊. The past of ευρισκω appears in several Greek manuscripts, 𝔼, 𝔸, 𝔊 (mg.), some of 𝕃, and Vg.
Barthélemy has pointed out the reading in 1 Kings 3:18 (against boc₂e₂𝔸; cf. DA, p. 66, n. 2).

51. Gen. 45:6; Hos. 5:14; Amos 5:6. In Gen. 45:6 the revision appears in Mfhi^amqrua₂. One is reminded of the primacy of irua₂ in Judges as representative of the καιγε recension, as well as the secondary relation of fmq; and the question is raised as to whether these manuscripts might show this relationship elsewhere than in Judges.

52. Both appearing in ϑ´ with ✶.

53. DA, pp. 69-78.

54. 5:3a; 8:5; 11:27, 35 (apparently ειμη of Bejqrs^a?z is an error for ειμι, which, in any event, is the reading of fimua₂), 37 (B only). A finite verb follows in 11:27, 35, and 37 (prior in position); and a participle in 8:5.

55. 5:3b (with 𝔊 [✶]); 6:15 (with A fam., K, 𝔊), 18 (with all but Mn, ∅^m [Ciasca's edition], 𝕃). A finite verb follows in 5:3b. Although the Hebrew of 16:17 is אני, not אנכי, the latter could have stood in the earlier Hebrew text toward which καιγε revision was made (the "proto-MT"). The καιγε reading appears in all Greek families except Gbcx of the A family and bears the asterisk in 𝔊.

56. 6:8; 17:9a; 19:18. The omission of εγω by Bq in 17:9a may be due to haplography, since both words begin with *epsilon*. It is, in any case, the distinctive word which appears. In 6:8, the omission of ος in iru leaves the full expression followed by a finite verb.

57. 6:37; 7:17, 18; 11:9; 17:9b, 10. In 11:9 Barthélemy suggests that the original Hebrew before eijmqrsuz was גם אני in light of their reading, και γε εγω (DA, p. 70, n. 2).

58. DA, pp. 81-88. In addition to these, one characteristic will be drawn from later in Barthélemy's work, number fourteen below.

59. DA, p. 84.

60. 9:17; 20:34.

61. DA, p. 84, n. 1.

62. 9:39; 16:25; 20:26a-b, 35.

63. 4:15 (vs. L); 8:28 (vs. A, ₡); 13:15 (vs. A); 20:32 (vs. L); 39 (vs. A fam., K).

64. 6:18; 11:9, 11; 20:23 (εναντιον in c), 28, 42; 21:2.

65. 4:23.

66. 2:14; 3:27; 4:14; 18:21.

67. DA, pp. 84-85.

68. 6:22; 15:19; 18:12. The only divergence in the latter 2 is in 15:19, where G reads δια το, likely an error for the common reading, as no substantive follows the article in G.

69. DA, p. 85.

70. 2:1.

71. DA, p. 86.

72. 6:33; 9:6; 11:20; 16:33; 19:15, 18; 20:11; 21:14.

73. 2:10; 10:17. In 2:10 the revision appears in efij mqrsuz, but not in Ba₂. (Also, the reading of i is singular; whereas that of the other is plural.)

74. 3:13.

75. 18:25.

76. 2:10 (with revision); 18:25 (without revision).

77. 3:13.

78. 10:17.

79. DA, p. 184.

80. CRDK, p. 115.

81. 13:10.

82. 9:48 (rendered by ταχεως).

83. 2:17 (מהר = ταχυ), 23 (מהר = το ταχος); 9:54 (מהרה = ταχυ [B fam.], το ταχος [A fam., L, K]).

84. "The Greek Translators"; and SJW, pp. 16-28.

85. CRDK, pp. 117-20.

86. These are presented in tabular form in "The Greek

Translators," p. 268 and in SJW, pp. 114-15.

While Thackeray's first characteristic is not included here, since Hebrew גרול does not appear as a substantive in Judges, the verbal root does. In the first of the 2 occurrences of the verb (11:2), all Greek witnesses employ a form of ηδρυνω (the καιγε root in Samuel-Kings); and in the second (13:24), the B family employs the καιγε root, whereas all other families have a form of αυξανω. This is likely another example of καιγε revision in the B family. This observation was made to the author by Leonard Greenspoon during the course of his work in the Greek text of Joshua for his Harvard dissertation.

87. 2:20.

88. This characteristic does give warning that the presence of a καιγε rendering in all Greek families should not be disregarded as evidence of καιγε revision. It appears that, in many cases, the revision has spread to all of the families and the OG has been lost. This phenomenon will be seen even more clearly in characteristic 22 (cf. also note 4 of this chapter).

89. 3:27; 11:5, 7; 18:10.

90. 11:35; 15:14, 17; 16:22.

91. 3:18.

92. Cf. DA, pp. 31-80 and especially p. 31.

93. Apart from 1 Samuel 1:24 (in Ab[mg.]cx), as Thackeray noted. In βγ and γδ there are a total of 7 instances.

94. According to H-R, the number of instances in the Heptateuch comes to a total of 57.

95. According to H-R, 9 times.

96. According to H-R, 7 times.

97. "Another Criterion for the καιγε Recension," *Biblica* 48 (1967), 443-45.

98. It is the reading of Aquila on 20 occasions, and only on 2 does he translate differently. More significantly, it appears in all 3 instances of the word in γδ as the καιγε rendering (2 Kings 12:3; 17:27, 28), on 2 occasions in the Quinta of Psalms (32:8 and 84:7), in 1 of the 2 preserved renderings of the Minor Prophets fragments (Hab. 2:18-19; the reading φω... appears in vs. 19), and in all of the 5 preserved readings of the sixth column (1 Sam. 12:23; Ps. 27:11; Prov. 5:13; Isa. 2:3; Mic. 3:11).

99. 13:8.

100. The reading is sound. Even the first two correctors of Vaticanus use the same verb, as noted by Smith (p. 445,

n. 3).

101. The only divergences are k with διδασκω and h with φωνεω.

102. Cf. R-T, p. vii, where Turner points out the possibility of later Hexaplaric influence, even in the best manuscripts.

103. In DA, pp. 113-26, Barthélemy discusses this phenomenon in βγ of Samuel-Kings.

104. The peculiarity of the B family of Judges within the καιγε recension as a whole will be the subject of chapter three. It is clearly discernible and makes a proposal such as this quite plausible. In this case confirming evidence may be found in Judges 13:23, where the verb φωτιζω is used by all other Greek families, 𝔖, 𝕃, and ϑ´ to translate the *hiphil* of ראה, but not by the B family.

105. SJW, pp. 34, 56, 69.

106. Cf. DA, pp. 102-10.

107. CRDK, pp. 13-17. Shenkel notes that Rahlfs had already pointed out this characteristic in Kings, but had not related it to recensional development. (The reference is Alfred Rahlfs, *Lucians Rezension der Königsbücher* [Göttingen, 1911], pp. 265-67.

108. 2:11; 3:7, 12a-b; 4:1; 6:1; 10:6; 13:1.

109. 14:3; 17:6.

110. 10:15; 14:7.

111. 6:17 (ενωπιον appears in 𝕃 and n and is conflate with the literal rendering in m); 19:24 (ενωπιον appears in L); 21:25 (Bdkmu have ενωπιον; this reading is interesting, for, whereas the B family as a whole has the καιγε reading, Bu [and m] from the family seem to show a reintroduction, or a preservation, of the OG).

112. CRDK, pp. 17-18.

113. 2:5; 16:23.

114. The respective equivalents in 𝔖 of the two Greek verbs are difficult to discern and may not be distinguished. A preliminary check of readings elsewhere has shown the D form of *dbḥ* (the *pa'el*) to be the normal cquivalent of ϑυσιαζω, but either the G (the *p'al*) or the D of the same verb to render ϑυω. Since the D form occurs in 2:5, where, as will be noted, the real variation occurs, nothing certain can be said about the alignment of 𝔖, although it likely stands with the A family and others against the B family, as is normal in Judges. (More will be said of this in chapter four.)

40

115. W. G. Lambert identifies q and o (in places) as a third cursive group of the B family (in his review of the work of Soisalon-Soininen on Judges in *VT* 2 [1952], p. 188).

116. CRDK, pp. 113-16.

117. Cf. above, p. 21.

118. 4:16, 22; 8:5.

119. 3:28; 7:25. The variation in tense in 3:28 is not significant, although a different verb, καταβαινω, is employed.

120. 7:23; 8:4; 9:40. In 8:4 the revision is from a form of πειναω, and in 9:40 only Bq have the καιγε word.

121. 8:12 (only Mtv have the OG reading); 20:43 (the B family is joined by K and stands against the A family, L, and ⑧ with forms of καταπαυω and adr with the normal OG equivalent).

122. 1:6.

123. The verb *rdap*, which is used in ⑧ for both διωκω and καταδιωκω, likely reflects καταδιωκω here and not κατατρεχω of the other witnesses.

124. 4:2, 7. The single additional occurrence of צבא in Judges (8:6) is rendered everywhere by στρατια/στρατεια, except in the B family. There δυναμις is employed, likely as καιγε revision, although without שר/αρχων. Greenspoon points out that αρχιστρατηγος δυναμεως is also common in OG ("Studies," p. 385).

125. 5:29.

126. The strange variant of q, εσομαι, is without textual significance and may be a corruption of αι σοφαι.

127. In addition to the fact that *sapientia* is singular, in accord with φρονησις rather than αι σοφαι, the greater proximity of Ƶ to the latter set of variants in L is seen in the singular *virtutis* (= ισχυος), the rendering of רחם רחמתים by *matri suae* (= μητρας αυτης), the rendering of צבעים שלל by *vulnerabant digitis* (= ετιτρωσκον δακτυλοις), and the entire remainder of verse thirty.

128. 16:2; 18:19. In 16:2, α´ (παρασιωπαω) and σ´ (ησυχαζω) differ.

129. 18:9.

130. 13:5, 7. Both of these can be taken as participial forms in the Hebrew.

131. 13:3.

132. These 3 instances are 2 Sam. 11:5a-b and 2 Kings 4:17. All of these references for Samuel-Kings may be found in CRDK, p. 116, nn. 14-15.

133. These instances are all in Isaiah (7:14; 33:11; 59:4, 13); and all but the first probably involve revision, though not from συλλαμβανω.

134. Cant. 3:4.

135. Gen. 16:4b, 5, 11; 25:21; 38:18, 24, 25; Exod. 2:2; 21:22; Num. 11:12; Isa. 7:14; 8:3; 26:18; Hos. 14:1; Amos 1:13; Job 15:35; 1 Chron. 7:23.

136. Apart from Judges, out of 33 instances of an imperfect form of הרה, 24 are rendered by a form of συλλαμβανω (Gen. 4:11, 17; 16:4a; 19:36; 21:2; 29:32, 33, 34, 35; 30:5, 7, 17, 19, 23; 38:3, 4; 1 Sam. 1:20; 2:21 [L and Hexaplaric manuscripts]; 2 Sam. 11:5a [L]; 2 Kings 4:17 [L]; Hos. 1:3, 6, 8; Ps. 7:15); 7 by a form of εν γαστρι εχω/λαμβανω (Gen. 25:21; 38:18; Exod. 2:2; 2 Sam. 11:5a; 2 Kings 4:17; Isa. 8:3; 1 Chron. 7:23); and 2 by another word (Isa. 33:11; 1 Chron. 4:17).

137. Since the adjective and the participle cannot always be distinguished on the basis of the consonantal text alone, these forms are always included in the present study if they are rendered by one of the Greek forms in question.

138. Gen. 16:4b, 5, 11; 38:24, 25; Exod. 21:22; Num. 11: 12; Isa. 7:14; 26:18; Hos. 14:1; Amos 1:13; Job 15:35. In 3 instances the verb συλλαμβανω is used (1 Sam. 4:19; 2 Sam. 11: 5b [L]; Ps. 7:15), and in 5 another word is employed (Isa. 26: 17; 59:4, 13; Jer. 3:18; Job 3:3).

139. Cf. chapter three for a development of the distinctive nature of the B family in Judges within the καιγε recension as a whole. Barthélemy has suggested that in be₂ in Chronicles there is καιγε intrusion (DA, p. 42). If this should be correct, and if the reading of bye₂ in 1 Chron. 7:23 should be such an instance (συνελαβε, in contrast to ελαβεν εν γαστρι), this would be a usage similar to Canticles 3:4. John A. Grindel, however, proposes that these manuscripts represent a later recension of Chronicles (and Ezra B´) on a Hexaplaric basis ("Another Characteristic of the kaige Recension: נצה/ νικος," *CBQ* 31 [1969], 508, 513).

140. Ibid., pp. 499-513.

141. TRE, pp. 286-91. His list of suggested characteristics comes to 36 in all; only those whose Hebrew equivalents appear in Judges will be considered in this study.

142. Ibid., pp. 5, 9-109, and especially 274-85.

143. O'Connell suggests three steps as a methodology for identifying καιγε revision in the Greek text. They call for the demonstration in the material in question of (1) its intermediary position between the OG and Aquila, (2) its tendency to revise the OG toward the Hebrew text (whether MT or proto-MT),

and (3) its sharing of known καιγε stylistic or translational characteristics (ibid., p. 291). It appears to the present writer that the second half of the third of these is the most objective, especially now that so many translational character- istics have been isolated and made known through publication.

Although the others are useful and observations will be made about the B family of Judges along these lines whenever appropriate, they are subject to complicating factors. Aquila does not always follow the recension. Sometimes he carries it further, but sometimes he goes his own way (DA, pp. 81-88). Whereas the καιγε revision was toward the developing MT, this movement from the OG is not always easy to trace. The OG may be difficult to discern, or later Hexaplaric influence may obscure the situation. Therefore, the positive identification of the B family in Judges as καιγε is carried out in this chapter on the basis of criteria already established in other καιγε material.

144. 4:5a-b, 17a-b; 5:11, 16, 27a; 9:23a-b; 11:10, 27a-b; 13:25a-b; 15:4; 16:25, 31a-b.

145. 5:27b. The A family is represented by Abcx. The reading of A and $ most likely represents an insertion of Ori- gen from Aquila (R-T, p. 156; Peter Katz, "Ein Aquila-Index in Vorbereitung: Prolegomena and Specimina I," *VT* 8 [1958], 267).

146. 1:29, 30, 32, 33; 3:5; 18:20.

147. 18:7.

148. He observes that Aquila employs the equivalent 12 times according to R-T.

149. 3:12; 16:28.

150. 9:24. Ł (Lug.) appears to have this reading as well, for there is a change from the verb employed in 3:12 for ενισχυω *(conforto)* to a form of *corroboro*. (In 16:28, Ł omits.)

151. 7:14, 20; 8:10; 20:2, 15, 17, 25, 35, 37, 46; 21:10.

152. 3:16, 21, 22. It is possible that καιγε revision to ρομφαια could have been avoided in these three cases, since they all have to do with a short sword (cf. 3:16).

153. 1:8, 25; 4:15, 16; 18:27; 20:48.

154. 7:22; 8:20; 9:54. In 9:54, K translates with the B family.

In these 3 instances, at least, it appears that the OG has been preserved. Ł is not useful in confirming the OG in this characteristic, since a form of *gladius* is used in all 18 of the surviving instances. The consistency of d and n in em- ploying a form of μαχαιρα should be noted (1:8, 25; 3:16, 21, 22; 4:16; 7:22; 8:20; 9:54 [not d]; 18:27 [only d]; 20:48 [only d]). Cf. on the fundamental importance of n for the Lucianic tradition throughout the Octateuch, Raymond Thornhill, "Six or Seven Nations: a Pointer to the Lucianic Text in the Heptateuch,

with Special Reference to the Old Latin Version," *JTS* 10 (1959),
233-46. However, cf. now, in contrast, THGG, pp. 158-75.

155. The 𝔊 equivalent of ρομφαια seems most likely to be
saypâ and that of μαχαιρα *sakînâ*. In 7:22; 8:20; and 9:54, the
reading of 𝔊 is *saypâ*. Why Rørdam departed from this clear
pattern only in these 3 instances is left unexplained in his
edition of the 𝔊 of Judges and its retranslation into Greek (cf.
T. Skat Rørdam, *Libri Judicum et Ruth secundum versionem Syriaco-
Hexaplarem* [Havinae, 1861]). Readings such as these, in which
𝔊 departs from its normal agreement with the other groups and
sides with the B family, will be discussed in chapter four.

156. 15:6; 19:5.

157. In the case of 𝔊, the situation is somewhat difficult to determine. From a study of the equivalents in 𝔊 in all
of the Old Testament, they seem to be *ḥatnâ* for both νυμφιος
and γαμβρος and *ḥmâ* for both πενθερος (?) and γαμβρος. If this
is accurate, 𝔊 in these 2 cases could side with either variant
tradition. In light of its general alignment with the A family,
it could be presumed to agree here also. Yet the rendering in
𝔊 of the Greek translations of חתן, especially in chapter nineteen, may suggest the opposite. In each case, *ḥmâ* is employed,
once for either γαμβρος or πενθερος (1:16) and otherwise clearly for γαμβρος (4:11; 19:4, 7, 9). In light of these clear
instances in 19:4, 7, and 9, the use of *ḥatnâ* in 19:5 would
probably represents νυμφιος of the B family and K, and not
γαμβρος of the A family and L. The same equivalence would seem
to stand, therefore, in 15:6 as well; and the agreement of 𝔊
would be with the B family throughout this characteristic.

158. 1:16; 4:11; 19:4, 7, 9.

159. In 1:16 the A family, L, and K have πενθερος. This
is a more precise rendering and may represent a later revision.
The same noun is employed for חתן throughout its usage elsewhere in the Old Testament by the group of manuscripts Fᵇ ᵐᵍdl
pᵇwᵇ. The references are: Exod. 3:1; 4:18; 18:1, 2, 5, 6, 7,
8, 12a-b, 14, 15, 17, 24, 27; Num. 10:29. In 3 of the other
references in Judges, it appears in some Lucianic witnesses
(19:4 [ow], 7 [lnow], 9 [lnw]).
𝔏 appears to follow MT in its rendering of both of these
Hebrew nouns in Judges, though in the case of חתן it is only in
chapter nineteen that a consistent equivalence is established
(for חתן: *gener* [15:6; 19:5] and for חתן: *gener* [1:16 - anoma-
lously], *cognatio* [4:11], *socer* [19:4, 9; in 19:7 𝔏 omits]).

160. Aquila's readings are preserved for Exod. 4:25, 26;
1 Sam. 22:14; and Isa. 61:10. His revision is in 1 Sam. 22:14.

161. Cf. DA, pp. 261-65 for such an understanding of σ´
in the Minor Prophets. The references are Exod. 4:25, 26;
1 Sam. 22:14; Ps. 19:6; Isa. 61:10.

162. 2 Sam. 10:19; 16:19a-b; 22:44.

163. 2 Sam. 15:8.

44

164. 1 Kings 22:54; 2 Kings 10:18a-b, 19a-b, 21, 22, 23a-b; 17:41; 18:7; 21:3; 25:24.

165. 2 Kings 17:12, 16, 33, 35; 21:21a-b.

166. 2 Kings 21:21a-b.

167. Job 21:15.

168. Jer. 25:14; 27:7a-b, 8, 12, 13, 17; 34:10.

169. Jer. 44:3. One usage of the *hiphil* shows an asterisked addition, but it is the verb αναβιβαζω (Jer. 17:4).

170. 2:11, 13, 19; 3:6, 7.

171. 2:7; 3:8, 14; 9:28a, 28c, 38; 10:6b.

172. 9:28b.

173. The references are: 10:6a, 10, 13, 16. In 10:13, K joins the B family. In 𝔊 the equivalent of λατρευω is *plaḥ*, and that of δουλευω is *plaḥ ʿabdûtâ*.

174. This pattern holds in 2:11, 13, 19; 3:6, 7 (all λατρευω) and in 3:8, 14; 9:28a-c, 38 (all δουλευω). It does not hold in 2:7 and 10:6b.

175. Cf. DA, p. 31 and CRDK, p. 12.

176. 2:8; 6:8, 27; 15:18.

177. 3:24.

178. The reference is 19:19. It appears that 𝔊 employs ʿabdâ as the equivalent of both δουλος (as in 2:8) and παις (as in 3:24). If so, it cannot be said assuredly, from this word alone, what 𝔊 is reading in 19:19.

179. This question will be dealt with in detail in chapter four. In this case, it is unfortunate that there is an omission in 𝕃, for in the other uses of noun forms of the root עבד, 𝕃 follows the Greek (*puer* in 3:24, but forms of the root *serv-* otherwise).

180. It appears that some such recension as that attributed by Jerome to Hesychius must be reckoned with. (Cf. Sidney Jellicoe, "The Hesychian Recension Reconsidered," *JBL* 82 [1963], 409-18 and Alberto Vaccari, "The Hesychian Recension of the Septuagint," *Biblica* 46 [1965], 60-66.) On the relationship of Vaticanus to Hesychius, cf. Jellicoe, *The Septuagint and Modern Study* (Oxford, 1968), pp. 146-56.

181. Of the group identified by Barthélemy as the most consistent representative of the καιγε recension, irua₂, a₂ most often goes its own way. Cf., for example, from the characteristics discussed in this chapter, 1--8:22a; 9:49b; 2--4:20; 7:21; 9:55; 3--3:21; 4--9:6 (γη); 5--7:18b; etc.

182. All of those characteristics which pertain only to Judges, or which have particular outworkings in Judges unrelated to καιγε material elsewhere, have been deferred until chapter three.

183. What was said earlier (cf. p. 13) should be repeated here. What is sought in the following classification is not total consistency. The presence or lack of this has been observed in the treatment of each separate characteristic. What is now sought, rather, is relationship. For example, with respect to both characteristics 1 and 2, the B family will be classified as καιγε because in both it clearly reflects that recension, although the consistency is total only in 2. Total consistency is not required in order to discern the presence or absence of a known recension in a manuscript or group for a given body of text.

184. The numbers of these characteristics are as follows: 1, 2, 3, 5, 8, 10, 13, 18, 19, 20, 22, 26, 27, 28, 29, and 30. Those resting on a base of only 1 or 2 instances are: 22, 26, 27 (all 1) and 29 (2).

185. 4, 6, 17, 24.

186. 4, 24.

187. 4 appears in 2 instances.

188. In characteristic 7, 5 instances are positive; and 5 are negative.

189. 9, 11, 12, 14, 15, 21, 23, 25.

190. 16.

191. Cf. pp. 16 and 20.

CHAPTER II

NEW KAIΓE CHARACTERISTICS FROM THE VATICANUS
FAMILY OF JUDGES

In the previous chapter, the Vaticanus family of Judges
was analyzed on the basis of the already established characteristics of the καιγε recension. Measured by these, this family
clearly stands as a member of the larger recension. If this
conclusion is accurate, new characteristics discovered in the
B family of Judges may be present in the καιγε material elsewhere as well. Such has proven to be true in several cases;
and this, in turn, adds confirmation to the conclusion that the
B family is καιγε in nature.

Not all characteristics of this family in Judges, however,
have been found to mark the rest of the καιγε recension. There
are traits of the καιγε text of Judges which are distinctive
within the larger recension. Therefore, instead of merely listing all characteristics discovered as new καιγε characteristics,
an effort will be made to distinguish those which are καιγε in
a broad sense from those which merely appear in the καιγε text
of Judges. The former will constitute the present chapter,
and the latter the following.[1]

The characteristics in this chapter and the following are
not presented as an exhaustive list from the text of Judges.
They will, in the case of this chapter, expand the present description of the καιγε recension and, in the case of chapter
three, present at least a partial description of the distinctive traits of the καιγε text of Judges within the entire
recension. Both sets of characteristics, but especially those
of this chapter, should be useful in the search for further
surviving parts of this early recension of the Greek Old Testament.

The characteristics described here will be presented in
alphabetical order, according to the Hebrew term(s) involved,
rather than necessarily in the order of their clarity and
consistency.[2]

48

1. גלה (and cognates)[3] = αποικιζω (and cognates)[4]

The discovery of this reading began with a single reference in Judges. There the B family shows a form of the noun
αποικια,[5] whereas the other groups show a form of μετοικεσια.[6]
The meaning of the Hebrew root in question is, therefore, that
of going into exile.

There is in the Minor Prophets as well only 1 reference
which is preserved in the καιγε fragments published by Barthélemy and labeled by him as R. In this reference, however,
the situation is the same as in Judges: the OG has a form of
μετοικεσια; but the R scroll has a form of αποικια (or αποικεσια; only the first four letters are preserved).[7]

In γδ the evidence is much more extensive. Out of a total of 18 references, a form of the verb αποικιζω, or a cognate
noun, appears 14 times.[8] In Jeremiah there is likewise a broad
base. Among a total of 12 Greek additions, all show the expected reading.[9]

This evidence seems to establish the equivalence of cognates as a genuine καιγε characteristic. The 2 readings of
Lamentations are mixed, 1 having the verb αποικιζω[10] and 1
μετοικιζω.[11] The 1 reference in βγ is negative, having a form
of μετοικεω.[12] These exceptions, however, do not change the
conclusion.

The group of cognates employed in the καιγε recension to
render the Hebrew verb גלה and its cognates is also the most
frequent rendering in the OG, appearing 41 times according to
H-R.[13] The verb μετοικιζω and its cognates, however, are frequent as well, appearing 13 times. Thus, as often in the
καιγε revision, a common OG rendering has been selected as the
preferred translation.

2. טוב (all forms of the root) = αγαθος (and cognates)

Again in the case of this reading, that which is being
proposed as a καιγε characteristic represents the most frequent
of the OG translations of the Hebrew root in question.[14] Nevertheless, a true characteristic does appear, for in many of the
instances revision from a different OG rendering is present.

This is clear in the Greek text of Judges. Here, out of
a total of 11 instances of the Hebrew noun/adjective, 9 of

these appear in the B family with the proposed characteristic. In 5 cases the characteristic is seen only in the B family,[15] in 1 in agreement with some other groups,[16] and in 3 with no variation.[17] In only 2 cases does the B family have a different reading. In the first of these, the characteristic does not appear at all;[18] and in the second, some of those manuscripts listed as the leading καιγε representatives by Barthélemy have the expected reading.[19]

In βγ the Hebrew word occurs 20 times. Of these, 17 have the expected translation; and 6 stand against a different rendering in L.[20] In γδ there are 16 occurrences of the Hebrew word; and 12 of these have the expected reading, though without certain revision.[21]

Of the 5 asterisked additions to Jeremiah, all show the same expected reading.[22] Although Aquila is not always consistent in his translation of this Hebrew root, in Jeremiah he does revise 5 times from another Greek word to a form of αγα-θος.[23]

In the Minor Prophets fragments from Naḥal Ḥeber, the 1 preserved reading has the expected translation; and it is in contrast to a form of καλος in the OG.[24] The 1 instance in which the Coptic versions are quoted by Ziegler shows the same revision.[25]

Of the 4 preserved readings of the Quinta of Psalms, all show the expected revision.[26] There are 15 preserved readings of Aquila in the Psalms, and in all of them he employs either αγαθος or αγαθοσυνη (on 5 occasions). In 11 cases revision is made from a different OG reading, and in 1 an OG omission is filled in.[27] There are 8 preserved instances of a Theodotionic reading, and 7 of them involve revision to the καιγε word.[28]

The 3 instances of the Hebrew word in Ruth are all rendered by the expected Greek adjective.[29] Of the 7 instances in Lamentations, 6 show the same word.[30]

From the foregoing collection of evidence it seems to be assured that a genuine καιγε revision is in view in this rendering. At first glance, the rendering might seem to be unlikely territory for discovering a revision, since the Hebrew word is so common and the Greek equivalent is the most frequent rendering.[31] Yet in a large number of the uses of the Greek word in

question, it stands against another term in the OG, apparently
as a revision. Thus, the most frequent OG equivalent has been
made even more consistent by καιγε revision. The frequency of
the Hebrew term then becomes an advantage, for it increases
the likelihood of its occurrence in material for which καιγε
revision is yet to be discovered.

The evidence of Job, Canticles, and Daniel is less clear,
but is thin in each case and does not diminish the force of the
conclusion already drawn. In Job, 2 Theodotionic additions are
positive;[32] and 1 is negative.[33] One of the 2 instances in
Canticles has the expected word,[34] and the other may be an am-
plified rendering.[35] Of the 2 instances in Daniel, 1 has the
expected rendering (in contrast to the OG);[36] and the other has
a revision, yet not to the καιγε term.[37]

It should be said that some of the many instances cited
above in which a καιγε text has a form of αγαθος and in which
another text has another word might call for a different, or
at least a more complicated, explanation than simply that of
καιγε revision from an OG reading. For example, S. P. Brock
has called attention to those instances in 1 Samuel in which
the Hebrew טוב, followed by בעיני, is rendered in the majority
text by a form of αγαθος, but in the L text by a form of αρεστος. He concludes that the revision in these cases is on the
part of L and that the same is true in 2 Samuel 19:39.[38]

This analysis may be correct, and if so it would account
for 2 Samuel 24:22 as well.[39] A reason for the revision could
even be apparent in the modification of the word in each case
by a form of the preposition בעיני with a suffix. Later Lucianic revision may have shown a preference for this Greek term
in expressing more precisely the idea of approval.

However, upon closer examination, this explanation seems
less than certain. For one thing, the supposed Lucianic revision is complete neither in 1 Samuel nor in βγ.[40] This would
not be conclusive, for, as has been observed already (cf. note
2 of the present chapter), full consistency is not always present in genuine revision.

More significant in opposition to the use of αρεστος by L
being a revision is the use of αγαθος in 1 Samuel. Out of a
total of 37 occurrences of the Hebrew word טוב in the MT, all

37 are rendered by a form of αγαθος in the majority Greek text, except for 1, which has the adverb αγαθως.[41] This kind of consistency is present nowhere else in the majority text translation of טוב in sections examined by the writer. These sections include γδ, Job, Psalms, Jeremiah, Lamentations, Daniel, and the Minor Prophets. The only exception has been the 3 references in Ruth (where the majority text is καιγε). Although αγαθος is the word employed most frequently by the OG, it is not normally employed in this exclusive fashion. It is possible that some kind of reworking has gone on in 1 Samuel to bring about such complete consistency and that these instances of αρεστος in the L text of 1 Samuel (and of βγ, vis-à-vis the καιγε text with αγαθος) do represent the OG after all. This must at least be considered a viable alternative explanation in light of the high degree of consistency in the OG of 1 Samuel.

Even if Brock's proposal were correct, however, it would primarily affect only the references in 1 Samuel.[42] Nor is an explanation of this sort likely in most of the instances in which a καιγε text has a form of αγαθος in opposition to a variety of other words, often in the majority text. The pattern is so clear that it seems to sustain only one explanation: that of καιγε revision from a varied OG rendering to a form of αγαθος as the translation of the Hebrew noun/adjective טוב.

Of the 32 instances of the Hebrew noun טוב, only 1 has clear significance for the present argument. The single Quinta reading in the Psalms confirms the characteristic being discussed, for it shows revision to a form of αγαθος from an OG rendering by a form of χρηστοτης.[43]

There is stronger confirmation of the characteristic in the rendering of the verb טוב, for out of 20 instances, 6 show the καιγε material with a form or a cognate of αγαθος in contrast to another reading in the OG. In 2 cases, the sixth column has the word αγαθος, in the first in contrast to a different OG rendering[44] and in the second against an OG omission.[45] In 1 of the 2 references in Judges, the B family has a form of αγαθος in contrast to a form of κρεισσων in all other Greek families, 𝕾, and 𝕷.[46] In the 3 references in βγ, the καιγε text has the expected rendering, in each case in contrast to a different translation in L.[47] In 2 of the remaining 3 renderings of the word in καιγε material, the expected root occurs, though without variation elsewhere;[48] and the other reference must be considered neutral evidence, due to omission.[49]

3. ישר (all forms of the root) = ευθυς (and cognates)

Here again the Greek translation which emerges as a καιγε characteristic represents the most frequent of the OG renderings.[50] It has simply been made more consistent by the καιγε recension.

In Judges there are 4 instances of the Hebrew root. All are rendered in the B family by a form of ευθυς or a cognate; and 3 of these stand against another selection, 2 on the part of all other groups and 1 on the part of L.[51]

In βγ there are 2 instances, and in both of these the καιγε text has the expected form in contrast to L.[52] The evidence of γδ is more extensive. There are 11 cases of the Hebrew root; and each has the expected form in the καιγε text, although no revision is certain.[53]

Revision to the expected word can also been seen in the 1 addition to Jeremiah,[54] in the 1 preserved translation in the R scroll of the Minor Prophets,[55] and in the 1 instance in the θ´ text of Daniel.[56]

Apart from Judges, the Theodotion column has the expected word or a cognate 19 of 20 times, 14 of them representing revision, or the filling in of an omission.[57]

The preserved readings of Aquila show 18 out of 19 with the expected reading, and 14 of them represent revision from the OG.[58]

The consistency in καιγε texts, especially when different from the OG, and the confirmatory evidence of θ´ and α´ indicate that καιγε revision has been in operation in these instances, giving greater consistency to the OG reading which was already the most common. No contrary evidence has appeared in this case.

4. לין = αυλιζω

There are 13 occurrences of this Hebrew verb in Judges.

Of these the B family alone translates by a form of the Greek
verb αυλιζω 6 times;[59] and the B family and others against L 2
times[60] and against L, the A family, and ℘ 1 time.[61] In 3 instances all groups have the expected reading;[62] and 1 case is
unclear, due to omission in the B family and K.[63]

The occurrences of the Hebrew verb in question in sections for which καιγε material has been identified are somewhat
limited outside of Judges, but they are sufficient to test the
characteristic, and they yield adequate confirmation. In 3 of
the 4 instances in βγ, the expected equivalent occurs; and in 2
of these it stands against a different rendering in L.[64] The
single θ´ addition to Job has the characteristic.[65] The 3 instances in Ruth are likewise consistent,[66] as are the 2 in
Canticles.[67]

Of the 6 instances of a preserved translation in Aquila,
5 show the expected verb; and 4 of these are in contrast to the
OG.[68]

The evidence of Theodotion, apart from Judges, is similar,
but not thoroughly consistent. Of the 3 cases in which readings are preserved, 1 is a revision to the καιγε word;[69] and 1
is a filling in of an OG omission with the καιγε word;[70] but 1
retains another OG translation (which was later revised by
Aquila).[71]

Secondary confirmation of this characteristic might be
seen in the consistency of the 3 instances in Nehemiah.[72] No
contrary evidence has appeared,[73] apart from the single instances in Aquila and Theodotion.

5. נצל = ρυομαι

In Judges this equivalence is clearly characteristic of
the B family, but not of the other groups. Out of a total of
6 instances, the B family has the equivalent 5 times. In 2
cases the revision is exclusive of other groups;[74] in 2 it is
shared;[75] and in 1 no variation appears.[76] In the final instance, the revision does not appear at all.[77]

The evidence is not consistent in the rest of the καιγε
material; but because of the positive evidence of βγ, Jeremiah,
and Aquila, the characteristic appears to hold more broadly
than merely in the B family of Judges.

In βγ out of a total of 9 occurrences of the Hebrew verb, the expected Greek verb appears 5 times. It is significant that each of these cases is in contrast to L.[78] The single addition in Jeremiah is attributed to ϑ´, α´, and σ´ and is a form of ρυομαι.[79] Of the 18 preserved readings of Aquila, 15 have the expected reading; and 12 of these stand in contrast to the OG, in 9 cases revising from a different OG reading[80] and in 3 filling in an OG omission.[81]

Unclear evidence stands in γδ and the Psalms. In the former, out of a total of 13 instances, the expected form appears only 4 times, though 1 of these does differ from that of L.[82] In the Psalms, only 1 instance of a Quinta reading is preserved. This agrees with Symmachus in using a form of εξαιρεω, a different form of which also stands in the OG, although Aquila, as has been mentioned, revises here to a form of ρυομαι.[83]

The evidence of Daniel is contrary. In the 2 instances of the Hebrew verb, the expected Greek equivalent occurs both times; but these are in the OG translation, the ϑ´ (καιγε) version having a form of εξαιρεω.[84]

The verb ρυομαι and the verb εξαιρεω are of virtually equal frequency in the OG translation of this Hebrew verb. The former occurs some 75 times, and the latter some 72 according to H-R. Although not with consistency, it seems that the former of these was employed as the καιγε rendering at least in the revision of Judges, βγ, and Jeremiah and in the work of Aquila. Its usage in γδ is inconsistent; in the καιγε revision of the Psalms, it is unattested; and in the ϑ´ version of Daniel, it was not present at all. It seems to be a καιγε characteristic beyond the text of Judges, but not throughout the recension.

6. שוב = επιστρεφω

Out of a total of 20 occurrences of the *qal* forms of this verb in Judges,[85] the B family shows the above rendering 14 times. In 9 of these cases, the translation is exclusively that of the B family;[86] in 1 it is shared with K;[87] and in 4 there is no variation in word choice.[88] In 2 instances the expected verb does not appear at all;[89] in 1 the situation is

unclear;[90] and in 3 the proposed καιγε rendering appears elsewhere, but not in the B family.[91]

The evidence of βγ and of γδ is positive also. In the
former there is a total of 19 instances of the Hebrew verb.
Of these, 11 show the expected translation; and 8 stand in
contrast to L.[92] In the latter there are a total of 44 instances. Of these, 29 show the expected rendering; and 6 of
these are in contrast to L.[93]

The occurrences of a translation of the Hebrew verb in
question in the καιγε fragments of the Minor Prophets are not
so extensive, but they are significant. There are 5 cases, and
2 of these have the expected verb in contrast to the OG, the
first filling in an omission[94] and the second revising
from a form of αποστρεφω.[95] The other 2 instances in the same
immediate context must be considered uncertain, since the stra-
tegic first part of each has not survived. Yet they can most
plausibly be restored as forms of επιστρεφω as well, as Barthélemy does, and would, in that case, also constitute καιγε
revision.[96] The final case is unclear as well; Barthélemy's
restoration to a form of συστρεφω is apparently based on the
OG.[97]

In Ruth, out of a total of 13 instances, the expected
verb occurs 8 times.[98] In Canticles all 4 instances have the
expected form (although they all occur in the same verse).[99]
In Lamentations, out of a total of 4, 3 have the expected
verb.[100] In Jeremiah, the 1 anonymous addition has the verb,[101]
as do 4 of the 5 θ´ additions.[102]

The evidence of Job and Daniel should be classified as
mixed. In Job there are 2 Theodotionic additions, 1 with the
expected verb,[103] and 1 with another.[104] In Daniel, 8 of the
11 instances show the expected verb in the θ´ version; and 7
in the OG version. However, whereas 2 of the θ´ cases are
supplying for an OG omission,[105] 1 in the OG stands against a
different verb in θ´.[106] The former of the OG omissions could
plausibly be supplied with a different verb in light of those
in Daniel 9:13 and 16, but the latter must surely be supplied
with a form of επιστρεφω in light of the immediate proximity
of this word both preceding and following (if some sort of haplography is assumed). In any case, the evidence of Daniel is

mixed.

The 4 readings of ϑ´ in the Psalms only produce 1 positive instance, and that is in agreement with the OG.[107] The
other 3 are negative and in each case are in contrast to a form
of επιστρεφω in the OG.[108] The only preserved Quinta reading
in the Psalms is identical with the single positive ϑ´ reference just cited.[109]

However, in spite of the mixed or ambiguous evidence of
Job and Daniel, and the apparently negative evidence of the
Psalms, the firm evidence of Judges, βγ, γδ, and R and the positive evidence of Ruth, Canticles, Lamentations, and Jeremiah
seem to establish επιστρεφω as the rendering of שוב employed
deliberately in at least a large part of the καιγε recension.[110]

1. It should be noted that characteristics 5 and 6 of the present chapter and 7, 8, and 11 of chapter three have already been pointed out for the text of Judges by Soisalon-Soininen (cf. pp. 66-68). He did not, of course, test them for the rest of the καιγε recension, since Barthélemy's work had not yet been published.

2. It must be emphasized again that absolute consistency is not a prerequisite for the recognition of a genuinely characteristic reading. What is required, rather, is sufficient consistency to indicate a trend. (If a reason can be ascertained for the revision, so much the better.) Very few of the characteristics described in chapter one showed full consistency. The nature of the Greek Old Testament is such as to make such consistency, in fact, an elusive thing. The backward influence of later revision, the mixing and exchanging of textual traditions, the inconsistency of scribes, and other factors make it unprofitable to impose on a text the requirement of such consistency. Cf. notes 24 and 183 of chapter one.

3. גלות גלה, גלה.

4. αποικεω, αποικεσια, αποικια, αποικισμος.

5. Or αποικεσια (efqsz).

6. 18:30. The Lucianic subgroup dptv has a form of μετοικια.

7. Nah. 3:10.

8. 2 Kings 15:29; 16:9; 17:6, 11, 23, 26, 28, 33; 18:11; 24:14a, 15a-b; 25:21, 27. The references with other readings are 2 Kings 17:27; 24:14b, 16; and 25:11. Among the former, there is revision to αποικιζω from μετοικιζω of the L text in 24:15a, omission in the L text in 24:16, and a form of μετοικεσια in A alone in 25:27. (Variation likewise occurs in 25:11, but without the expected verb in the καιγε text, and in 24:15b, but without significance [L has απωκισμω, in contrast to αποικεσιαν of the καιγε text].)

9. Jer. 27:20; 28:4; 29:1, 14, 16, 20, 31; 39:9; 40:1; 52:27, 28, 30. All of these additions are θ´ except 28:4, which is anonymous, and 40:1, which is α´. Aquila likewise has 29:1 and 31.

Whereas Barthélemy's delineation of the members of the καιγε recension has been followed in the present study (cf. DA, p. 47), the sixth column has been consistently checked only for the texts of Daniel and the additions to Job and Jeremiah (the anonymous additions to which Barthélemy identifies in particular as καιγε). Although the sixth column in general is postu-

lated as being καιγε in nature (apart from βγ and the Minor
Prophets scroll, cf. DA, p. 47, n. 1), detailed study is needed
to bear this out for each section of the Old Testament (such as
has been carried out by Kevin G. O'Connell for the book of
Exodus [TRE]). This will be discussed further in chapter four.

    10. Lam. 4:22.

    11. Lam. 1:3.

    12. 2 Sam. 15:19.

    13. Actually 21 of these instances are found in Chroni-
cles (2), Ezra B´ (17), and Nehemiah (2); whereas μετοικιζω
and its cognates do not appear at all in Ezra B´ and Nehemiah,
although they do in Chronicles (5). Generally in the tabula-
tions of OG statistics for this study, Chronicles and Ezra B´
have not been distinguished from the rest of the non-καιγε
material; nor have they seemed to show a significant difference. There is, however, evidence that the Greek text of the
Chronicler does diverge from the OG (as seen in Ezra A´) and
represents, rather, local development in Palestine (Ralph
Walter Klein, "Studies in the Greek Texts of the Chronicler,"
Th.D. dissertation, Harvard University, 1966). If these statistics were removed from the total count for OG usage, it
would stand at 20; and the comparison with the most frequent
alternate group of cognates would be much closer. (Cf. also
note 139 of chapter one and the references given there).

    14. In the treatment of this characteristic, the dis-
tinction between the Hebrew noun/adjective and the Hebrew verb
of the same spelling generally follows the concordance of
Lisowsky. The present discussion will deal with the noun/
adjective, the cognate noun טוב, and the verb in that order.

    15. 9:2, 16; 10:15; 15:2 (in the comparative degree);
18:19. In 9:16, there was, apparently, an omission in the OG
(preserved in L and Ł); Ƨ, the A family, and K have restored
the text with καθως, which makes good sense in the verse, and
could represent an error for טובה = καλως.

    16. 19:24. Ł (with a form of placeo) is in agreement
with the reading of L in this case (αρεσκη), confirming it as
the OG rendering (cf. Ł in 10:15, where it has a form of placeo
also).

    17. 8:35; 9:11; 18:9. In 8:35, καιγε revision may be
present; but the alternate reading is the cognate noun αγαθω-
συνη.

    18. 8:2. The only variation here is in the spelling of
the adjective.

    19. 8:32. In this case, the translation of the entire
Hebrew phrase בשיבה טובה must be considered. It is rendered
correctly by all groups but the B family as εν πολια αγαθη.
(According to H-P and Field, only Alexandrinus itself has
πολεια.) The B family has, rather, εν πολει αυτου. From the

family, however, ir have πολια with the other groups; and irua₂ have αγαθη.

This variation could represent simply inner-Greek corruption. In the case of πολια/πολει, the loss of only one letter would be involved; and that would have been facilitated by the fact that the next word (whether αγαθη or αυτου) began with the same letter, thus producing haplography. (The confusion of *iota* and ει was a common mistake, cf. Peter Walters [Katz], *The Text of the Septuagint: Its Corruptions and Their Emendation*, D. W. Gooding, ed.[Cambridge, 1973], pp. 29-58.) In the case of αγαθη/ αυτου, the change is not, however, so easy to explain.

There is, moreover, evidence to suggest that a different Hebrew *Vorlage* may have lain behind the variant. In the text of Pseudo-Philo, both readings are represented (see Daniel Joseph Harrington, "Text and Biblical Text in Pseudo-Philo's *Liber Antiquitatum Biblicarum*," Th.D. dissertation, Harvard University, 1969, pp. 135-36). Whereas the counterpart of εν πολει αυτου, *in civitate sua*, stands after the following verb, it has no justification at that point in the present Hebrew text or in any Greek manuscript cited by B-M or H-P. Assuming this to have been an earlier form of the verse, the B family reading could have come about through the haplography of πολια/ πολει, with the intervening verb being restored later. This would still, in effect, represent inner-Greek corruption in the B family, although the variant preserved there would represent an earlier Hebrew reading.

Confirmation that this Pseudo-Philo reading represents an earlier Hebrew form of the text may exist in Josephus, who has the phrase τη πατριδι at the same location as *in civitate sua*. This would be to assume that the reading of Josephus is his way of expressing בעירו/εν πολει αυτου. It could, however, be his way of expressing the phrase בקרב יואש אביו/εν τω ταφω Ιωας του πατρος αυτου, which would not otherwise appear in his text.

Whatever the correct explanation of this variant may be, it does not alter the conclusion regarding the translation generally of the noun/adjective טוב by the B family of Judges. It is by a form of αγαθος or a cognate.

20.   The 6 references are 2 Sam. 14:17, 32; 15:3; 18:3; 19:39; and 24:22. The others are 2 Sam. 10:12; 13:22; 16:12; 17:7, 14a-b; 18:27a-b; 19:28, 36; and 1 Kings 1:42. The 3 references with another reading are 2 Sam. 11:2; 19:19; and 1 Kings 1:6.

21.   2 Kings 2:19; 3:19a-b, 25a-b; 5:12; 10:3, 5; 20:3, 13, 19; 25:28. The references with another reading are 1 Kings 22:8 (where L has αγαθα), 13a-b, and 18. It may be significant that they are all in the same chapter.

22.   Jer. 15:11 (α´, σ´); 22:16 (θ´); 29:10; 33:14 (θ´); 40:4b. In 22:15 Field is apparently wrong in listing an omission for the OG, for the reading is βελτιον, though out of order. On the contrary, there is omission in the OG of verse 16; and in his apparatus Field does give the asterisked addition of Codex 88, although he does not, as Ziegler, list the attribution to α´ and θ´.

23.   Jer. 12:6; 22:15; 26:14; 33:11; 40;4a. An exception

may be Jeremiah 32:39, but the Hexaplaric apparatus in Ziegler questions this.

24. Zech. 1:13. Though this is the only word preserved in the verse, the revision is virtually certain, for there is no other word in the Hebrew or OG of the verse for which αγα-[θα] could stand.

25. Mic. 3:2. Barthélemy identifies the Coptic versions, especially the Achmimic and the Sahidic, as being primarily influenced by the καιγε text in the Minor Prophets (DA, pp. 228-34). It is noteworthy that the one secondary translation which comports with the B family in Judges is the Sahidic (cf. Moore, *Judges*, p. xlvi and Soisalon-Soininen, p. 20-21).

26. Ps. 23:6; 25:8; 38:21b; 119:65. In Psalm 38:21b the revision is from δικαιοσυνη to αγαθοσυνη. There is some question about the reading in Psalm 119:65 according to the apparatus of Field, where it is cited. If it is a valid Quinta reading, it also involves the use of αγαθοσυνη, here in contrast to χρηστος of the OG.

27. The 11 cases of revision are Ps. 25:8; 35:12; 38:21b; 68:11; 86:5; 104:28; 106:1; 119:65, 68; 128:2; and 133:1. Omission is filled in in Ps. 133:2. Aquila is in agreement with the OG in Ps. 16:2 (though he uses αγαθοσυνη instead of αγαθων); 39:3 (though with αγαθου instead of αγαθων); and 147:1.

28. Ps. 35:12; 38:21b; 68:11; 86:5; 104:28; 106:1; 119:68. Omission is retained in the eighth instance, Ps. 133:2, the same omission which Aquila filled in with the καιγε word.

29. Ruth 2:22; 3:13; 4:15. In ℤ of 3:13, there is omission.

30. Lam. 3:17, 25, 26, 27, 38; 4:1. The exception is in 4:9.

31. In the OG, according to H-R, αγαθος is employed some 219 times, καλος some 92, κρεισσων/κρατιστος 28, χρηστος 23, χρηστοτης 13, and so on.

32. Job 9:25; 36:11.

33. Job 34:4.

34. Cant. 1:2.

35. Cant. 1:3. For טובים the rendering is apparently υπερ παντα τα αρωματα. This could also represent a Hebrew *Vorlage* different from MT.

36. Dan. 1:15.

37. Dan. 1:4. The καιγε word does not appear in the OG here either. In the θ´ text, a form of καλος is used; in the OG, a form of ευειδης.

38. S. P. Brock, "Lucian *redivivus*: Some Reflections on Barthélemy's *Les Devanciers d'Aquila*," *Studia Evangelica* 5 (1968), 179-80.

39. This same revision could also be seen in 2 Samuel 19:19, though not from a form of αγαθος.

40. It fails to appear in 1 Samuel 29:6a-b; 29:9; 2 Samuel 10:12; and 19:28.

41. The references are 1 Samuel 1:8, 23; 2:24; 3:18; 8:14, 16; 9:2a-b, 10; 11:10; 12:23; 14:36, 40; 15:9, 22, 28; 16:12, 16, 23; 19:4a-b; 20:7 (αγαθως), 12; 24:18, 19, 20a-b; 25:3, 8, 15, 21, 30; 26:16; 27:1; 29:6a-b, and 9.

42. He discusses the Lucianic text in terms of recensional activity aimed at producing a more readable Greek text (Brock, pp. 177-81), but the text opposing the καιγε recension in the translation of טוב is Lucianic alone only in βγ. In βγ, furthermore, Brock's explanation will not stand, for in 2 Samuel 24:22, the 𝕃 (*placet*-Vercellone) concurs with the reading of L (αρεστον) and, thus, demonstrates the reading to be pre-Lucianic. This strongly suggests that the same is true for 1 Samuel as well. Added confirmation may be seen in the 2 references in Judges in which the Hebrew term is followed by בעיני and is rendered in the non-καιγε texts by the verb αρεσκω (the root of αρεστος of 1-2 Samuel). In both of these instances (10:15; 19:24), the non-καιγε reading is the reading of L; and in both it is demonstrably earlier than Lucian's own time, appearing also in 𝕃 as a form of *placeo* in both and in 𝔊 in 10:15. That *placeo* of 𝕃 renders αρεσκω/αρεστος is indicated by 2 Samuel 3:19, where the Hebrew verb טוב is rendered in all Greek witnesses by a form of αρεσκω and in 𝕃 by a form of *placeo*.

43. Ps. 119:66. Aquila shows revision to a form or a cognate of αγαθος from a different OG root in Psalm 25:7; 31:20; and 119:66. Yet he is not consistent in Hosea 10:11, where he has the noun καλλος.

44. Deut. 5:33.

45. 2 Sam. 3:36.

46. Judg. 11:25. Here *melior* of 𝕃 must represent κρεισσων or simply render the MT, but does not represent the B family reading, εν αγαθω αγαθωτερος, which renders more literally the Hebrew הטוב טוב.

47. 2 Sam. 13:28 (L = ευ εχη); 15:26 and 19:38 (L = το αρεστον). In these latter 2, L most likely represents the OG reading (cf. above, note 42).

48. Judg. 16:25; 2 Kings 10:30.

49. Cant. 4:10.

50. In the OG, ευθυς and its cognates are used a total

of 65 times to render the forms of the root ישר. (In the
Psalms, 28 of these occur, with only 1 other rendering appearing in this corpus.) The other most frequent translations,
in order of frequency, are by ορθος and cognates (16 times, 11
in Proverbs), αρεσκω/αρεστος (11, 6 in Deuteronomy), αληθινος
(7, all in Job), and δικαιος (7).

51. In Judges 14:3 and 7, all other groups, 𝔊, and 𝔏
have a form of the verb αρεσκω. In 17:6, L (and 𝔏, apparently,
according to B-M) has a form of αρεστος. In 21:25 all witnesses employ a form of ευθης (except q, which has αγαθον).

52. 2 Sam. 17:4; 19:7.

53. The references are 1 Kings 22:43; 2 Kings 10:3, 15,
30; 12:3; 14:3; 15:3, 34; 16:2; 18:3; and 22:2. In 2 Kings 15:
3, the reading αγαθον would seem to be a later Hexaplaric alteration, since it stands in 𝔊 and in the Hexaplaric witnesses
Ax𝔐, but in no L witness at all. It should also be noted that
in all but 2 Kings 10:3 and 5 there is the use of a set phrase,
the Greek adjective followed by בעיני and an object. This
could be said to account for the consistency, though the choice
of words is still significant.

54. Jer. 40:4.

55. Hab. 2:4. The OG has ευδοκει.

56. Dan. 11:17. The OG has συνθηκας.

57. The references showing revision, or the filling in
of an omission, are Deut. 6:18; Josh. 10:13; Jer. 40:4; Ezek.
1:23; Prov. 11:3, 6, 11, 24; 12:6; 14:2; 15:8(?), 19; Job 33:3; and Dan.
11:17. The others which have the καιγε rendering, but without
revision from the OG, are Isa. 45:13; Ps. 5:9; 11:2; 94:15; and Prov.
20:11. The 1 instance with a different reading is Jer. 27:5.
(The sixth column for Judges will be discussed in chapter four;
it must be dissociated from the καιγε recension. In the present discussion, Judges 14:3 and 7 are illustrative.)

58. Those references showing revision are Deut. 9:5;
12:28; Jer. 26:14; Mic. 2:7; Hab. 2:4; Job 1:8; 6:25; 33:3;
Prov. 4:11; 11:6; 12:6; 14:2; 15:19; and 17:26. The references
with a καιγε reading, but no demonstrable revision, are Ps. 5:9;
25:21; 33:1; and 94:15. The 1 exception is Jer. 27:5. (The
majority text of Ecclesiastes 7:29 and 12:10 shows the expected
reading, in keeping with Barthélemy's identification of that
text with the work of Aquila himself [cf. DA, pp. 21-30].)

59. 18:2; 19:4, 15a-b, 20; 20:4.

60. 19:6, 13.

61. 19:9b. The 2 instances in 19:9 must be considered
together (cf. below and note 63). The omission of a rendering
of the first imperative (לינו) in the B family, L, and K seems
clearly to be due to haplography, with the consequent loss of
לינו נא הנה חנות היום. This haplography likely occurred in the

OG, where the second imperative (ל֖וּ) was rendered as καταλυσον. Later καιγε revision of this singular verb seems to
have been carried out to the singular αυλισθητι. Still later,
Origen supplied the omitted verb by the plural μεινατε (which
appears after ※ in 𝔖 as wqawaw), though he did not establish
the proper word order.
    If the above reconstruction is correct, L alone would
retain the OG rendering; the B family would represent the καιγε
revision of καταλυσον to αυλισθητι; and 𝔖 and the A family
would contain the Origenic addition, μεινατε. K accords with
the B family in both cases; and 𝔏 seems to follow MT, judging
by the number of the verbs. This reconstruction is dependent
on the Hebrew of MT. Had a different Hebrew *Vorlage* been before
earlier translators, the explanation would be different. In any
case, the evidence is clear for the present argument that αυλιζω is the characteristic καιγε rendering of Hebrew ל֖וּ.

    62. 19:7, 10, 11.

    63. 19:9a.

    64. 2 Sam. 17:16 (where L is confirmed as OG by 𝔏^V and
𝔏^b); 19:8. The verb αυλιζω also appears in 2 Sam. 12:16, possibly as revision there as well (cf. QTSJ, pp. 100-1). The
exception is 2 Sam. 17:8.

    65. Job 29:19.

    66. Ruth 1:16a-b; 3:13.

    67. Cant. 1:13; 7:12.

    68. Deut. 21:23; Isa. 1:21; 65:4; Prov. 15:31 (OG omits).
Aquila has the word in Ps. 91:1 in agreement with the OG; but
in Ps. 59:16, he follows the OG in a different rendering. (It
should be noted that in 2 of the 3 preserved Aquila renderings
of the cognate nouns מלון and מלונה he uses the noun αυλιστηρι-
ον, and both instances represent revision from a different OG
[Isa. 1:8; 10:29; the exception is Jer. 9:1].)

    69. Isa. 1:21.

    70. Prov. 15:31. Job 29:19 has already been noted.

    71. Deut. 21:23.

    72. Neh. 4:16; 13:20, 21. (Cf. DA, pp. 43-44.) The
same revision appears in bye₂ for 1 Chron. 9:27, but cf. note
139 of chapter one regarding this group in Chronicles.

    73. In this case, the word chosen for consistent use in
the καιγε recension appears clearly in the OG a total of 9
times; κοιμαω appears 15 times; and καταλυω 13 times. The
καιγε word is only one of those frequently used in the OG, and
in this case it is not the most frequent.

    74. 6:9; 18:28. In 6:9 Alexandrinus shares the revision,
but no other members of the A family have it.

75. 9:17 (with K); 11:26 (with all but L, though in a different person and number in the A family, K, and ∅).

76. 8:34.

77. 10:15. It should be noted that ∅ stands against the B family in 6:9; 9:17; 11:26; and 18:28, though B-M do not indicate this. The equivalents in ∅ are clear from 8:34 and 10:15, in both of which cases there is no Greek variation. For ρυομαι, ∅ employs *praq*; and for εξαιρεω, *pṣâ*.

78. The cases of revision are 2 Sam. 12:7; 14:16; 19:10; 22:18, and 49. In each case but the last, L has a form of εξαιρεω; there it has a form of διατηρεω. The instances without the καιγε verb are 2 Sam. 14:6; 20:6 (an unusual usage); 22:1 and 23:12.

79. Jer. 15:21. This single instance is especially significant, since for all 10 instances of Hebrew נצל in Jeremiah, not a single occurrence of ρυομαι is attested in the OG.

80. 1 Sam. 30:22; Isa. 57:3; Jer. 7:10; 42:11; Ezek. 33:9; Zech. 3:2; Ps. 31:3; 33:16; Job 5:19.

81. Exod. 5:23a; Isa. 37:11; Jer. 15:21 (all of these with ※). Aquila agrees with the OG in having a form of ρυομαι in Isa. 36:20b; 38:6; and Ps. 34:5 (though here he, rather, employs a form of the compound αναρρυομαι). The 3 exceptions are Isa. 44:20 (where οι λ′ may be a mistake); Ezek. 3:22 (where α′ is said to be the same as σ′); and Prov. 19:19 (where a form of ρυομαι is an alternate reading for both θ′ and α′).

82. The instances with a form of ρυομαι are 2 Kings 18:32, 33a-b; and 19:11. The divergent L reading is a form of εξαιρεω in 18:32. The cases in which the καιγε reading does not appear are 2 Kings 17:39; 18:29, 30a-b, 34, 35a-b; 19:12; and 20:6. (A form of ρυομαι does appear in 18:34 in the miscellaneous group Ndefmpqstwz and in 20:6 in L.)

83. Ps. 31:3. If, as Grindel has proposed, the Quinta represents the καιγε recension of the Psalms which was employed by Aquila, then this instance could represent a revision missed in the Quinta, but carried out later by Aquila (cf. "Another Characteristic," pp. 506, 512).

84. Dan. 8:4, 7.

85. A preliminary check of the *hiphil* of this verb seemed to indicate less consistent renderings; so the study, in this case, has been limited to the *qal* forms. Also, only those references for which καιγε material has been identified have been cited, since this collection of data seems adequate to demonstrate the characteristic.

86. 7:3a-b; 8:13, 33; 11:8, 35 (B only), 39; 18:26; 20:48.

87. 21:14.

88. 6:18; 8:9; 11:31; 15:19. In 11:31 there is variation in the form of the verb used, but not in the root; and
in 8:9 the B family employs the cognate noun επιστροφη.

89. 2:19; 3:19.

90. In 19:7 the evidence could also be omitted, since
the B family renders by a form of καθιζω, taking the verb to
be, rather, from the root יש׳. (The A family, L and ℊ show the
adverb παλιν, reflecting a precise understanding of Hebrew
idiom.) Such cases, in which the root is taken to be יש׳,
will be omitted in the discussion of remaining sections of the
text.

91. 7:15; 14:8; 21:23. In each of these instances, the
proposed reading occurs in the A family and L (and in K in 7:
15); whereas the B family has a form of υποστρεφω. It is possible that this might be the OG preserved, with later revision
on the part of Origen showing itself in the other families.
On the other hand, these uses of υποστρεφω (which is a rare
translation of the qal of שוב, appearing only 12 other times
throughout the Old Testament according to H-R, cf. also note
110 below) may represent later revision imposed on the B family.
In light of the common usage of υποστρεφω in 3:19, however, it
is safest to regard that case and these as OG; and this does
not alter the pattern in Judges. The normal choice of the B
family is a form of επιστρεφω to render the qal of שוב.

92. The cases of revision are 2 Sam. 10:15; 12:31; 15:19,
20, 27, 34; 19:16 (against b´o), and 40. Those with the expected verb, but without apparent revision, are 2 Sam. 15:8;
17:3; and 19:15. Those without the expected verb are 2 Sam.
10:14; 11:4, 15; 12:23; 17:20; 18:16; 20:22; and 22:38. In 2
of these cases, a form of επιστρεφω appears in L contrary to
the καιγε text (18:16 and 20:22).

93. The cases of revision are 2 Kings 1:6; 4:31; 19:8,
9; 20:9; and 23:20 (in 19:8 the contrary rendering is common to
all but Bir, not only to L). Those with the rendering, but
without apparent revision, are 1 Kings 22:28a-b; 2 Kings 1:5a-b;
2:25; 3:27; 4:22, 35, 38; 5:10, 14, 15; 7:8, 15; 8:3, 29; 9:36;
13:25; 20:5, 10; 21:3; 23:25; and 24:1. In 2 Kings 1:5a the
expected verb appears in BAbiyc₂e₂, and a form of αποστρεφω
stands in all of the other Greek witnesses. This could be an
instance of revision as well. Since L, however (the surest
guide here to earlier Greek translation, however that be defined [cf. DA, p.91]), agrees with the καιγε text, revision
cannot be clearly identified.
Those without the expected verb are 1 Kings 22:17, 33;
2 Kings 1:11, 13; 9:15, 18, 20; 14:14; 15:20; 17:13; 18:14;
19:7, 33, 36; and 23:26. There is 1 contrary instance, in
which L has the expected verb against the καιγε text (2 Kings
9:15). This, however, and those contrary instances in the case
of βγ do not override the force of the greater number of positive examples. The omissions in B in 2 Kings 2:13 and 18 have
not been included in this enumeration.

94. Jonah 3:9a. Apparently the form μετανοησει of the

OG is for the following בּנֹֹֹ of MT, which R revises to παρα-
κληθησεται (to follow Barthélemy's reconstruction).

95. Jonah 3:10. This entire verb is preserved.

96. Jonah 3:8, 9b. The verb of the OG is a form of
αποστρεφω in each case.

97. Mic. 1:7. There are several variants to this in
other Greek witnesses. According to Ziegler, there are forms
of επιστρεφω (0 22[c] C-68), καταστρεφω (lI Cyr.[F] Hi. [destrux-
it]), αποστρεφω (239), and συντριβω (764 Thph.[P]).

98. Ruth 1:7, 10-12, 15b, 22a-b; 4:3. The cases with
another verb are 1:6, 8, 15a, 16; and 2:6.

99. Cant. 7:1a-d.

100. Lam. 3:3, 40; 5:21. The exception is 1:8.

101. Jer. 34:11.

102. Jer. 22:27a; 29:14; 30:10; 48:47. The negative case
is 15:7.

103. Job 36:10.

104. Job 39:4.

105. Dan. 9:25; 11:29. The others with a form of επιστρεφω in θ´ are 10:20; 11:13, 28a-b, and 30a-b. Those with
a different verb are 9:13, 16; and 11:9.

106. Dan. 11:9. The others with επιστρεφω are 10:20;
11:13, 28a-b, and 30a-b. Those with a different verb are 9:13
and 16; and those with omission are, as mentioned above, 9:25
and 11:29.

107. Ps. 56:10.

108. Ps. 7:8; 119:79; 146:4.

109. Cf. note 107.

110. In the OG outside of Judges, επιστρεφω is the most
frequent translation, occurring some 201 times according to
H-R. However, αποστρεφω occurs some 168 times, and αναστρεφω
some 66.

CHAPTER III

CHARACTERISTICS PECULIAR TO THE VATICANUS
FAMILY OF JUDGES

In chapter one, it was established that the Vaticanus
family of Judges does, as Barthélemy proposed, stand within
the καιγε recension. In chapter two, the description of that
recension was expanded by the addition of six characteristics
discovered in the book of Judges. The purpose of this chapter is to present another aspect of the B family of Judges.
It will deal with peculiarities of that family within the
entire καιγε recension.[1]

Such a discussion is necessary in order to present an
accurate description of the Vaticanus family of Judges in relation to the καιγε material elsewhere. It also constitutes
strong evidence for proposing a general observation about the
entire καιγε recension. If this segment of the material has
such a broadly based individuality, then the same is likely
true for other parts of the recension as well.[2]

In any case, the likelihood of the entire καιγε recension
being attributable to the work of one man is called into seri-
ous question by the Vaticanus family of Judges. Whereas the
correspondences are so extensive as to firmly establish it as
a member of the καιγε recension, the inner peculiarities[3] are
so full as to make the hypothesis of one reviser for the whole
of the καιγε material extremely unlikely.[4] The more likely
explanation is that the καιγε recension was prepared by a
body of individuals united in a common purpose, i.e., to revise
the earlier translation of the Old Testament into Greek[5] so as
to bring about greater conformity to the Hebrew text in current use.

Those characteristics thus far discovered by the writer
which are peculiar to the Vaticanus family of Judges will be
presented in a way similar to that of the two preceding chapters. The characteristics will be described, and the data
from Judges and elsewhere will follow.

67

68

1. אבה (לא) = ευδοκεω

This characteristic is in continuity, and also in contrast, with that isolated in the καιγε sections of Samuel-Kings by Shenkel.[6] He found there a tendency for the OG to translate the above Hebrew term by the verb βουλομαι and for the καιγε revision to employ θελω instead.

In Judges the contrast between the B family and all other groups is consistent. In all 4 instances, the B family translates by the verb ευδοκεω, while the others employ θελω.[7] Thus, the καιγε material in Judges employs a distinctive term to render this Hebrew verb. In fact, the term is not used anywhere else in the Old Testament to translate the verb אבה.

At first glance, the term employed by the other groups, θελω, may seem to create a problem, for it is the same as that of the καιγε material in Samuel-Kings, as pointed out by Shenkel. However, closer examination reveals that, whereas there does appear to be καιγε revision at work in Samuel-Kings, the term employed there in this revision is also common to the OG throughout the Old Testament. It appears a total of 18 times;[8] and βουλομαι occurs only 4 more, a total of 22 times.[9] The use of θελω in the OG is even apparent in the material in which Shenkel isolated the καιγε revision, for there θελω occurs in the non-καιγε material 3 times.[10]

The contrast in 6 instances in Samuel-Kings between καιγε and L is sufficient to indicate a recensional difference, and the exclusive use of θελω by the καιγε material there confirms that καιγε revision has been at work.[11] A common, but not consistent, OG term has been made consistent in the καιγε revision of βδ, as in many cases in Judges already examined in the previous two chapters.

In Judges there is likewise full consistency within the καιγε material; and there the opposing witnesses are united and thus, presumably, represent the OG reading.[12] Again καιγε revision is apparent; but here the revision is to a different and, in this case, entirely distinctive word, suggesting the distinctiveness of the καιγε revision of Judges.[13]

2. אור = διαφαυσκω

This usage is peculiar to the book of Judges within the
καιγε recension. There it occurs 2 times, once as the exclusive reading of the B family[14] and once as the reading of B
and several other leading members of the family, joined by A
and some other minuscules, and standing against L, K, and 𝔊.[15]

This Greek verb is used for this Hebrew verb on 3 other
occasions in the Old Testament, each in the OG.[16] This is out
of a total of at least 42 uses of the Hebrew verb outside of
Judges. On the other hand, the Hebrew verb is translated elsewhere in presently identified καιγε material only in the ϑ´
version of Daniel once (where it is rendered by a form of επιφαινω[17]) and on 8 other occasions in the sixth column (6 of
which show a form of φωτιζω[18]).

Thus, it is impossible, at least at present, to say anything assuredly about the καιγε rendering of this Hebrew verb
outside of Judges. Whether there would have been a consistent
equivalent must remain uncertain. It does appear, however,
that there was such in the B family of Judges.

3. הביא = φερω/εισφερω

The *hiphil* of this Hebrew verb seems to have a deliberate
translation equivalent in the καιγε text of Judges in the verb
φερω and a compound thereof. Out of 8 instances, this verb or
a compound from it appears in the B family 6 times. In 1 of
these it is shared by the other groups as well,[19] but in 5 it
is exclusive to the B family.[20] In the 2 remaining instances,
the καιγε reading does not appear at all.[21]

Nowhere else in the καιγε recension, as it is presently
identified, does this peculiar translation pattern clearly
appear, although traces may be present. The *hiphil* of this
Hebrew verb is not used in any of the passages preserved in
Barthélemy's Minor Prophets fragments. However, the usage can
be checked in βγ and in γδ. In the former, out of 6 instances,
the first 2 have the verb φερω with no variation;[22] and the
last has the same verb with a form of εισαγω in L,[23] apparently
the same pattern as in Judges. But the verb does not appear
in the other 4 references.[24] Neither is the pattern clear in

γδ. Although the Hebrew verb is translated there 19 times, only 8 of these are by a form of φερω;[25] the other 11 have a simple or compound form of αγω.[26]

In Jeremiah none of the 5 asterisked additions shows the καιγε verb of Judges.[27] On 2 occasions, α΄ does employ a form of φερω;[28] but on the other 4, he uses a form of επαγω.[29] Furthermore, according to R-T, φερω and 2 of its compounds vie with 4 other verbs for Aquila's choice in translating this Hebrew verb in the *hiphil* throughout the Old Testament.[30] In the 1 asterisked addition of θ΄ to Job, the verb is επαγω.[31]

In the remaining material, there may be traces of the same revision; but this is doubtful. There is nowhere, in any case, a clear pattern. In the Psalms there are 3 Quinta readings preserved; 2 show other verbs,[32] and 1 may have φερω.[33] Neither of the 2 θ΄ readings have the verb φερω.[34] In Canticles, 2 of 5 instances show a form of φερω.[35] In Lamentations, 1 of 3 instances has the verb.[36] In the θ΄ version of Daniel, the verb occurs 4 out of 10 times; and 2 of these do show variance from the OG.[37]

4. בעיני = εν οφθαλμοις

Although this characteristic, discussed by Shenkel in regard to its occurrence in Samuel-Kings, was treated in chapter one,[38] it must also be mentioned here. Whereas its occurrence in Judges does demonstrate the continuity of the Judges B family with the καιγε recension, its peculiarity within Judges also sets off this body of text as distinctive from the καιγε material of Samuel-Kings. In Samuel-Kings the literal rendering is employed by the καιγε revision for all uses of the Hebrew preposition. In Judges the literal translation does not occur when the object is explicitly יהוה,[39] thus setting off this textual tradition as distinctive within the καιγε recension. Its continuity with that recension is demonstrated by the use of the literal translation when the object is a suffix equivalent to יהוה,[40] in contrast to the OG in Judges, as elsewhere.

5. צעק/זעק = βοαω

In Judges this equivalence seems to represent a characteristic of the B family. Out of a total of 19 occurrences of
1 of the 2 Hebrew alternates, 6 are rendered by βοαω in the B
family alone,[41] and 2 by the B family and some other groups.[42]
In 4 instances the same rendering occurs in all groups,[43] and
in 4 others it appears nowhere.[44] The remaining 3 cases are
unclear due to omissions in the B family in the first 2[45] and
a possible error in transmission in the third.[46]

Outside of Judges the picture is not so clear, although
traces of the revision may appear. In βγ the exact opposite
appears 3 times,[47] but the same reading as in Judges is present 2 times.[48] In γδ, out of 9 instances, the καιγε word of
Judges appears 8 times, 1 of these showing conflation with an
alternate (possibly the OG) reading in L.[49] In 1 case, the
word does not appear.[50]

In Jeremiah the 1 addition which appears does show a
form of βοαω.[51] In Job the 1 addition which appears has a
form of κραζω.[52] In Lamentations there are 2 instances, 1
with a form of βοαω[53] and 1 with a form of κραζω.[54]

This characteristic might actually have been placed in
chapter two as a general καιγε trait. However, since the evidence is mixed outside of Judges, it is discussed here. It
could, nevertheless, be useful in searching for new καιγε
material,[55] but only if revision appears, since it is a common
OG word as well.[56]

6. חרה אף = οργιζομαι θυμω

Out of the 7 instances in which this Hebrew expression
occurs in Judges, all appear in the B family with the rendering given above. In 4 cases no variation is seen elsewhere,[57]
but in 3 the B family stands against all of the other groups.[58]

This Greek rendering, which is the consistent choice of
the καιγε material in Judges, appears as 1 of the 2 major alternatives in the OG for translating the Hebrew expression.
It occurs 14 times in the OG according to H-R; and the other
most common rendering, θυμουμαι οργη, occurs exactly the same
number of times.[59]

It does not appear that the καιγε rendering in Judges is characteristic of the recension elsewhere. On 1 occasion in γδ, it does appear, against the same alternate reading in L as in the opposing groups in Judges.[60] Once, however, in βγ,[61] once in γδ,[62] and once in an addition to Job,[63] the reading opposed to the B family in Judges appears as the καιγε reading. These are the only other preserved instances in the presently identified καιγε material in which translations of the Hebrew expression can be consulted, so the evidence outside of Judges is scant. What there is seems to indicate that this is another case in which the καιγε revision of Judges shows its distinctiveness within the larger recension.

7. נלחם = παρατασσομαι

This rendering is clearly characteristic of the B family of Judges. Out of a total of 32 occurrences of the Hebrew verb, 24 are so translated by the B family, 19 against all other groups,[64] and 5 against some other groups.[65] One case is unclear due to omission, but is likely an exclusive rendering of the B family as well.[66] In 7 cases the B family shows the alternative rendering, a form of πολεμεω; but only in 1 of these does the verb παρατασσομαι appear at all.[67]

It is striking that this translation characteristic of the B family in Judges never occurs in καιγε material elsewhere. Of the 20 clear instances in βγ and γδ, πολεμεω is always employed.[68] One addition to Jeremiah[69] and 2 renderings of the θ´ text of Daniel[70] both show the same verb.

The verb which always appears in the καιγε material elsewhere is the normal OG rendering of Hebrew נלחם. It appears as the translation in the OG outside of Judges some 93 times[71] according to H-R; whereas παρατασσομαι occurs 8 times,[72] as does πολιορκεω. Thus, a reading infrequent elsewhere appears as the characteristic of the B family in Judges, but distinctively so, for it is employed nowhere else in the presently recognized καιγε recension.

The very first instance of the Hebrew verb in βγ offers a possible explanation of the absence of παρατασσομαι outside of Judges. It does occur there, immediately preceding the verb πολεμεω and translating the Hebrew verb ערך.[73] Throughout

Samuel-Kings, this equivalence is maintained in 8 of the 10 occurrences of ערך.[74] Prior to Judges and Samuel-Kings, this rendering appears on only 1 of 14 occasions.[75] However, in the 5 instances of ערך in Judges chapter 20, it is the reading of all groups except the B family.[76] It may be that this equivalence, which begins at the end of Judges in non-καιγε material, is adopted by the καιγε reviser(s) of βγ and γδ, forcing the abandonment of the נלחם/παρατασσομαι rendering of Judges. After this the Judges rendering never appears again in the καιγε recension.[77] Whether the process was exactly like that outlined here, however, is of secondary importance. The reading of the B family in Judges is clear in this case and equally clear in its distinctiveness within the καιγε recension.[78]

8. מלחמה = παραταξις

This characteristic will be dealt with here, rather than in alphabetical order, because of its relationship to the one preceding. It is a clearly delimited feature of the B family of Judges, appearing in no Greek tradition elsewhere, καιγε or otherwise.

In Judges the equivalence occurs 15 of the total of 20 times the Hebrew word is used. Of these the B family alone has it 12 times,[79] and the B family and K have it 3 times.[80] In 2 instances the B family has an omission and is, therefore, unclear.[81] The general OG word, πολεμος, appears in the remaining 3 cases in all Greek witnesses.[82]

Outside of Judges παραταξις does not occur at all in καιγε material and only appears 3 times in the OG as a translation of the Hebrew word in question.[83] On the other hand, πολεμος appears in the καιγε revision elsewhere at least 36 times and in the OG elsewhere some 179 times. Etymologically related words appear 2 more times in the καιγε material and 34 more in the OG.[84]

A similar situation is present in this case as in the preceding. Here the noun מערכה, occurring before the book of Judges, is rendered by different words.[85] As in the preceding case, though only in 1 reference, this noun appears in Judges with the same rendering on the part of all witnesses (including the B family) as is characteristic in the Judges B family for

the noun מלחמה.[86] The noun מערכה does not appear elsewhere in
καιγε material; but out of 16 instances in 1 Samuel, it is
rendered 14 times by παραταξις.[87] Thus, the equivalence can be
demonstrated, as can that of ערך/παρατασσομαι, within Judges
itself and may account for the absence of the characteristic in
question outside of Judges in καιγε material.[88]

9. לקראת = εις συναντησιν

In Judges this rendering, as observed by Barthélemy,[89]
is clearly characteristic of the B family. Out of a total of
11 instances of the Hebrew expression, the B family has εις
συναντησιν against all other groups 8 times.[90] The same rendering is shared by all groups without certain revision 2
times.[91] The 1 final instance is unclear because the B family
employs a different Greek word, υπαντησις; however, the situation is similar to the 8 instances of clear revision, for
here also the variant is found only in the B family.[92]

Outside of Judges, εις συναντησιν is the standard OG
equivalent in the preceding books, occurring some 30 times,
whereas εις απαντησιν does not appear at all prior to Judges.
On the other hand, the latter becomes the more common OG
equivalent after Judges, occurring some 22 times; whereas the
former continues to appear, occurring some 12 times.[93]

O'Connell has suggested that this feature of the καιγε
revision in Judges, vis-à-vis the Greek traditions in Exodus,
could indicate that the OG of Exodus served as the basis of
the καιγε revision of Judges.[94] Actually, this suggestion
should be broadened to include the OG of all of the Hexateuch,
for εις συναντησιν is standard throughout the OG prior to
Judges. That the OG of Exodus, or of the Hexateuch, served as
the basis of the καιγε revision of Judges, however, seems unlikely, as a comparison of the characteristics discussed thus
far will demonstrate. Such a relationship does not appear to
exist generally.

It does appear that the OG underwent a change at the
point of Judges and that the common reading of all groups but
the B family represents the OG of Judges. This is the most
frequent OG reading subsequent to Judges.

In any case, the B family of Judges is consistent in

rendering this Hebrew expression in a way unlike the καιγε revision elsewhere. In Samuel-Kings, as Barthélemy has indicated, the καιγε reading is εις απαντην. In the single clear
occurrence of the expression in the remaining καιγε material,
a different reading occurs.[95] Thus, the distinctiveness of
the καιγε revision of Judges within the recension as a whole
is again demonstrated.

10. נתץ = καθαιρεω

This translation characteristic appears clearly in the B
family of Judges, but nowhere else in the καιγε material with
consistency. In Judges out of a total of 8 uses of the Hebrew
verb, this translation is employed by the B family 6 times.
Of these, 5 are apparently in common with Ɓ only,[96] and 1 is
without any variant.[97] Another reading appears in the B family
in the remaining 2 instances, but without any appearance of
καθαιρεω in the other groups.[98]

Outside of Judges the same reading does appear 3 times
in γδ[99] and 2 times in additions to Jeremiah.[100] On the other
hand, it appears in the L text of γδ 3 times, 2 of these standing against another reading in the καιγε text.[101] Likewise in
Jeremiah, there is 1 addition which is contrary.[102]

In the OG outside of Judges, the reading occurs 13
times.[103] Other frequent translations are κατασκαπτω (4)[104]
and κατασπαω (4).[105] The latter also appears as the reading of
γδ 4 times.[106]

Thus, this characteristic rendering of the B family in
Judges is the most common OG reading, but does not appear as a
καιγε characteristic elsewhere.[107]

11. סרן = αρχων

This Hebrew noun appears 8 times in the book of Judges;
and in 7 of these the B family shows a form of αρχων against
the other groups, which have the common OG reading σατραπης.[108]

It is this latter translation which appears for 10 of
the 12 other occurrences of the Hebrew word outside of
Judges.[109] In 1 case the related noun σατραπεια is used;[110]
once the noun στρατηγος is used;[111] and once the καιγε word of

Judges appears.[112]

Whereas the καιγε revision of the OG equivalent to a new one by the B family of Judges is clear, it is impossible to speak of this revision in relation to the rest of the recension, for the Hebrew word does not appear in any other passage for which καιγε material has been identified. Thus, it must be presented as a distinctive feature of the καιγε text of Judges.

12. פגע = συνανταω

This rendering occurs 3 times in the text of Judges, each in the B family against all other groups with a form of απανταω.[113] The only other instances of a translation of the Hebrew verb in καιγε material are the 2 in Ruth, both showing the non-καιγε verb of Judges.[114] In the OG these 2 words are the most frequent translations of the Hebrew verb, απανταω occurring 10 times[115] and συνανταω 8 times.[116] Thus, 1 of these OG words was chosen for the καιγε revision of Judges; and the other appears in Ruth, possibly representing revision there as well.[117]

13. קצין = αρχη

Of the total of 12 occurrences of this Hebrew noun in the MT, 2 occur in Judges and 1 in the θ´ text of Daniel. In Judges the B family use of αρχη stands against all other groups in both cases, the latter reading a form of ηγεομαι.[118] In Daniel the OG reading is unique (a form of οργη), whereas the θ´ reading is a form of αρχων.[119] Thus, the B family of Judges shows a reading which cannot be identified as καιγε in any other material.

There is no consistent OG translation of this Hebrew word. The καιγε word of Judges appears in 2 other cases as the OG reading.[120] In 2 instances a form of αρχων appears;[121] in 2 a form of καταλοιπος;[122] and on 1 occasion each, forms of 4 other words.[123]

14. רעה = πονηρια

This Hebrew word appears 10 times in the text of Judges. In 3 of these instances, the Greek text is united in its translation, 1 having πονηρια,[124] 1 κακος,[125] and 1 κακια.[126] In the other 7 cases, the B family shows a form of πονηρια, while the other groups show a form of either κακια[127] or κακος.[128] Thus, the καιγε text of Judges stands apart from the others in its rendering of this noun.

In βγ and γδ, out of 18 instances of the Hebrew noun, a form of πονηρια (or of πονηρος) does not occur at all. Each rendering shows a form of κακια or κακος.[129] The same is true of the 3 additions to Jeremiah,[130] of the 3 occurrences of the noun in Daniel,[131] and of the 3 instances in Lamentations.[132] Thus, the characteristic καιγε rendering of רעה in Judges appears nowhere else in the καιγε recension as presently identified. It is a peculiarity of the καιγε text of Judges.[133]

With the conclusion of this chapter, the treatment of the B family of Judges in relation to the καιγε recension as a whole has been completed.[134] It was demonstrated in chapter one that the B family of Judges is, in fact, a genuine part of that recension. The basis upon which this identification was established is the body of characteristics already identified in texts other than Judges and already published. Chapter two has confirmed the conclusion of chapter one by presenting new characteristics discovered in Judges and verified in other καιγε material. It also adds new criteria to those employed in chapter one, which may now be used in the search for further surviving parts of this ancient Greek recension. Finally, chapter three has shown the distinctiveness of the Judges B family within the καιγε recension by presenting characteristics which appear in that family but not in the entire recension.

CHAPTER III

1. Again, as in chapters one and two, attention will be placed upon vocabulary choices which characterize the καιγε material. The analyses thus far published have dealt primarily with these specific translation correspondents and not with other aspects of style. Therefore, these correspondents constitute at present the most objective basis for the identification and analysis of καιγε material. As the extant members of the recension are more firmly identified, its description should be broadened to encompass other stylistic features. For the present, it seems best to proceed toward that objective by building on the foundation already laid. An appendix to this study will present an initial discussion of several other features of the καιγε text of Judges in addition to its characteristic vocabulary selections.

2. Such a proposal can only be introduced in this study. Its demonstration for other parts of the καιγε recension is not essential to the present argument, and the possibilities are manifold. It could be that a large part, or even all, of the rest of the καιγε material might prove to have a more thoroughgoing homogeneity. It seems more likely that such differences will appear among other sections; but whether that is, in fact, the case can and must await future study.

3. Those peculiarities are most significant for this point which appear as correspondents to words which likewise have characteristic καιγε renderings elsewhere, but different ones. When this is the case with a specific rendering, it will be noted in the presentation that follows.

4. Barthélemy is somewhat ambivalent on this point. The emphasis of his discussion is placed on the work of one man, Theodotion, whom he equates with Jonathan ben Uzziel (DA, pp. 144-57). Yet he does grant that "Jonathan Theodotion" may have done several successive revisions of one and the same book himself, or that he may have formed a school or had predecessors. Still he states that little light will be brought to bear by being able to attribute to or deny to this Jonathan the production of individual elements of the καιγε recension.
Whereas several specific facets of Barthélemy's hypothesis about the origin of the καιγε recension are open to question (cf. Cross, "The History of the Biblical Text," p. 283, n. 11) and thorough analysis is needed in order to define precisely the number and nature of the layers in the Theodotionic sixth column, this much can now be said assuredly. The καιγε recension is almost certainly not the work of one reviser in its entirety. Light, moreover, will be brought to bear as individual segments of the recension are analyzed, not only in their positive relation to the whole, but in their peculiar differences within that whole. Such distinctiveness has already been proposed for the θ´ text of Daniel (cf. Armin Schmitt, *Stammt der sogenannte "θ"-Text bei Daniel wirklich*

von Theodotion? [Göttingen, 1966]). The present chapter will
demonstrate the distinctiveness of the Judges καιγε text within
the larger recension.

5. Whether the basis of this revision should be regarded as the OG itself, or as the earlier stratum of the Lucianic
revision, need not be discussed here. In chapter four, what
can be said about the Lucianic family in Judges from the
writer's study thus far will be presented. The thrust of the
present work is not in the direction of this still vexed
question.
An introduction to the question of proto-Lucian may be
found in Cross, "The History of the Biblical Text," esp. pp.
292-97 and "The Contribution of the Qumran Discoveries to the
Study of the Biblical Text," *IEJ* 16 (1966), 81-95. A different
position is presented by George Howard in "Frank Cross and
Recensional Criticism," *VT* 21 (1971), 440-50 and "Lucianic
Readings in a Greek Twelve Prophets Scroll from the Judaean
Desert," *JQR* 62 (1971-72), 51-60. A more moderating position,
but with distinctives, is that of Emanuel Tov, "Lucian and
Proto-Lucian," *RB* 79 (1972), 101-13.
Cross prefers to speak of the early layer of the Lucianic
material as a "drift," rather than as a systematic recension
("The Evolution of a Theory of Local Texts," *1972 Proceedings:
IOSCS and Pseudepigrapha,* ed. Robert A. Kraft [Missoula, 1972],
p. 119).

6. CRDK, p. 116.

7. The references are 11:17; 19:10, 25; and 20:13. In
11:17, m and in 20:13, Ay read ακουω; but there is no variance
among the groups opposed to B.

8. Gen. 24:8; Deut. 1:26; 2:30; 10:10; 23:6; 25:7;
29:19; Josh. 24:10; 1 Sam. 26:23; 2 Sam. 2:21; 1 Kings 20:8;
Isa. 1:19; 28:12; Ezek. 3:7a; 20:8; Prov. 1:30; 1 Chron. 11:18;
19:19. These references and those in the following note are
apart from the book of Judges. In Deut. 13:9 the compound
συνθελω is used. In Isa. 1:19 the negative is lacking.

9. Gen. 24:5; Exod. 10:27; Lev. 26:21; 1 Sam. 15:9;
22:17; 31:4; 2 Sam. 6:10; 12:17; 13:14, 16, 25; 23:16, 17
(all in L in 2 Sam., except 6:10); Isa. 30:9, 15; 42:24; Ezek.
3:7b; Job 39:9; Prov. 1:10; 1 Chron. 10:4; 11:19; 2 Chron.
21:7. In Job 39:9 the negative is lacking.

10. 1 Sam. 26:23; 2 Sam. 2:21; 1 Kings 20:8.

11. This also supports the position, assumed in this
paper, that the καιγε material is a revision of the earlier
Greek translation, represented here by L, however one may
define the relationship of L and OG. In a review of DA, Kraft
raised the question of whether Barthélemy had demonstrated
sufficiently that the R scroll was a conscious and deliberate
recension (Robert A. Kraft, "Review of Dominique Barthélemy,
O. P.: *Les devanciers d'Aquila,*" *Gnomon* 37 [1965], 477-78).
At least for Exodus this particular aspect of καιγε studies
has now been specifically demonstrated in the work already
frequently cited by O'Connell (TRE). Each study which has

expanded Barthélemy's initial description of the καιγε material
has, in fact, confirmed its recensional nature.

Aside from βδ and Judges, the only rendering of אבה (לא) in
presently identified καιγε material is the ϑ´ reading of Prov.
1:30, which reads, in contrast to a form of ϑελω in the OG, a
form of εκδεχομαι. Aquila agrees with the OG of Josh. 24:10 in
using a form of ϑελω, but revises with Theodotion away from
ϑελω in Prov. 1:30.

12. In a case such as this, in which all other groups, ℊ,
and ℤ are united against καιγε, it seems to be axiomatic that
the OG reading is present, unless there is some strong reason
to the contrary. No variants occur (except ακουω in 11:17 [m]
and 20:13 [Ay]), and the word employed is one of the two common
OG words.

13. It should be said that other explanations are possible for this and many of the other readings presented in this
chapter. That they are not characteristic of the καιγε recension in general can be said assuredly; that they, in fact,
represent καιγε revision in Judges cannot always be shown with
certainty. The possibility is open that some of these peculiar
characteristics may represent later revision imposed on the
καιγε text. (Cf., for example, note 180 of chapter one and the
possibility of later Hesychian influence in the Judges καιγε
text.) In those cases in which the reading also appears in
some other segments of the καιγε recension, e.g., number 5 of
this chapter, or in which the same revision is being accomplished as elsewhere in the recension, but with differences,
e.g., number 4 of this chapter, their καιγε nature is virtually assured. Other peculiarities must be regarded with less
certainty, unless other factors lead to a sure conclusion.

This situation indicates the need for further detailed
study of the B family of Judges so as to identify, not only
the other aspects of its nature as a καιγε text, but also those
features not attributable to καιγε revision, wherever such
may be present. Because some of the characteristics presented
in this chapter clearly represent καιγε revision and the others
potentially so, the primary argument of the chapter stands,
i.e., that the B family of Judges is both an authentic part of
the καιγε recension and also a distinctive member of that
recension.

14. 16:2. Here the B family has some division as to the
tense of the verb, but is united in using a form of διαφαυσκω.

15. 19:26. The B family is actually divided between
διαφαυσκω and διαφωσκω, which L-S list as the Ionic form of
the former. One of the forms of these 2 appears in Bmrua₂ and
is shared by Abklo, 71, 84, and M (mg.). In opposition, with
the verb διαφωνεω, are efjqsz from the B family, Gacx from the
A family, M, the rest of the minuscules, and ℊ. Thus L, K,
and ℊ clearly read a form of διαφωνεω, with the A family being
divided.

16. Gen. 44:3; 1 Sam. 14:36 (where L shows a form of
διαφωτιζω); and 2 Sam. 2:32 (where L apparently has a form of
διαφωσκω [oc₂e₂, but διαφωτιζω in b]).

17. Dan. 9:7. This stands in contrast to the OG, which has a form of επιβλεπω. The word in the θ´ version is quite frequent in the Psalms as a rendering of אור, occurring some 7 times out of 15, with φωτιζω occurring 6 times and simple φαινω 2 times. The references are επιφαινω: Ps. 31:17; 67:2; 80:4, 8, 20; 118:27; and 119:135; φωτιζω: Ps. 13:4; 18:29; 19:9; 105:39; 119:130; and 139:12; and φαινω: 77:19 and 97:4. Whether this has any significance must await further study, but one is reminded of Barthélemy's suggestion as to the possibility of a καιγε type revision appearing in the Psalms (DA, pp. 41-43). Surely as the main outlines of the extent and nature of the καιγε recension become clearer, subgroups will appear; and phenomena such as this can signal their discovery. (Elsewhere in the OT επιφαινω translates אור only in Num. 6:25.)

18. Job 33:30; Ps. 13:4; Prov. 4:18; 29:13; Isa. 27:11 (taking minuscule 86 to be correct, cf. Ziegler and Field); 60:1. A form of φαινω appears in Exod. 13:21, and a form of αναπτω in Mal. 1:10.
Aquila employs the verb φωτιζω in 7 of the 8 readings which are preserved from his translation (Exod. 14:20; 1 Sam. 14:27; Ps. 13:4; Prov. 29:13; Isa. 27:11; 60:1, 19). The exception is a form of φαινω in Gen. 1:15.

19. 7:25.

20. 12:9; 18:3; 19:3, 21; 21:12. The alignment of 𝔊 is difficult to determine in this case, since a form of the verb 'etâ is used for both αγω (e.g., 1:7; 2:1) and φερω (e.g., 7:25). Presumably its agreement is with the others against the B family, as is generally the case in Judges.

21. 1:7; 2:1.

22. 2 Sam. 13:10a-b.

23. 1 Kings 1:3.

24. 2 Sam. 14:10, 23; 17:14; 23:16.

25. 2 Kings 4:20 (in L only), 42; 5:6, 20; 10:8; 12:5; 20:20; 21:12. In none of these is there a different verb in L.

26. 2 Kings 9:2; 10:24; 11:4 (this and the preceding have variation in L only in the type of compound formed from αγω); 17:24; 19:25; 22:16, 20; 23:8 (again here and in the final 2, L varies in the type of compound used), 30; 24:16; 25:7.

27. Jer. 11:8 (θ´); 18:22 (οι γ´, cf. Ziegler); 28:3; 39:7 (θ´); 42:17.

28. 17:21 (εκπορευομαι in the OG); 33:11.

29. 18:22; 35:17 (φερω in the OG); 49:8, 32 (φερω in the OG).

30. The other verbs used by Aquila are αγω, εισαγω, επαγω, and λαμβανω.

83

31. Job 34:28.

32. Ps. 43:3 (αγω); 66:11 (εισαγω).

33. Ps. 90:12. Field renders 'etâ of 𝔖 (attributed to α´) back to a form of φερω, but this and *venio* of Jerome could as well represent αγω (in Judges 'etâ of 𝔖 renders both; cf. above note 20).

34. 43:3; 74:5.

35. 1:4 (εισφερω); 8:11. The other references are 2:4; 3:4; and 8:2.

36. Lam. 5:9 (εισφερω). The others are 1:21 and 3:13.

37. Dan. (ϑ´) 1:2a-b (b varied); 11:6 (varied), 8. The references without a form of φερω are 1:3, 18a-b; 9:12, 14, and 24.

38. Cf. above, pp. 20-21 and CRDK, pp. 13-17.

39. 2:11; 3:7, 12a-b; 4:1; 6:1; 10:6; 13:1.

40. 6:17; 10:15. The same revision appears in 14:7; 19:24; and 21:25 (cf. the discussion in chapter one, p. 21), though the suffixal object is not equivalent to יהוה.
The single instance of חשה = ησυχαζω (also discussed in chapter one, p. 23) could furnish a similar example of a distinctive B family rendering.

41. 4:10; 6:6; 10:10, 12; 12:1; 18:22.

42. 6:34 (vs. L, 𝔏) and 18:23 (vs. K, 𝔖). In the latter of these, the A family is divided, but seems most clearly aligned with K and 𝔖.

43. 7:23, 24; 10:14; 12:2.

44. 3:9, 15; 4:3, 13. In the last of these, L and 𝔏 employ a form of παραγγελλω, whereas a form of καλεω appears elsewhere.

45. 6:7, 35. Both of these omissions seem to have been due to haplography of entire clauses. If so, the B family word could be assumed to be a form of βοαω in both cases in light of the proximity of its occurrence in 6:6 and 34. (In 6:34, B and q have a form of φοβεομαι; but the B family has the verb βοαω.)

46. 10:17. The form ανεβησαν, appearing here in the B and A families, L, and K, may be an error for ανεβοησαν. The latter form actually appears in mx and, surprisingly, 𝔖. Compound forms of verbs meaning "to go" also appear in 𝔏 and σ´.
It should be said that the apparatus of B-M does not accurately represent 𝔖 in this case. The equivalents seem to be z'aq for βοαω and q'â for κραζω, the most frequent alternate reading. The agreement of 𝔖 with groups other than the B family should be noted in 10:10, 12; 18:22 and 23.

47.   2 Sam. 13:19; 19:5, 29.   In all 3 of these instances, the καιγε material has a form of κραζω; but boc₂e₂ have a form of βοαω.

48.   2 Sam. 24:4, 5.   Here the verb of L is παραγγελλω.

49.   2 Kings 2:12; 3:21; 4:1, 40; 6:5, 26; 8:3, 5.   In 3:21, L has παρηγγειλαν και εβοησαν.   In 2 of these cases, a form of the compound αναβοαω is used (3:21; 4:40).

50.   1 Kings 22:32.   A form of αναβοαω does appear in u.

51.   Jer. 30:15 (ϑ´).

52.   Job 35:12.

53.   Lam. 2:18.

54.   Lam. 3:8.   Here a form of βοαω appears in immediate proximity to translate the Hebrew verb שׁוע.

55.   This is true, at least theoretically, for all of the characteristics in this chapter.   New καιγε material, when discovered, could prove to have closer ties with the B family of Judges, or with some other parts of the entire recension, inasfar as it is known.   Subgroups within the recension have yet to be identified and clearly differentiated.

56.   This has been true of many of the characteristics thus far discussed.   In the OG material, according to H-R, βοαω occurs for the Hebrew verbs in question 33 times, and κραζω appears 31 times.

57.   2:14, 20; 3:8; 6:39.

58.   9:30; 10:7; 14:19.

59.   In the other OG translations of the Hebrew expression outside of Judges, the verb ϑυμοω is used 5 times, οργιζω 3, παροξυνομαι ϑυμος 2, οργη ϑυμου 1, and οργη 1.

60.   2 Kings 13:3.   The reading of borc₂e₂ here is εϑυμωϑη οργη.

61.   2 Sam. 12:5.

62.   2 Kings 23:26.

63.   Job 32:5 (ϑ´).

64.   1:3, 5; 9:17, 39, 45, 52; 10:9, 18; 11:5, 6, 8, 9, 12, 20, 27, 32; 12:1, 3, 4.

65.   5:19a (with A family, K, Ⴚ against L), 20a-b; 8:1; 9:38 (all after the first in agreement with K against the others).

66.   11:4.   The cause of omission appears to be haplography.

In the verses immediately following, the B family alone revises to παρατασσομαι (cf. 11:5, 6, 8, 9, 12). The situation in 11:5 is somewhat uncertain also, since only Bfq have the revision; but since the reading of the B family is clear throughout Judges, Vaticanus and these two minuscules should likely be followed here as well.

67. The references are 1:1, 8, 9; 5:8, 19b; and 11:25a-b. In 5:19b παρατασσομαι appears, anomalously, in L alone (glnw). The form in 5:8 is problematic, but is included here, since it is translated as a finite verb by all Greek text groups except the A family and ɢ, which treat it as a noun.

68. 2 Sam. 10:17; 11:17, 20; 12:26, 27, 29; 21:15; 1 Kings 22:31, 32; 2 Kings 3:21; 6:8; 8:29; 9:15; 10:3; 12:18; 14:15, 28; 16:5; 19:8, and 9. 1 Kings 22:46 and 2 Kings 13:12 have omissions.

69. Jer. 32:5.

70. Dan. 10:20; 11:11. The OG of 10:20 has a form of διαμαχομαι; in 11:11 the verb is the same.

71. This includes compounds of the verb formed with εκ, κατα, συν, and συνεκ. The simple verb occurs some 81 times.

72. In Zech. 14:3, the noun παραταξις translates the verb in question.

73. The reference is 2 Sam. 10:17.

74. The other references with ערך, in addition to 2 Sam. 10:17, are 1 Sam. 4:2; 17:2, 8, 21; 2 Sam. 10:8, 9, 10; 23:5; and 1 Kings 18:33. The 2 exceptions are 2 Sam. 23:5 and 1 Kings 18:33. Thus, the equivalence of παρατασσομαι and ערך has been established, at the outset in the material of Samuel-Kings.

75. Gen. 14:8 is the only occurrence. The other 13 reveal 7 different verbs (επιτιθημι [Gen. 22:9], καιω [Exod. 27:2; Lev. 24:3, 4], προστιθημι [Exod. 40:4], προτιθημι [Exod. 40:23; Lev. 24:8], επιστοιβαζω [Lev. 1:7, 8, 12], στοιβαζω [Lev. 6:5; Josh. 2:6], and ετοιμαζω [Num. 23:4]). Thus, an equivalence is initially established in the OG of Judg. 20 which extends through Samuel-Kings. It also holds in 1 and 2 Chron. (8 out of 10 cases) and occurs in Jer. (3 out of 5 times) and in Joel (in the only instance). On the other hand, it does not appear at all in Job (8), Pss. (6), Prov. (1), Isa. (4), Ezek. (1), or Zech. (5). These statistics, after Samuel-Kings, are based on H-R.

76. The references are Judg. 20:20, 22a-b, 30, and 33. The reading of the B family in each case is a form of the verb συναπτω. In verse 33 Alexandrinus itself omits, but the A family otherwise shows the verb παρατασσομαι.

77. Cf. above notes 68-70.

78. This case, in and of itself, could be accounted for nicely by assuming only one reviser behind the καιγε material. The other distinctive renderings of the Judges B family will not, however, due to the sheer force of their multiplicity, permit such an assumption. One individual, attempting the consistency in revision which does mark the καιγε recension, would not have employed such variety as the characteristics of this chapter indicate.

In contrast to this reading representing καιγε revision, it, the following one, and the first one discussed in this chapter may constitute, rather, evidences of later revision imposed upon the καιγε text of Judges. Due to their uniqueness and especially to their less literal conformity to the Hebrew words in question, they may well be a part of a post-καιγε stratum of the Judges B family. The positive identification and description of such material must await further study and will not affect the conclusions being presented here, since the characteristics of the Judges B family discussed in chapters one and two and some of those discussed in the present chapter are clear in their relationship to other καιγε material (cf. also note 13 above).

79. 8:13; 18:16; 20:17, 18, 20a, 22, 23, 28, 34, 39a-b; 21:22.

80. 18:11; 20:14, 42.

81. 18:17 (likely a case of haplography of the verb באו in vss. 17 and 18); 20:20b.

82. 3:1, 2, 10.

83. 2 Chron. 13:3; 20:15; Isa. 36:5.

84. These figures are all from H-R, except that the renderings of the Hebrew word in presently identified καιγε material have been checked directly.

85. The translation in Exod. 39:37 is by a form of καυσις, and in Lev. 24:6a-b and 7 is by a form of θεμα.

86. The reference is Judg. 6:26.

87. 1 Sam. 4:2, 12, 16b; 17:8, 10, 20, 21a-b, 22, 23, 26, 36, 45, 48. The exceptions are 1 Sam. 4:16a and 23:3.

88. This case is not as clear, however, since the conflicting word, מערכה, does not occur in the καιγε material outside of Judges.

89. DA, pp. 78-80.

90. 4:18, 22; 6:35; 11:31; 14:5; 19:3; 20:25, 31.

91. 7:24; 15:14. In 15:14 the situation is complex. To begin with, L is not simply at variance, but rather omits the later reading εις συναντησιν, together with the verb εδραμον, both of

which occur in all other Greek families. The B family and K, on the other hand, omit the phrase εις απαντησιν, which appears in the A family and 𝔊. The latter two have the fullest text. The variant text forms seem to be as follows:

MT	*hry'w*	*lqr'tw*		
A fam.	ηλαλαξαν	εις	απαντησιν	αυτου
𝔊	"	"	"(*lpeg'â*)	"
B fam., K	"	--	--	--
L	"	εις	απαντησιν	αυτου

MT	--	--	--	--	--
A fam.	και	εδραμον	εις	συναντησιν	αυτου
𝔊	⸓ "	"	"	"(*l'ûr'â*)	"
B fam., K	"	"	"	συναντησιν	"
L	--	--	--	--	--

The following reconstruction of the development of this situation is offered only suggestively. It appears that the A family and 𝔊 preserve an ancient doublet. To honor the obelus sign of 𝔊 (and G) would be to regard the last clause as an early reading. It would appear that the καιγε reviser retained the two verb forms, but eliminated one of the two prepositional phrases, retaining the one in keeping with his characteristic rendering of the Hebrew elsewhere in Judges. K later followed the καιγε rendering; and L, anomalously, eliminated one of the two variants. Were it not for the obelus in 𝔊 and G, one would be tempted to regard L as the OG reading. This is possible, of course. Since the Hexaplaric signs are known to have suffered corruption in the process of transmission (cf. Max L. Margolis, "Hexapla and Hexaplaric," *AJSL* 32 [1915-16], 134-35), such could be the case here; or Origen could have had a Greek *Vorlage* with an expansion, or conflation, which was later than the text of Lucian. On the other hand, neither is it inconceivable that an earlier form of the Hebrew text may have had the longer reading, including forms of both רוע and רוץ.

The first explanation fails to account for the choice of συναντησις in the second OG variant, since this word does not appear elsewhere as an OG rendering in Judges. It is, however, common elsewhere in the OG, as will be noted in the following discussion in the text. It also fails to give a reason for the elimination of one of the two members of the doublet in L, contrary to the general tendency of Lucian to be conflate (Metzger, p. 25).

It does, however, acknowledge the obelus sign of 𝔊 and G; and
it identifies the καιγε selection of the second prepositional
phrase as being in keeping with καιγε revision elsewhere in
Judges. This latter consistency stands, whether the first reconstruction is correct or not.

One further complication exists in this verse, and that
is the variation of 𝔊 between *lpeg'â* for εις απαντησιν and
l'ûr'â for εις συναντησιν. Whereas otherwise in Judges 𝔊 always reads *l'ûr'â*, it would seem at first glance that the
agreement is, rather, with the B family elsewhere. This might
not be the case. Outside of Judges, *l'ûr'â* is employed in 𝔊
for both εις συναντησιν (e.g., Exod. 4:14, 27) and εις απαντησιν (e.g., 1 Kings 2:8, 19). Nevertheless it remains difficult to explain why in 15:14 *lpeg'â* would have been chosen
first for the common reading of the A family and then *l'ûr'â*
used subsequently for the B family word. The alternation is
understandable, but not the choice of alternates, if 𝔊 agrees
otherwise with the A family. Further evidence that 𝔊 may side
with the B family throughout in this reading is found in 7:24,
where *l'ûr'â* is used, clearly for εις συναντησιν, for there is
no Greek variant in this case.

92. Actually, the variant appears only in Bq. The reference is Judg. 11:34. The minuscules kmx do have the reading
εις συναντησιν.

93. All of these figures are according to H-R.

94. TRE, p. 282.

95. In Ps. 35:3, both ϑ´ and ε´ read εξ εναντιας, as does
the OG. (In Ps. 59:5, the OG is εις συναντησιν; but σ´ has
εξ εναντιας, possibly a retention of καιγε revision.)

96. 2:2; 6:28, 30, 31, 32. The situation with 𝔊 seems
clear because of 2 references in which different Greek translations appear in all witnesses. These are in 8:9 (κατασκαπτω)
and in 9:45 (καθαιρεω). The equivalents in 𝔊 are forms of
hpak and *'qar* respectively. To follow this lead would be to
conclude that the reading of 𝔊 in the 5 references given above
is always in agreement with the B family against the other
groups. This is out of keeping with the normal pattern in
Judges, but it seems to be the only sound analysis in this
case. (More will be said of the nature of 𝔊 in Judges in
chapter four.)

97. 9:45.

98. 8:9, 17. In 8:17 the B family has the verb καταστρεφω; whereas the A family, K, and 𝔊 have κατασκαπτω. The
witnesses to L are divided in this instance.

99. 2 Kings 23:7, 8, 12.

100. Jer. 18:7 (σ´); 39:8 (ϑ´).

101. 2 Kings 10:27b; 23:15; 25:10. The latter 2 are a-
gainst the καιγε text; in the first there is an omission in

the majority text. Actually, in the last Vaticanus also omits; but the reading of all other witnesses, apart from boc₂e₂, B, and A (κατελοσαν), is κατεσπασεν.

102. Jer. 31:28 (𝔊). This usage is somewhat difficult to identify, precisely because a form of καθαιρεω does appear as 1 of the 2 forms in the OG; and among the 5 forms which appear after the addition, καθαιρεω also appears. However, according to the order given, κατασπαω is the equivalent of נתץ.

103. Exod. 34:13; Lev. 11:35; 14:45; Deut. 7:5; 2 Kings 10:27b; 23:15; 25:10 (all these references from 2 Kings being in L); Isa. 22:10; Jer. 33:4; 52:14; Ezek. 16:39; 26:12; Ps. 52:7.

104. Deut. 12:3; Jer. 1:10; 2 Chron. 34:4 (though different in B); 36:19.

105. 2 Kings 23:12 (L); 2 Chron. 23:17; 33:3; 34:7.

106. 2 Kings 10:27a; 11:18; 23:15; 25:10.

107. The reading of the groups opposing the B family in Judges is one of the other most common OG renderings, κατασκαπτω. It appears in the A family, L, and K 6 times (Judg. 2:2; 6:28, 30, 31, 32; 8:17).

108. The 8 instances are Judg. 3:3; 16:5, 8, 18a-b, 23, 27, and 30. In 3:3 all witnesses have a form of σατραπια. This noun also appears in 16:18b in the A family, K, and 𝔊, although L maintains a form of σατραπης. In 16:23, K sides with the B family.
According to B-M, 𝔏 divides in this reading, holding with the A family and others in 16:23, 27, and 30 and with the B family in 16:5, 8, and 18a-b. Such division in 𝔏 in Judges is quite unexpected, as is agreement with the B family against the others. (The citations of 𝔏 by B-M in these cases have been confirmed in the text of Codex Lugdunensis in the edition of U. Robert.)

109. 1 Sam. 5:8, 11; 6:4a, 12, 16, 18; 7:7; 29:2, 6, 7.

110. Josh. 13:3. This noun also appears in miscellaneous witnesses in 1 Sam. 6:4a and 16.

111. 1 Chron. 12:20 (be₂ have σατραπαι).

112. 1 Sam. 6:4b. With the confirmation of 𝔏 and the total lack of any divergent witnesses, this appears to be the genuine OG word here.

113. 8:21; 15:12; 18:25.

114. Ruth 1:16; 2:22. In the former of these, L shows a form of γινομαι; and in the latter, the καιγε word of Judges (each witnessed by glnowe₂).

115. Gen. 28:11; 1 Sam. 10:5; 22:17, 18; 2 Sam. 1:15; 1 Kings 2:32, 34; Job 21:15; 36:32; Jer. 34 (27):18. These references and those in the following note are drawn from H-R.

116. Gen. 32:1 (2); Exod. 5:3, 20; 23:4; Num. 35:19, 21; Josh. 2:16; Isa. 64:5 (4).

117. There may have been a relationship between this choice by the καιγε reviser(s) of Judges and that of εις συναντησιν as the translation of לקראת, over against εις απαντησιν of the OG. (Cf. above in this chapter the discussion of reading number 9.) Such preferences of words per se apart from Hebrew counterparts, however, have not thus far come to the writer's attention with any frequency in Judges.
The usage by 𝔖 of a form of *pga'* in each case in Judges would seem to indicate its agreement with the non-καιγε text groups in this reading, in light of the words employed in 15:14 (cf. note 91 above).

118. 11:6, 11.

119. Dan. 11:18.

120. Isa. 3:6, 7.

121. Isa. 1:10; 22:3.

122. Mic. 3:1, 9. In these references, the readings of ϑ´ are αρχη (with α´) and εξουσιαζοντες, respectively.

123. Josh. 10:24 (εναρχομαι, L having the καιγε word of Judges); Prov. 6:7 (γεωργιον [*vid.*]); Prov. 25:15 (βασιλευω); Dan. 11:18 (οργη).

124. 11:27.

125. 2:15.

126. 20:34.

127. 9:56, 57; 20:3, 12, 13, 41.

128. 15:3.

129. 2 Sam. 12:11, 18; 13:16; 15:14; 16:8; 17:14; 18:32; 19:8a-b; 24:16; 1 Kings 1:52; 22:23; 2 Kings 6:33; 8:12; 14:10; 21:12; 22:16, 20.

130. Jer. 28:8; 44:11 (ϑ´), 29 (ϑ´,α´).

131. Dan. 9:12, 13, 14. In verse 14, the ϑ´ text omits; so this is actually unclear; but in context the word may be assumed to have been the same as in the 2 preceding references, if it was ever present at all.

132. Lam. 1:21, 22; 3:38.

133. The treatment of related Hebrew words (רַע, רֹע, רעע) does not seem to reveal any characteristic differences in the text groups of Judges. All are united in translating רַע by a form of πονηρος, as is the rest of the Heptateuch and Samuel-Kings. The verb רעע appears once in Judges (9:23) and there is translated by a form of κακοποιεω in the B family and by a form of πονηρευομαι in the other groups. But 1 instance does not reveal a characteristic in itself; and, according to H-R, these 2 Greek verbs do not form a pattern anywhere else.

It should be noted that πονηρια does appear as the characteristic rendering of רעה in Nehemiah. It is employed in 5 of the 7 instances, 1 of the others having an omission and the other a form of κακος. The references are Neh. 1:3; 2:10 (omission), 17; 6:2; 13:7, 18 (κακα), 27. This single strand of evidence, however, against all of the other firmly identified καιγε material, does not alter the conclusion. If Nehemiah were to prove to be a genuine part of the καιγε recension, this would merely be a case in which it would share an inner-recensional peculiarity with the B family of Judges.

134. Characteristic 23 of chapter one also reveals, in part, a peculiarity of the Judges B family. Characteristic 5 of chapter two is an example of a peculiarity of Judges and some, but not all, of the other members of the καιγε recension generally.

CHAPTER IV

OTHER RECENSIONAL DEVELOPMENTS
IN THE GREEK TEXT OF JUDGES

The conclusion which has been established regarding the
B family of Judges affords a basis for a fresh examination of
the book's other recensional developments. The present chapter aims to provide an initial discussion of this sort. In
some cases, previous understanding will not be essentially
changed; in others new understanding is indicated.

The evidence for this discussion will consist first of
all of a series of variant Greek readings which will give op-
portunity for comparing and contrasting the different text
groups. These readings have been drawn from a word-by-word
analysis of six chapters of the book.[1] The criteria for their
selection have been that they reveal differences among the
major Greek families and that they potentially represent recensional differences within the Greek tradition.[2] Further
evidence from the translation characteristics discussed above
in chapters one through three and from the rest of the book of
Judges has also been employed in some cases.

As in chapters one through three, the major Greek textual
families, $\mathcal{B}$, and $\mathcal{L}$ have been cited for each of the variants
presented below. The other versions cited by B-M, except for
$\mathcal{B}$ and $\mathcal{L}$, have not been included. It has been concluded in
past study that, of these, only the Sahidic follows the B fam-
ily of Judges; whereas the others concur in general with the
other groups.[3] Because of the importance of $\mathcal{L}$ in identifying
OG readings[4] and of $\mathcal{B}$ in discerning readings of Origen's revision,[5] these two witnesses have been quoted throughout.[6]

On occasions when one of the variant text forms can be
detected in the writings of Josephus, this author will be quoted in the commentaries to follow. Josephus' use of the biblical text of Judges is quite free, in contrast to that of
Samuel, in which the nature of his text can be more clearly discerned. Nevertheless, the type of text he used for Judges can
be identified in certain instances. The significance of these

will be considered in the following discussion. In certain
cases, Jerome's Vulgate will also be cited (when it throws
potential light on an OG reading as possibly mediated via the
𝕷 through the Vulgate), as will Targum Jonathan and the Syriac
Peshitta (when they potentially preserve a non-MT reading).[7]

The variants to be used as evidence in the chapter will
first be given in tabular form with a textual commentary.[8]
Then an examination of the Greek textual families will follow
in an effort first of all to identify those that best preserve
the OG, then to analyze the revision of Origen and the sixth
column in relation to the OG and the καιγε recension,[9] and
finally to discern the place of the remaining major families
in the recensional development of Judges.

A preliminary explanation should be made of the principles
followed in classifying various readings. The starting point
in the analysis was the identification of what may represent
an OG translation. In many cases it is not possible to say
whether such a reading is truly early or late, e.g., those in
which L has a divergent reading and stands alone. (These
instances may represent an early rendering, or may be the work
of Lucian himself.) Such readings have been regarded as potentially OG. In these cases those groups agreeing with MT
have simply been classified as such,[10] and no conclusions have
been based solely on this evidence.

In other instances, however, in which there is corroborating evidence that the reading is early,[11] an effort has been
made to identify later recensions. If the B family, for example, is in agreement with MT, but stands against L and the
earlier witness of 𝕷, then the B family and those agreeing with
it have been identified as καιγε. If an early reading at variance with MT is indicated elsewhere, but the text of 𝔖 conforms to MT, or if 𝔖 has an asterisk, then 𝔖 has been regarded
as the revision of Origen. When, however, in cases such as
this, the B family and 𝔖 agree, then both have been classified
as καιγε, unless 𝔖 has an asterisk.[12] 𝕷 itself has been classified either as following the OG or as being in agreement
with MT, apart from those cases in which an inner-Greek change
seems to be preserved. More detailed study would be required
to speak of the relation of 𝕷 to whatever recensions were

extant at the time of its translation.

A more specific explanation of the treatment of individual
variants will be given in the commentary following the table.
As in the first three chapters above, the A and B families will
serve in each case as the primary points of comparison. Since
the purpose of the present chapter has to do with identifying
and describing the OG and subsequent recensions, the question
of what Hebrew text ultimately lay behind the Hebrew *Vorlagen*
that can be identified now, i.e., the question of an "Ur-
Hebrew," will not be discussed, except as it may pertain to the
matters being considered here.

Table of Readings

MT	B Fam.	𝔊	A Fam.	L	K	Misc.
1:6 את בנתה ויהוה ידיו ורגליו	τα ακρα των χειρων αυτου και τα ακρα των ποδων αυτου	= L	? = B-Ackx = L-ab	τα ακρα των χειρων αυτου και των ποδων αυτου	= B	𝔏 - *summas manus illius et summum pedum illius*
1:7 בנתה ויהוה ורגליהם	τα ακρα των χειρων αυτων και τα ακρα των ποδων αυτων	= L	? = B-Ack = L-abx	τα ακρα των χειρων αυτων και των ποδων αυτων -glnw, p	= B	𝔏 - *summitatis manum eorum et pedum*
1:13a מבוא	-- So: 𝔏	= A (✻)	υπερ αυτον -Abcx	--	--	
1:13b --	Χαλεβ	--	-- So: 𝔏	= B	= B	
1:14 --	Γοθονιηλ	= B	-- -Abcx So: 𝔏	-- -glnw	= B	
1:15 --	δη	--	-- So: 𝔏	-- -glnw	= B (MN- different order)	

	MT	B Fam.	𝔊	A Fam.	L	K	Misc.
1:16a	מדבר יהודה אשר בנגב	εις την ερη- μον την ου- σαν εν τω νοτω Ιουδα	= A (※ Ιουδαι γ)	εις την ερη- μον Ιουδα (Abc) την ουσαν εν τω νοτω	εις την ερη- μον την ου- σαν εν τω νοτω So: 𝔏	εις την ερη- μον η εστιν εν τω νοτω Ιουδα	
1:16b	וילך וישב	και επορευ- θησαν και κατωκησαν (B = κατωκησαν)	= A	και επορευ- θη και κατω- κησεν -Acx (abk = B Fam.)	και κατωκησαν -glnow So: 𝔏 (et habitavit)	= B Fam.	
1:21	בירושלם	εν Ιερουσα- λημ So: 𝔏	= B	= B (A = L)	-- -glnw	= B	
1:23	בית יוסף	--	(missing)	οικος Ισραηλ	οι υιοι Ιωσηφ (gn)/Ισραηλ (lptvw)	= A	𝔏 - filii Istrahel
1:24	--	και ιδου	(missing)	-- So: 𝔏	--	--	
1:27	הזאת	ταυτη So: 𝔏	(missing)	= B	-- -glnw	= B	

	MT	B Fam.	𝔊	A Fam.	L	K	Misc.
1:30	--	αυτω (imra₂= αυτου)	(missing)	-- So: 𝔏	ο Χαναναιος... αυτω/αυτου/ αυτου -glw (ptv -diff. order)	= B	
1:35a	בית יוסף	οικου Ιωσηφ	= B	= B	Ιωσηφ -glnw So: 𝔏	= B	
1:35b	--	αυτοις	--	--	αυτω So: 𝔏	= B	
1:36	--	--	= A (÷)	ο Ιδουμαιος So: 𝔏	= A	--	
2:1a	--	ταδε λεγει	--	-- So: 𝔏	--	= B	
2:1b	אעלה	ανεβιβασα So: 𝔏	= A/L ?	ανεβιβασεν (A -pr. Κυριος)	ανεβιβασεν ανηγαγεν	? = B-hb₂ = A-MNy	
2:1c	ואביא	και εισηγαγον So: 𝔏	= A	και εισηγαγεν	= A	? = B-hb₂ = A-MNy	

	MT	B Fam.	𝔊	A Fam.	L	K	Misc.
2:1d	אמר בנעמי	ην ωμοσα So: 𝔏	= A	ην ωμοσεν	= A	? = B-hb2 = A-MNy	
2:1e	--	--	= A (÷)	του δουναι υμιν So: 𝔏	= A	= A	
2:1f	ואמר	και ειπα	= A	και ειπεν υμιν	= A	και ειπεν	𝔏 - et dixi uobis
2:2	בקלי	της φωνης μου So: 𝔏	= B	= B	της φωνης αυτου	= B	
2:3a	אמרתי	ειπον	= A/B	ειπα	φησιν	= A	
2:3b	לא אוסיף	ου μη εξαρω	= L (÷ ου- ειπον γ)	= L (ειπα, του εξολε-θρευσαι -Acx)	ου προσθησω του μετοικισαι τον λαον ον ειπον του εξωσαι So: 𝔏	= L + B (om. του 1°, ειπα)	
2:4	רבי	υιους	= B	= B (A = L)	-- -glnw So: 𝔏	= B	

MT	B Fam.	𝔊	A Fam.	L	K	Misc.
2:11 את הבעלים	τοις Βααλειμ So: Ł	= B	= B	τοις Βααλειμ και τη Ασ-ταρτη	= B	
2:13 את יהוה	αυτοιν	-- So: Ł	τον Κυριον	= B	= B	
2:14a ויחר אף יהוה / בישראל	και ωργισθη θυμω Κυριος εν τω Ισραηλ So: Ł	= L	= B (om. εν)	= B (επι τον)	και ωργισθη θυμω Κυριου	Soιοθη Κυριου ωργισθη θυμω Κυριου
2:14b עוד לעבד	ετι αντιο-τηναι So: Ł	= A Fam.	αντιστηναι (A = B)	= A Fam.	= A Fam.	θ΄- ετι στηναι
2:15 להם	αυτοις	= B	= B (Aa = L)	--	--	Ł missing
2:16a ויקם יהוה	και ηγειρεν αυτοις Κυρι- So (B = K)	και ηγει-ρεν αυτοις ος αυτοις (※ αυτοις ʸ)	? = 𝔊 -bcx = K -Aak	= B Fam.	και ηγειρεν Κυριος So: Ł	
2:16b --	-- -imru So: Ł	= A Fam.	Κυριος (A = B Fam.)	= A Fam.	= A Fam.	
2:17a שפטיהם	των κριτων	= A Fam.	των κριτων αυτων (των αυτων - A)	= A Fam.	αυτων	θ΄- των κριτων αυτω, Ł - iudicio sou [sic]

	MT	B Fam.	𝔊	A Fam.	L	K	Misc.
2:17b	--	-- -Bimrua₂	= A (÷)	και παρωργι-σαν τον Κυρι-ον So: 𝔏	= A	= A	𝔏 – *et non recesserunt a uia sua dura* .
2:19	הקשה מדרכם	και τας οδους αυτων τας σκληρας	= L	και απο της οδου αυτων της σκληρας (A = 𝔏)	και απο της οδου αυτων της σκληρας ουκ απεστρεφον	απο της οδου	
2:21	יהושע	Ιησους υιος Ναυη εν τη γη (efjmrsuzb-diff. order, i = K)	= A	Ιησους So: 𝔏	= A -glnw (doptv = K)	Ιησους υιος Ναυη	
2:22	הם	-- So: 𝔏	= A	αυτοι -bcx	--	--	
10:1a	ויקם	και ανεστη So: 𝔏	= B	= B	και ανεστησεν ο θεος	= B	
10:1b	בן דודו	υιος πατρα-δελφου αυτου (πατρος αδελ-φου -efijmr suza₂)	= B	= B	υιον Καριε (Καρηε -gtv) πατραδελφου αυτου	= B (πατρος αδελφου -MNb₂ diff. order -y)	𝔏 – *filius Charreon fratris patris eius*
10:1c	איש יששכר	ανηρ Ισσαχαρ So: 𝔏	= B	= B	--	= B	

	MT	B Fam.	𝔊	A Fam.	L	K	Misc.
10:2	--	-- So: 𝔏	--	--	ο θωλα	--	
10:3	אחריו	μετ αυτον So: 𝔏	= B	= B	μετα τον θωλα	= B	
10:4	להם יקראו	και εκαλουν αυτας	και αυτας εκαλεσαν So: ϑ´	και αυτας εκαλεσεν -Gabc (A = L)	και εκαλεσεν αυτας So: 𝔏	= ϑ -MNh (εκαλεσεν -y, αυται -b₂)	
10:6a	את אלהי ארם	και τοις θεοις Συριας -eijrua₂ (Αραδ -B) So: 𝔏	= B (*)	= B (Σιδωνος -A)	-- -glnow, Thdt.	= B	
10:6b	בני עמון	υιων Αμμων So: 𝔏	= B	= B	Αμμων -glno,d,Thdt.	= B	
10:8a	את בני ישראל	τους υιους Ισραηλ So: 𝔏	= B	= B	τον Ισραηλ -glnow	= B	
10:8b	השנה ההיא	εν τω καιρω εκεινω So: 𝔏	= A	εν τω ενιαυτω εκεινω	-- -glnow	= B	

	MT	B Fam.	𝔊	A Fam.	L	K	Misc.
10:9a	ובדיה	και προς	= A	και εν τω οικω So: ϑ´, 𝔏	= A	= A	
10:9b	ואתר	και εθλιβη So: 𝔏	= A	και εθλιβησαν οι υιοι	= A	= A	
10:10a	לי	οοι So: 𝔏	= B	= B	-- -glnow	= B	
10:10b	--	-- So: 𝔏	--	--	θεος εστι και ελατρευ-σαμεν	--	
10:11a	מהמצרים והמ האמרי ומן ועמון	εξ Αιγυπτου και απο του Αμορραιου και απο υιων Αμμων	= A	οι Αιγυπτιοι και οι Αμορ-ραιοι και οι υιοι Αμμων So: 𝔏	= A	= A	σ´ - απο Αιγυπτου και απο των Αμορ-ραιων και απο των υιων Αμμων
10:11b	--	-- So: σ´	= A (÷)	και Μααβ So: 𝔏	= A (ptv - diff. order)	= A	
10:11c	ומן פלשתים	και απο Φυ-λιστιειμ	= A	και (οι) αλλοφυλοι So: 𝔏	= A	= A	σ´ - και απο των Φυλισ-τιαιων

	MT	B Fam.	𝔊	A Fam.	L	K	Misc.
10:12	צידונים	και Σιδωνιων	= A	και Σιδωνιοι	-- So: Ḻ	= A	
10:15a	אתה לך	συ ημιν So: Ḻ	= B	= B	ημιν Κυριε συ	= B	
10:15b	--	--	= A (ⸯ)	Κυριε So: Ḻ	= A	--	
10:15c	נא	δη (Bqa₂ = L) So: Ḻ	= B (※)	= L (cx = B)	--	= B	
10:16a	--	-- So: Ḻ	--	--	οι υιοι Ιοραηλ	--	
10:16b	--	μονω So: Ḻ	--	--	--	= B	
10:16c	--	-- So: Ḻ	= A (ⸯ)	και ουκ ευηρεστησεν εν τω λαω	= A (pr. μονω -δρτιν)	--	
10:16d	--	-- So: Ḻ	--	--	Κυριος	--	

	MT	B Fam.	𝔊	A Fam.	L	K	Misc.
10:18	שרי העם	ο λαος οι αρχοντες	οι αρχον-τες	οι του λαου αρχοντες (A - diff. order)	= A	? / = B-Mhb₂ / = 𝔊-Ny	𝔏 - *principes populi uiri*
11:4	ויהי מימים וילחמו בני עמון עם ישראל	--	= A	και εγενετο μεθ ημερας και επολεμησαν οι υιοι Αμμων μετα Ιστραηλ So: 𝔏	= A	= A	
11:11	אתו העם	αυτον ο λαος	= B (※ ο λαος)	= B (Abx - 2-3-1)	αυτον -glnow So: 𝔏	= B	
11:12a	--	-- So: 𝔏	= A (⸓)	ου	? / = A-low, ptv / = B-gn, d	--	
11:12b	--	--	= L (⸓)	? / = L-Aab / = B-ckx	με So: 𝔏	--	
11:13a	--	--	--	--	μοι So: 𝔏 (diff. place-ment)	--	

MT	B Fam.	𝔊	A Fam.	L	K	Misc.
11:13b ―	και πορευσομαι	= A (÷)	και αποστρε- ψαν οι αγγελοι προς Ιεφθαε So: 𝔏	= A	= B	
11:14 ויוסף עוד יפתח וישלח מלאכים	και προσεθη- κεν ετι Ιεφ- θαε και απεστειλεν	= A/B Fam. (* ετι ×)	και Ιεφθαε και απεστειλεν -abcx	και παλιν απεστειλεν Ιεφθαε -ǧlo(n)	= A Fam.	𝔏 - et misit *Iepthe iterum*
11:15 את ארץ מואב ואת ארץ בני עמון	την γην Μοαβ και την γην υιων Αμμων So: 𝔏 (nec)	= B	= B	την γην σου ουδε την γην υιων Μοαβ	= B	
11:16 כי	οτι	―	―	―	―	𝔏 - sed
11:17a וכן	δη	―	― So: 𝔏	―	= B	
11:17b ―	― So: 𝔏	= L	―	αυτου	―	
11:17c ―	― So: 𝔏	= L (÷)	―	ουδε ουτος ανειναι αυτω παρελθειν	―	

	MT	B Fam.	𝔖	A Fam.	L	K	Misc.
11:18	את ארץ אדום ואת ארץ מואב	την γην Εδωμ και την γην Μωαβ So: 𝔏	= B (※ και την γην Μωαβ ✓)	= B	την γην Μωαβ -ginow	= B	
11:19a	מלך חשבון מלך האמרי	βασιλεα του Αμορραιου βασιλεα Εσεβων	= B	= B (Aa - om. των Αμορραιων) 1-3, bcx - των Αμορραιων)	βασιλεα Εσ- σεβων του Αμορραιον - ginow (diff. spellings)	= B	𝔏 - Amorreorum regem Esebon
11:19b	לא	δη	= B	? = B -akx = L -Abc	-- So: θ´, 𝔏	= B	
11:21	--	-- So: 𝔏	= L	? = B -Aak = L -bcx	αυτου	--	
11:22a	ותאכל כל גבול וירשו את	--	= A	και εκληρονο- μησεν παν το οριον του Αμορραιου So: 𝔏	= A	--	
11:22b	--	-- So: 𝔏	--	--	Ισραηλ	--	

	MT	B Fam.	𝔖	A Fam.	L	K	Misc.
11:22c	מן הגלעד ומן הגלעד עד	του Ιαβοκ και απο της ερημου Σω3	= B (※)	= B	--	του Ιαβοκ	𝓛 - usque Ia- boe et usque ad fines fili- orum Ammon et a deserto us- que ad
11:22d	ומן הגלעד ועד הירדן	και απο της ερημου του Ιορδανου So: 𝓛	= B	= B	= B	--	
11:23	--	-- So: 𝓛	= A/L (־)	επι σου	επι σου	--	
11:24a	--	-- So: 𝓛	= L (־)	-- (A - σοι)	ημιν	--	
11:24b	--	-- So: 𝓛	--	--	εθνη	--	
11:24c	--	-- So: 𝓛	--	--	και εξηρεν	--	
11:25	מבלק	υπερ Βαλακ So: 𝓛	= B	? = B -Ack = L -abx	Βαλακ	= L	

	MT	B Fam.	𝔖	A Fam.	L	K	Misc.
11:26a	וּבְנוֹתֶיהָ	και εν τοις οριοις αυτης So: 𝔏	= A	και εν ταις θυγατρασιν	-Kglnow, d	= A	ριν - και εν τοτ πεσι Σιαι Σιων Σιαι ριων αυτης Σιων
11:26b	--	-- So: 𝔏	--	--	αι πασαι πλησιον Μωαβ	--	
11:27	--	-- So: 𝔏	--	--	και ηλθεν Σιηυ	--	
11:28	מַלְכֵּי בְנֵי עַמּוֹן	βασιλεως υιων Αμμων So: 𝔏	= B	= B	-Kgln	= B	
11:30	--	-- So: 𝔏	= A	μοι	= A	= A	
11:31	לִקְרָאתִי	ο εκπορευομε- νος	= B (*)	= B	-glnow So: 𝔏	= B	
11:35a	כִּרְאוֹתוֹ אוֹתָהּ	ως ειδεν αυτην αυτος	= A	ηνικα ειδεν αυτην So: 𝔏	ηνικα ειδεν αυτην Ιεφθαε	ηνικα ειδεν αυτην αυτος	ηνικα ειδεν αυτος αυτου

110

	MT	B Fam.	𝔊	A Fam.	L	K	Misc.
11:35b	בתי	θυγατηρ μου	= B	= B	θυγατηρ -glnow So: 𝔏	= B	
11:35c	ואת היית בכרעי	και συ ης εν τοις ταραχου μοι	= A	εγενεθη εν τω εμποδισμα εν εμποδισμα νου So: σ´ (λον), 𝔏 ο´, -(μοι)	= A	= A	
11:36	—	-- So: 𝔏	—	—	η θυγατηρ αυτου	—	
11:37	עשה לי	ποιησατω δη ο πατηρ μου	= A	και ποιησον μοι So: θ´	πλην ποιησον μοι	= A	𝔏 – fac mihi
11:38a	—	-- So: 𝔏	—	—	αυτη	—	
11:38b	—	-- So: 𝔏	—	—	ο πατηρ αυτης	—	
11:38c	—	-- So: 𝔏	—	—	απεστειλεν	—	

	MT	B Fam.	𝔊	A Fam.	L	K	Misc.
11:38d	על ההרים	επι τα ορη	= B	= B	-- -glnow (dptv - επι των ορεων)	= B	𝕷 - *in montibus*
11:39a	--	So: 𝕷	--	--	η θυγατηρ Ιεφθαε	--	
11:39b	ויעש לה	και εποιησεν (εν) αυτη	= A	και επετελεσεν Ιεφθαε So: θ´, 𝕷	= A -gnow (dptv - + Ιεφθαε)	= B (om. εν)	
17:4	מאתים	διακοσιους	= B	= B	-- So: 𝕷	= B	
17:5a	והאיש	και ο οικος	= A	και ο ανηρ So: 𝕷	= A -gl(ανην) no,d(w - om.)	= B	
17:5b	--	So: 𝕷	--	--	Μιχα	--	
17:7	מבית לחם יהודה ממשפחת יהודה	εκ Βηθλεεμ δημου Ιουδα	= A Fam.	εκ Βηθλεεμ Ιουδα εκ της συγγενειας Ιουδα (A - δημου Ιουδα 1°) So: θ´, 𝕷	εκ Βηθλεεμ δημου Ιουδα κ3 συγγενειας Ιουδα της συγγενειας Ιουδα	= A Fam.	

	MT	B Fam.	𝔊	A Fam.	L	K	Misc.
17:8	—	τοπω	—	-- So: 𝕷	—	—	
17:9a	—	-- So: 𝕷	= L	—	συ	—	
17:9b	—	τοπω	—	-- So: ϑ´, 𝕷	—	—	
17:10	וילך הלוי	και επορευθη ο Λευειτης	= B	= B	και ηυδοκησεν ο Λευειτης και επορευθη	= B	𝕷 - et coegit eum et abiit Leuites
17:12	הנער	—	= A	το παιδαριον So: 𝕷	= A	? = A-My = B-hb₂ (N missing)	
18:2a	מקצותם	—	= A (※)	απο μερους αυτων So: 𝕷	= A (diff. order)	—	
18:2b	אנשים	-- So: 𝕷	= A Fam. (※)	ανδρας (Gbcx, G-※)	—	—	

MT	B Fam.	𝔊	A Fam.	L	K	Misc.
18:2c ומאשׁתאל	και απο Εσθαολ	= A	και Εσθαολ So: 𝔏	και εξ Εσθαολ	= A	
18:2d --	-- So: 𝔏	= L (∸)	--	οι ανδρες	--	
18:3a המה עם בית מיכה	αυτοι εν οικω Μειχα	= A	αυτων οντων παρα τω οικω Μειχα	--	αυτων οντων εν τω οικω Μειχα	𝔏 - et cum ibi essent in domo Micha
18:3b אתה	ου -Befjmsz So: 𝔏	= B	= B -bckx (AGa=L)	-- -Kzglnow,d	= B	
18:6 --	-- So: 𝔏	--	--	Κυριου υγιαινοντες	--	
18:7a בארץ	εν τη γη So: σ´	= B (✳)	= B (G-✳)	-- So: 𝔏	--	
18:7b יושׁב לבטח	κληρονομους εμπιεζων ησαυρου	= B (om. εμπιεζων)	? = 𝔊 -G(✳)bx = L -Aak	-- So: 𝔏	--	

	MT	B Fam.	𝔊	A Fam.	L	K	Misc.
18:7c	מצרים	Σιδωνιων	= A	απο Σιδωνος So: σ´, 𝔏	= A	= A	
18:9	--	--	= A (÷)	(Long addition - cf. B-M, G÷) So: 𝔏	= A	--	
18:10	ידים	--	= x of A Fam. (✳)	χεροιν -x (diff. order -G[✳]bc) So: 𝔏 (diff. order)	--	--	
18:11a	משם	εκειθεν	= B (✳)	= B (G - ✳)	-- -KZglnow So: 𝔏	= B	
18:11b	ואשתאל	και απο Εσθαολ	= B/K	και Εσθαολ So: 𝔏	= A-KZgnow	και εξ Εσθαολ	
18:12	--	-- So: 𝔏	= L (÷)	--	και κατελυσαν εκει	--	

	MT	B Fam.	𝔊	A Fam.	L	K	Misc.
18:13	הר	ορους -Βfgsz (pr. εις - imrua₂)	= A (÷ και ηλθον γ, so G)	και ηλθον εως του ορους (A- ηλθαν, a- εις) So: Ḳ	εως του ορους Σοδο - K(uid.)Zgn, dptv (low = A Fam.)	= L	
18:14	ש׳ל	Λαισα	= B (*)	= B (G - *)	-- So: Ḳ	--	
18:15a	--	-- So: Ḳ	--	--	(Long addition οι εξακοσιοι - τερα)	--	
18:15b	ב׳ת	οικον	= A	εις τον οι- κον -AGckx So: Ḳ	= A	= B	
18:16	מלחמתם	της παραταξεως αυτων	= A	πολεμικα αυτων (G - * αυτων)	πολεμικα- K(uid.)Zglnow So: Ḳ	= A	
18:18a	ואלה	--	= A	ουτοι So: Ḳ	= A	= A	

	MT	B Fam.	𝔊	A Fam.	L	K	Misc.
18:18b	--	εκει	--	-- -Ackx So: 𝕷	--	--	𝕷- et cogna- tionis unius in Istrahel
18:19a	--	-- So: 𝕷	--	--	σοι (σου go)	--	
18:19b	ולמשׁפחה בישׂראל	και οικον εις δημον Ιοραηλ	= A	και συγγε- νειας εν Ιοραηλ So: ϑ´	και σκηπτρου ενος εν Ιοραηλ -KZ glnow (om. εν -no)	= A	
18:21	וישׂימו	και εδηκαν	= A Fam.	και επαταξαν -bcx (Aa = B, k- confl.)	και εταξαν -Zgnow (dptv = A Fam.) So: ϑ´, 𝕷	= A Fam.	
18:23	אל בני דן דן לי	-- So: 𝕷	= A	και εβοησαν προς τους υιους Δαν -Abcx	--	--	
18:24a	--	--	= L	? = B -Aab = L -ckx	εμαυτω So: ϑ´, 𝕷	= L	

	MT	B Fam.	𝔊	A Fam.	L	K	Misc.
18:24b	הנה הז	και τι τουτο So: Ḷ	= B	= B	-- -zglnow	= B	
18:24c	--	-- So: Ḷ	= A	τουτο	= A -zglno(w)	--	
18:25	--	-- -efimqrua₂ So: Ḷ	--	-- -abkx	δη	= L	
18:26	ולקח	-- So: Ḷ	= A	και εξενευσεν	= A	--	
18:27a	וישלח	και οι υιοι Δαν	= A	και αυτοι So: Ḷ	= A	= A	
18:27b	באש	εν πυρι So: Ḷ	= B	= B (om. εν -bcx, om. -Ak)	--	--	
18:30a	--	--	= A (⁘)	Μειχα So: Ḷ	= A	--	

MT	B Fam.	𝔖	A Fam.	L	K	Misc.
18:30b	υιος Γηρσομ υιος Μανασση αυτος (υιος 2° = υιου -efijsz a₂)	= L (*, υιου 2° = υιος)	= B (Γηρσομ- diff. spell- ings, υιος 2° = υιου)	υιος Μανασση υιου Γηρσαμ υιου Μωση αυτος	--	𝔏 -filius Gessam filii Moysi ipse

MT column Hebrew:
בן גרשם
בן משה
בנא

Commentary[13]

1:6   The presence of what would be the rendering of a second בהנות in Ɫ (though in the singular), the καιγε text, and K suggests that an OG reading has been preserved. 𝔖 and L conform to MT;[14] and the A family, both in this instance and even more clearly in the following, is divided. Moore points to Exodus 29:20 as possible evidence of a Hebrew basis for the addition.[15]

1:7   Here Ɫ does not support the plus in the B family and K; otherwise the situation is the same as in 1:6. It may be noted that Ɫ also omits the second of the possessive suffixes, which has the combined support of all of the Greek witnesses and the MT.

The plus (1:10) και εξηλθεν Χεβρων εξ εναντιας will not be included in this discussion for two reasons. For one thing, as Pretzl observed,[16] it seems more likely that this clause is an alternate rendering of the following ושם חברון לפנים than that it represents a different Hebrew *Vorlage*. Although it is difficult to see a connection between ושם and και εξηλθεν (Schreiner suggests ויצא[17]), the similarity of the rest of the two clauses is striking. Still more important, however, is the observation that no Greek family shows revision to MT in this case. The loss of the first three words in L is most likely due to haplography of Χεβρων. Instances in which all Greek families show the same variant and none have revision to MT will not be included in the present study.

1:13a   Here the absence of the prepositional phrase in an earlier Hebrew *Vorlage* is uncertain. As Schreiner observes, the comparative and its reference are adequately expressed by the Greek without υπερ αυτον.[18] Nevertheless, the OG reading seems clear and is affirmed by the asterisk of Origen. Moore calls attention to the parallel in Judges 3:9.[19] There the most literal rendering appears only in the καιγε text; a translation by simple αυτου followed by an OG addition (with an obelus) stands in all of the other Greek families and 𝔖; and an omission of the phrase appears in Ɫ. In this latter

instance, the καιγε reading is clear; whether the OG involved
a simple αυτου or an omission is not so clear. Nevertheless,
it confirms the usefulness of such a reading (which may or may
not involve a different *Vorlage*) for identifying a recensional
difference.

    1:13b   The addition of a second Χαλεβ in the B family, L,
and K may not be a genuine OG reading. If so, it would be expected to be retained in the text of Origen (cf. note 11).
Such instances are included here as being potentially OG,
although in no case will a conclusion depend on them.

    1:14   This addition has much greater claim to being an
OG reading, since it stands in Origen's text, though without
an obelus (cf. note 11). Whereas in the discussion to follow
it will be shown that the L text, especially when supported by
Ⱬ, most consistently preserves OG readings, this instance
illustrates what has been frequently affirmed about the Greek
text of Judges, i.e., that an eclectic approach must be
followed for the recovery of the OG.[20] The early nature of
this addition is confirmed by its appearance in the Ⱬ of
Sabatier.
    The addition of the Lucianic manuscripts gw and ptv
before και 2° in the verse and the variant translation of
והצנח מעל החמור later in the verse are not included in the
chart, since in both cases a double rendering of the same
Hebrew text is involved, rather than a different *Vorlage*.[21]

    1:15   The presence of this particle in the B family and
K may reflect only a stylistic tendency. Yet the same Hebrew
particle (נא) is in question in the six chapters being presently analyzed in 4 other instances,[22] and in at least 3 of
these a genuine OG variant seems to be present.[23] Therefore,
it seems best to include each of these cases as potential
examples of OG variation.

    1:16a   The variant in question here is the treatment of
the Hebrew יהודה. That its absence in L represents an OG
reading is confirmed by the agreement of Ⱬ and the asterisk

which precedes it in 𝔖. Its restoration in the B family,
though at a different location, can be taken to represent
καιγε revision; and its more exact restoration in 𝔖 would be
the work of Origen, as the asterisk demonstrates.

1:16b The reading of the primary Lucianic witnesses
glnow is also that of 𝕷 and is, therefore, demonstrably early.
The restoration of וילך in the B family would represent καιγε
revision, and the more exact rendering of the verbs as singular in 𝔖 would reflect Origen's work.[24]

The doublets in verses 17, 19, and 20 will not be included
in this study, since no variant Hebrew *Vorlage* is indicated.[25]

1:21 The omission in L and Alexandrinus may well represent the OG here, although this cannot be assured without
further evidence. The phrase בירושלם in MT may itself be a
secondary harmonization with Joshua 15:63.[26] Since, however,
there is no confirming evidence that the reading of L is an
early one, the other groups are simply classified as being in
agreement with MT in this case.[27]

Because יהודה would be such an easy corruption of יהוה,
the variant near the end of verse 22 is not included.[28]

1:23 Moore suggests that the subject is superfluous
here and may not have been original in any form.[29] It would
seem, rather, that the omission in the B family should be
explained as haplography. The reading of 𝕷 may represent the
primitive Greek rendering. If so, it would be preserved in
lptvw of the L text, and in the A family and K with only partial revision to MT. It should be noted that בית יוסף of verse
22 is rendered by all Greek witnesses and by a number of Hebrew
manuscripts as בני יוסף.[30]

The αυτων which is added later in the verse in Boqℓ is not
a clear reading of the B family and has no other support, so
it is disregarded in this study.

1:24 This addition of the B family, which should represent והנה, has no early support.

122

1:27 This omission in glnw of the L text could be a
primitive Greek reading, or it could be an inner-Greek corruption due to homoeoteleuton in the Greek text. Were the
omission primitive in a Hebrew *Vorlage*, it could have been
restored later through harmonization with Joshua 17:12. As
has been stated, the conclusions to be drawn in this chapter
will in no case be dependent upon variants such as this which
lack corroborating evidence that they are early.

The B family addition of ουδε τα περιοικια αυτης is not
included, since it appears to be an alternate rendering of
ואת בנותיה.[31]

1:30 At least this pronoun, if not the noun as well, may
represent the OG; but there is no early confirmation. On the
other hand, it could represent harmonization with verses 29
(L), 33 (plural except in K), and 35 (L, Ƚ, plural in the B
family and K, lacking in Ṣ and the A family). Judging from
the general conformity of the A family to Ṣ,[32] and from verse
35, if Ṣ had been preserved here it would presumably have
omitted the pronoun in accord with MT.

The addition in L at the end of verse 33 is not included
because it seems to be a restoration of the same clause which
is lost in L (glnw) in the midst of the verse (likely through
haplography of [י]וישב).

1:35a The reading of L (glnw) and Ƚ is an early variant, and the conformity of the other families and Ṣ to MT is
most likely to be attributed to καιγε revision.[33]

1:35b Here an early Greek addition has been preserved
in L and Ƚ, and, with a difference in number, the B family and
K. The addition is missing in Ṣ and the A family, apparently
indicating its absence in Origen's base text. Therefore, in
this case either the OG reading is not preserved in L and Ƚ;
or it was not represented in Origen's base text; or it has been
lost from Origen's revision.

1:36 This OG addition is confirmed by Ƚ and Ṣ (with an
obelus).

2:1a   This addition in the B family and K appears to have been deliberately made in order to adhere to the person of the following Hebrew verbs. In any case, there is no confirming evidence that it is early.[34]

2:1b-d   In each of these variants, the καιγε family conforms to MT in the person of the verb; and the L text, 𝔖, and A family diverge. The K text divides, and Ⱡ also agrees with MT. Thus, the antiquity of the variant forms cannot be confirmed. It is a case in which the first divergence would have set the pattern for the entire passage, whenever that may have occurred.[35]

2:1e   The presence of this Greek addition in Origen's base text is attested by the obelus, and its antiquity is confirmed by its appearance in Ⱡ. Such readings will be regarded as OG in this analysis. Its absence in the B family is to be attributed to καιγε revision.[36]

2:1f   The additional pronoun here is an OG reading, being attested by Ⱡ and 𝔖 (though without an obelus), as well as L and the A family. Again καιγε revision appears in the B family. The person of the verb in Ⱡ, however, could suggest that the third person readings here and in 2:1b-d are not OG, but rather are a later alteration (cf. the discussion above).

2:2-3a   The third person perspective of the first verse is maintained here only by the L text, again suggesting that it is not primitive in the Greek tradition, though it does precede the work of historical Lucian in verse one.

2:3b   That the text of the OG in this verse was longer is confirmed by the obelus and by the agreement of Ⱡ. The B family shows the καιγε reading, and K is conflate.

2:4   An ancient omission in L is confirmed here by Ⱡ. The addition of L in 2:10 has no early confirmation. Its virtual identity with 3:5-6 and the similarity of the following verse in each case probably account for its interpolation here.[37]

2:11   This addition in L may be due to the use of the
two nouns together in verse thirteen.[38]   In any case, there is
no early confirmation.

2:13   It may be that the αυτov of the B family, L, and K
is primitive in the Greek tradition.   It is the reading of the
Vulgate, which could indicate its presence in an 𝔏 text.   The
loss of the entire phrase closing with the variant in question
in 𝔏 and 𝔖 could be due to haplography of the preceding Kυρι-
ov,[39] or to the similarity of the verbs ויעזבו and ויעבדו.

2:14a   The omission of בישראל is attested among the
Greek families only by K, but it is also the reading of the 𝔏
of Sabatier.   The restoration is most literal in the καιγε
text, and L agrees with 𝔖 (ʿal).

2:14b   The omission of עוד in 𝔖, L, the A family, and K
could be due to a haplography of ετι and αντι, but it is perhaps better to see this as the OG reading.   The Vulgate, which
agrees, could represent an Old Latin rendering with the same
omission.   In that case this would be an instance in which
Origen did not fill in the omission.   The B family would represent revision to the Hebrew text, and ϑ´ would constitute a
still more literal revision.

2:15   The omission of להם in L and K has no early confirmation as an OG reading, although 𝔏 has a break at this point.

2:16a   The OG of this verse apparently included an αυτοις
not reflected in MT.   Presumably the asterisk of 𝔖 should be
an obelus.   Of the B family, only B agrees with the Hebrew;
but this could represent καιγε revision.[40]

2:16b   The addition of Kυριος (as well as the change of
ויושיעום to the singular) has wide support, being preserved
in 𝔖 as well as in all of the Greek families.   Of the καιγε
family, however, imru[41] reveal partial revision to the Hebrew

in the deletion of the noun. The Greek addition appears to be primitive in this case.[42]

  2:17a   The variants in this case are difficult to classi-fy. Since the Vulgate agrees with K in reading only the pro-noun, this can be seen as potentially OG.[43] The καιγε text has the noun of the MT, but not the pronoun. The other Greek texts have the full Hebrew reading.

  2:17b   This obelized OG addition has been suppressed by καιγε.[44]

  2:19   The verb which is added at the end of the phrase in 𝔊 and L and at the beginning in 𝕷 and A is best regarded as an OG reading. The initial *mēm* of ממעלליהם could have easily been overlooked by haplography in the OG translation, so that the preposition of ומדרכם necessitated the second verb. The καιγε text has suppressed the addition, though in the process the second object has been aligned with the first as an accu-sative plural without a preposition.[45]

  2:21   The addition in the B family, which appears in part in K and the Lucianic subgroup dptv, may well be a later explanatory insertion.[46] There is no confirmatory evidence that it is early.

  2:22   The restoration of הם in the text of 𝔊 and in bcx of the A family is to be attributed to Origen, though an aster-isk does not appear in the extant sources.

  10:1a   The Lucianic addition of ο θεος as the subject, in keeping with the rendering of the verb as a *hiphil*, has no ancient support.[47]

  10:1b   The Lucianic addition of the proper name Καριε has been ascribed to a Hebrew *Vorlage* with קָרָח.[48] While many have objected to this explanation,[49] the 𝕷 text does support the L reading; and the inclusion of the following איש יששכר in 𝕷 militates against Καριε being merely a corruption from the latter part of this expression.[50]

 10:1c There is no supporting evidence for this omission in L; and it may well have been made to relieve the difficulty in the L text, in which הוהי cannot be taken as a proper name.[51]

 10:2 No other evidence supports this addition in L.

 10:3 It is likely that the same tendency to clarify is seen here as in the preceding L addition.

 10:4 The reading of L, 𝕷, and Alexandrinus is to be regarded as the oldest Greek extant. The verb was read as singular, and a word order different from that of the MT was employed. The καιγε text shows revision in the number of the verb, and the texts of 𝕾 and ϑ´ also show revision in the word order.

 10:6a Here is a case in which only L preserves the reading of the text which Origen used as his base. The reading which Origen supplied under an asterisk is also that of the best representatives of the καιγε text as well as the A family and K.

 10:6b-8a These L omissions have no supporting evidence that they are early.

 10:8b Here there are three variants among the Greek families. The reading of the B family is also that of 𝕷 and may presuppose a different *Vorlage*.[52] The omission of L has no firm confirmation that it is early.[53] The texts of 𝕾 and the A family conform to MT.

 10:9a The omission of בים by the B family may be early. Although there is no firm evidence, the Vulgate also omits.

 10:9b Since this addition appears in 𝕾 (though not in 𝕷) and in all Greek families but καιγε, it seems best to take it as the OG reading and to see the καιγε text as a revision to MT.

10:10a-b   Neither the omission of לך nor the longer addition near the end of the verse in L has any other support.

10:11a   That the reading of all Greek families except καιγε is probably the OG here is confirmed by the agreement of Ƶ and possibly also by the following variant (in which the preposition is likewise omitted and the addition is further confirmed as OG by the obelus of Origen). This, then, would be a case in which Origen did not revise to MT. In both cases, καιγε revision would be seen in the B family.[54]

10:11b   Cf. the preceding comment.

10:11c   The absence of מן in all Greek texts but καιγε and in Ƶ is in keeping with the pattern in the two previous instances and is the reason for the inclusion of this variant. It appears that καιγε revision has also been at work in the change from αλλοφυλοι to Φυλιστειμ.[55]

10:12   This L omission is confirmed by Ƶ.

10:15a-c   Although the Lucianic addition of 15a has no confirmation, that of 15b is confirmed as OG by Ƶ and the obelus of Origen; and the omission of 15c is confirmed by the asterisk.

10:16a,c   16a and c are Lucianic additions with no other support.

10:16b   Three text forms appear in 10:16b. That of the B family and K has the support of Ƶ; that of the A family, L, and Ƨ has the support of the obelus; and both differ from MT. The second of these variant Greek forms has been plausibly explained as a double rendering of (ל)בעמ נפשו ותקצר,[56] in which case the B family reading would be best seen as the genuine OG, and the other as an early doublet which arose before the work of Origen and stood in his *Vorlage*.

10:18 The only variant here which could involve a difference in *Vorlage* is the omission of העם in 𝔖. This is more likely an inner-Syriac corruption,[57] since Origen did not delete OG plusses.

11:4 The omission in the B family here has no other support and may be an inner-Greek error due to homoeoteleuton.[58]

11:11 L is supported by 𝕃 and by the asterisk of Origen in this omission.

11:12a-b The agreement of 𝕃 in 12b and the obelus of Origen in both cases confirm both of these readings as being OG. In 12a, L is divided, as is the A family in 12b. In both cases K agrees with the καιγε text.

11:13a This L addition also appears in 𝕃, though there it follows the subsequent pronoun of L.

11:13b The addition of L and the A family has the support of 𝕃 and 𝔖 with an obelus and so is to be regarded as an OG reading. The shorter addition of the B family and K has no other support and may represent a partial stage of revision to the Hebrew of MT (or exact revision to a proto-MT reading).

11:14 The variant at issue here is the omission of עוד in L and 𝕃, which can be seen as the OG rendering. The less idiomatic and more literal rendering of ויוסף in the other families also restores the עוד and, thus, shows revision to the Hebrew in both respects.

11:15 The reversal of מואב and the substitution of σου for בני עמון in L has no other support.

11:16 This omission is not demonstrably early.

11:17a-c　These three variants all have sufficient support to be regarded as OG readings: 17a in Ƚ, 17b in ʃ (though without an obelus), and 17c in ʃ (with an obelus).[59]　In each case, the καιγε text conforms to MT.

11:18　The omission of L is likely reflected in the asterisk of ʃ (which is probably misplaced).

11:19a　Although arranged differently, the readings of L and Ƚ agree in the omission of the מלך which stands in MT with האמרי.

11:19b　The omission of נא has the support of Ƚ.

11:21　This L addition has the support of ʃ (without an obelus).

11:22a-b　No other evidence supports the omission in the B family and K[60] or the addition in L.

11:22c　This and the following variant are written separately, although the text overlaps.　Here the variant in question, the L omission, has the support of the asterisk of Origen, indicating that the reading did not stand in Origen's base text.[61]

11:22d　The omission here on the part of K has no other support.[62]

11:23-24a　Both of these additions are confirmed as being early by the obelus of Origen.

11:24b-28　In none of these L variants (or in K in 25) is there confirming evidence that the reading is early.

11:30　This addition is attested by the text of Origen (though without an obelus).

11:31　This omission has the support of Ƚ and is also

found in the text of Pseudo-Philo, which has been analyzed as a witness to a Palestinian Hebrew text and has been dated to somewhere before A.D. 100 and probably before A.D. 70.[63]

11:35a   Here the omission of the pronominal subject may be the OG (which Origen did not correct), in which case the literal rendering by αυτος in the B family would represent καιγε revision. The addition of Ιεφθαε in L would simply be a clarification, possibly made by Lucian himself.

11:35b   The omission of the pronoun in L is supported by *Ł*.

11:35c   A different Hebrew text seems to have lain behind this variant,[64] which is supported by *Ł* and *Ş*.

11:36   This L addition has the support of the early witness of LAB.[65]
The OG reading ει εν εμοι, later in this verse, was evidently based on Hebrew הבי (real or assumed).[66] The addition of πατερ in the B family (and the omission of ει εν εμοι in B itself) would, thus, represent καιγε revision to MT. The variant is not included in the present study, but it is mentioned here to point out another instance of καιγε revision in the text of Vaticanus alone.

11:37   The variation in the person of the verb and the addition in the B family can be treated together, since the latter appears to have been necessitated by the former, which would represent καιγε revision.[67]

11:38a-b   Both of these Lucianic additions seem to appear in the text of LAB, though 38b is in a different location.[68] The first also appears in, the Vulgate.

11:38c - 39a   These three L variants have no other support, though in the case of 39a, *Ł* omits the entire clause and so cannot be consulted.

11:39b   Here the Hebrew text read by the OG translator
apparently had יפתח (as in 𝔊, the A family, L, ϑ´, and 𝕷),
while the MT reads לה (as in the B family and K). In any case,
the addition is clearly OG; and its suppression represents
καιγε revision.

17:4   This L omission is confirmed by 𝕷.

17:5a   This variation in the B family and K could be due
to the context, since οικος both precedes and follows,[69]
though it is potentially OG.

17:5b   There is no other support for this addition of L.

17:7   The B family could preserve the OG reading here,
although there is no confirming evidence. If so, 𝔊, the A
family, and K would represent revision to MT; and L would be
conflate.[70]

17:8,9b   The addition of τοπω in the B family in both of
these cases has no other support.

17:9a   This addition of L also stood in the base text of
Origen (though an obelus does not appear in 𝔊) and would,
therefore, appear to be OG. It appears as well in Targum
Jonathan, which normally agrees with MT in the readings tabulated here.

17:10   An OG addition may well be reflected here in the
texts of L and 𝕷, though the verb presumed would seem to have
been different in each case.

17:12   The omission of the B family appears elsewhere
only in the Syriac Peshitta.

18:2a-b   In both of these cases, the B family preserves
an omission which Origen filled in under an asterisk. In 2b,
𝕷 and L also omit; and in both the Vulgate omits.

132

18:2c   The preposition is omitted in 𝔊, the A family, 𝕃, and K. This is a Greek minus which Origen did not fill in.

18:2d   This addition has the support of 𝔊 with an obelus.

18:3a - 6   Although these variants have no early support, the Vulgate shares the omission in 3a and in 3b.

18:7a-b   These two variants could have been treated as one, except that σ´ is only preserved for the first and the A family divides in the second. 𝕃 and the asterisk indicate the early nature of the full omission.

18:7c   There is no early support for the omission of the preposition in the B family.

18:9   This addition appears in 𝕃 and did stand in Origen's base text, since it bears the obelus.[71]

18:10   This OG omission is restored only by Origen (with an asterisk, followed by some of the A family) and by 𝕃.

18:11a-b   Both of these omissions are confirmed by 𝕃, and the first by the asterisk as well.

18:12   The obelus of Origen confirms this addition of L.

18:13   The full OG text apparently stands in the A family, 𝔊, and 𝕃. Most of the addition is suppressed in L (except for low) and K, but full conformity to MT is found only in B and some other manuscripts of the καιγε family.

18:14   This omission is confirmed by 𝕃 and the asterisk.

18:15a   This addition has no early support.[72]

18:15b   The elimination of the Greek preposition in the B family seems to represent καιγε revision.

18:16   The omission of the pronoun is confirmed by Ⅼ and the asterisk.

18:18a - 19a   None of these variants from MT have early support. (In 19a, the Vulgate has the pronoun.)

18:19b   The addition of ενος in L is confirmed by Ⅼ as an early reading. It is missing in the B family, but an οικου has intruded (possibly under the influence of the context[73]). Virtual conformity to MT appears in the other groups and witnesses. Since suppression of an OG plus appears to be involved, the Ⅹ reading is not attributed to Origen's own revising work, but is simply classified as being in accord with MT.

18:21   Contrary to the procedures followed thus far in this selection of variants, this one is included even though it involves only a difference in vocabulary, because here a different Hebrew *Vorlage* could be indicated by the reading of Ⅹ, the A family, and K. The verb of L, ϑ´, and Ⅼ is actually a more precise rendering of ערך, but could render שׂים. The καιγε translation is exact.[74]

18:23   This variant involves a correction in the apparatus of B - M.[75] The omission of L and Ⅼ is preserved also in the καιγε text and K and is presumably OG. The reading of Ⅹ and the A family would be, therefore, the restoration of Origen (though without an asterisk).

18:24a   This addition is supported by Ⅼ and Ⅹ (without an obelus).

18:24b   This omission has no early support, though it does appear in the Vulgate.

18:24c   This addition is supported by Ⅹ (without an obelus).

18:25   This has no early support.

18:26   Here the B family preserves an early omission.

18:27a-b   These have no early support.

18:30a   This addition is supported by 𝕃 and 𝕊 (with an obelus).

18:30b   The reason for the inclusion of this variant is the omission of the entire reading in K and the asterisk of Origen which indicates that it was not in his base text (though his restoration, like that of L, is apparently conflate).

The Survival of the Old Greek

Lucian. A conclusion of primary importance from the study of the variants given above is that the Lucianic text of Judges is the most consistent representative among the Greek families of the earliest Greek translation extant for that book. For convenience, this will be referred to simply as the Old Greek, without an effort in general to distinguish proto-Lucianic readings such as those identified by Cross in Samuel.[76]

In those cases in which L shows a text which diverges from MT but stands alone among the Greek witnesses, the primacy of L as a witness to the OG of Judges is clearly seen. There are 59 such cases.[77]

Some of these instances, of course, may not be OG at all, but the work of Lucian himself. It is commonly recognized that Lucian's own revision involved interpolation and conflation, as well as the filling in of omissions in the older Greek.[78] Somewhat under half of these variations (25) do constitute additions of some sort in the Lucianic text over against the other Greek witnesses.[79] However, the larger half (34) consists of variations of other types, mostly short readings (32), which are not regarded as typical of Lucian.

More significant still is the number of these Lucianic variants which are confirmed as pre-Lucianic by their presence in another source which antedates the martyr Lucian.[80] Of

these 59 variants found exclusively in L, 25 have such confirmation.[81] This is more than the total number of variants
found exclusively in any of the other Greek families.[82]

Those cases in which the L text preserves a potential OG
reading in agreement with one or more of the other Greek text
types also constitute primary data for the present argument
that L is the most consistent witness to the OG of Judges. In
56 instances such a reading stands in L, and in 47 of these
the reading has early confirmation.[83] This latter figure is
more than the total number of readings of this type in any of
the other families or witnesses.[84]

Therefore, the evidence pointing to a preservation of the
OG indicates the Lucianic text as the most reliable guide to
that source. In those potentially OG readings which appear in
only one of the Greek families, L has the overwhelming majority; and even those of this type which are demonstrably prior
to Lucian himself surpass the totals of the other families.
In those potentially OG readings which are common to two or
more of the Greek families, L again has the majority, with
those which are demonstrably early again surpassing the total
figure of this type of reading in any other family or witness.
It is to the L text that one must turn in Judges for his first
recourse in seeking the rendering of the Old Greek.

This recognition of the ancient material in L has been
common to many students of the Greek text of Judges. Billen
has pointed out that, more specifically, the group glnow is
the best witness to the OG, dptv including a large number of
Hexaplaric insertions.[85] Barthélemy has observed that the L
text of Judges most consistently resists the καιγε revision of
the B family.[86] Soisalon-Soininen has found that the L text
(his A II) preserves the most ancient material, and he sees
this confirmed by its close relationship to ʟ.[87] This tradition must now be considered, for it appears to represent in
Judges a carrier of the OG second only to the L text in consistency.

The Old Latin. Billen has called the agreement of ʟ
with L "one of the most remarkable characteristics of the LXX
text of Judges";[88] and in his article on the ʟ of Judges, he
suggests that it may prove to be one of the primary authorities

for the OG ("LXX" in the article).[89] This is the conclusion
to which the present writer is led by the readings tabulated
above.

Of those potentially OG readings which appear in only one
of the Greek families, Ł also has the reading 19 times.[90]
This is more than the totals of the other Greek families in
this type of reading, except for L.[91]

With respect to those potentially OG readings which are
found in at least two of the Greek families, Ł (38) comes behind all of the other groups except the B and A families in
total count.[92] In each case, however (except for L and Ș, the
latter of which is equal to Ł), the total of Ł is higher than
the total number of readings in the other groups which are
demonstrably early.[93]

Finally, not only does the number of OG readings in Ł
(57) surpass the total number of potentially OG readings in
every group except L,[94] it also surpasses the total number of
demonstrably early readings in every group except L.[95]

It should be added that these are likely not all of the
instances in which Ł retains an OG reading. There are cases
in which a reading divergent from MT and plausibly reflecting
the OG is shown by Ł, but in which that reading is not witnessed by any of the Greek families. These cases have not
been classified in the present study. They would, however,
require treatment in any thorough analysis of Ł[96] and would
add support to the present description of Ł as a primary
avenue to the OG of Judges, second only to the L text.[97]

The Hexapla with Special Reference
to the Fifth and Sixth Columns

The Fifth Column. Apart from 4 of the readings tabulated
above which are included in the section of chapter one of
Judges lost by the Syro-hexapla,[98] this translation preserves
all of the other readings dealt with in this chapter. The
alignment of these 146 readings of the Syriac translation of
Origen's fifth column[99] is strongly suggestive of the nature
of his Greek *Vorlage*.

It appears that the text which Origen used as his base was a form of the OG. In the readings tabulated in this chapter, he shows agreement with the OG a total of 42 times; and 40 of these have confirmation that they are early. This exceeds the number of OG readings with early confirmation in K (32), A (29), and B (12). Only L (72) and Ḻ (57) have more.[100]

To be sure, this OG *Vorlage* has been extensively revised toward MT in the fifth column as it is preserved to us. The total number of readings in Ş which are in agreement with MT is 99. Of this total, 60 could not be more precisely defined; whether they reveal revision is questionable.[101] The revising work of Origen himself does seem to appear in at least 26 of these readings.[102] Finally, in 13 of the readings which accord with MT, the text of Ş is in agreement with the καιγε family.[103] This evidence seems sufficient to indicate that the base text used by Origen was a form of the OG.[104]

In his study of the βγ section of Samuel-Kings, Barthélemy concluded that Origen used the καιγε revision of that section in his fifth column instead of the OG.[105] This is not the case in Judges. The basic agreement of Ş is clearly not with the B (καιγε) family, but with the other groups. More, however, must be said. For, whereas the καιγε text did not furnish the base for Origen's revision, καιγε influence on his work can be identified.

For one thing, the 13 readings in which Origen shows agreement with the καιγε text suggest the possibility of καιγε influence on his revision.[106] These readings, however, because of their small total, could be regarded simply as the coincidence of what was actually discrete revision in the καιγε text and in Origen.

More significant indication of καιγε influence on Origen's work is found in the characteristics discussed in chapters one through three above. Of the total of 430 readings in which Origen's revision could be compared with the καιγε text, 230 show the OG reading, either with the B family (85),[107] or apart from the B family (which would, in these cases, show καιγε revision - 145).[108] These totals, especially the latter, confirm the conclusion stated above, i.e., that Origen's base text was a form of the OG.

However, the total number of instances in which Origen's revision shows a καιγε characteristic (200) would seem adequate to demonstrate that καιγε influence is present in his fifth column. Although some of these latter readings could represent, rather, the OG in need of no καιγε revision,[109] 58 of them stand with the καιγε family against OG renderings elsewhere and are, therefore, confirmed as καιγε readings.[110] The 133 instances in which 𝔖 agrees with the B family in a καιγε reading, but without the OG appearing elsewhere, likely represent καιγε revision as well in many cases.[111] The 9 remaining instances in which 𝔖 shows a καιγε reading stand in contrast to the B family, which in these cases may retain the OG.[112]

Perhaps the best place to look to discover the nature of the sources which Origen used in the revision of his Greek *Vorlage* is that series of readings which are explicitly labeled by Origen as constituting such, i.e., those readings bearing the asterisk. In the entire book of Judges, there are 104 asterisked readings which can be significantly compared with the other Greek families.[113] The distribution of these readings in relation to the καιγε family both confirms the presence of καιγε influence on the work of Origen and gives further indication of the source(s) on which he drew.

The 64 readings from this total of 104 in which the asterisked additions of Origen agree with the καιγε text[114] add confirmation of the influence of this recension on his revision. Although these readings could theoretically be construed as discrete revision in the καιγε text and in Origen's work, this explanation is even less likely in cases in which a recognized καιγε characteristic is involved. In the 5 cases in which this is true, Origen has the characteristic.[115] Nor is this explanation likely in the other 59 instances.

These three lines of evidence (the 13 readings from the preceding table in which the text of 𝔖 agrees with the καιγε text in a revision to the Hebrew, the 200 instances in which Origen's text shows a recognized καιγε characteristic [especially the 58 of these which stand against an OG rendering elsewhere], and the 64 asterisked readings in which Origen agrees with καιγε) converge to establish the presence of καιγε influence in the formation of Origen's revision.

This conclusion concerning Origen's revision in Judges was anticipated somewhat by Cooper in his observation that the A and B texts were both cited in the fifth column of the Hexapla.[116] Stated more precisely now, the OG (which is generally reflected in the A text, cf. the discussion later in this chapter) and the καιγε recension (which is found in the B text and its congeners) both appear in Origen's fifth column, the former constituting the base text and the latter being somehow connected with the revision he carried out.

In pursuit of a more precise identification of the source or sources of Origen's revisional work, several clues appear which help to point the way. First it should be observed that 27 of the remaining asterisked readings show revision to MT in Origen's fifth column, but not in accord with the καιγε text. The pattern in these readings is significant, for the great majority (21) are more Hebraizing, i.e., closer to MT, than is the καιγε text.[117]

Perhaps even more significant are the remaining 13 asterisked readings. These involve what is probably the most distinctive characteristic of Aquila, the use of συν to render the definite object marker את.[118] Although the evidence is not completely clear, it can be analyzed as follows.

Of the 13 asterisked passages in Judges which render the object marker, the first appears as συν in ϭ.[119] All but the final 1 of the remaining 12 appear as lamad.[120] Furthermore, whereas only the first, second, and fourth of the 13 have an asterisk in ϭ, all bear the asterisk in Colberto-Sarravianus (G) except the first and second, for which the uncial is not extant.[121]

The apparent inconsistency of ϭ in this rendering has been clarified by Rørdam in his study of the work of Paul of Tella in Judges and elsewhere in the Old Testament. He has observed that it was characteristic of the bishop to render συν by lamad;[122] and this is most strikingly confirmed in Ecclesiastes, in which the Greek version[123] frequently has συν and ϭ has lamad.[124] The usage in Judges is thereby clarified; and in this connection, Rørdam himself concluded that Origen inserted συν into his revision for the object marker את and that he drew this insertion from Aquila.[125]

Another indication pointing to Aquila as a source for
Origen's revisions is the asterisked addition of επι τουτω for
כן על in 6:22. This is a distinctive characteristic of Aquila
which has been identified by Barthélemy.[126]

Still another indication comes from the rendering of בין
in 5:27b as μεταξυ in $ and the A family. It has already been
noted that this is also a characteristic of Aquila.[127] These
renderings converge and point to Aquila as one of the sources
upon which Origen drew as he did his work of revision.

Another of his sources is suggested by the asterisked
addition in 11:21, which is in agreement with the sixth
column.[128] This indication is amply confirmed by the agreement of the fifth column with the following sixth column citations, all of which seem to show revision to MT (although
without an asterisk): 2:17a(?); 3:18; 4:7; 10:18; 11:24;
14:18b; 16:7 (≠ α´ ≠ σ´), 12, 19; 18:19c, 24, 28a. The following references show agreement with others of the Three as well
as ϑ´: 2:14a (σ´), 17b (λ); 5:27b (α´); 11:26 (λ); 15:11 (παντ).

The following conclusions have been reached, therefore,
in this study of Origen's fifth column in Judges. His base
text was a form of the OG; his revisions indicate a significant
degree of καιγε influence; and he drew specifically on both
the third and the sixth columns in the course of these revisions.[129] The possible relationships between the second and
third of these conclusions will be discussed after the following study of the sixth column.

The Sixth Column. Several studies of the sixth column of
the Hexapla should be mentioned in preparation for the following analysis of the Judges sixth column. Barthélemy has included the sixth column as a whole in his catalog of members
of the καιγε recension.[130] He has, however, indicated the
exclusion of the sixth column of Samuel-Kings and of the Minor
Prophets. The former he characterizes as the otherwise lost
Septuagint for that section,[131] and the latter as late and
eclectic.[132] Furthermore, he has proposed the identification
of Theodotion with Jonathan ben 'Uzziel,[133] thereby denying
the work of the traditional Theodotion of the second century.
The sixth column of Daniel has since been studied, and Schmitt

has denied its relationship to the Theodotionic material elsewhere.[134] Still more recently, O'Connell has confirmed the
καιγε nature of the sixth column of Exodus and has indicated
the lack of an identifiable role in its formation on the part
of the traditional Theodotion.[135]

Against this background, the sixth column of Judges can
now be examined. A study of the material leads to two primary
conclusions. One is that the Judges sixth column has a form
of the Old Greek as its base. Out of a total of 341 readings
which are preserved for the entire book of Judges,[136] the
sixth column contains at least 124 which are best classified
as OG. These include those which are shown to be pre-Origenic
by the obelus, or which stand against a known καιγε characteristic in the B family or a revision to MT elsewhere. Also to
be included are the readings which are in agreement with L and
𝕃, but which differ from other major families (almost always
from the καιγε text). Since these often involve vocabulary
selections which are not demonstrably more removed from MT
than their variants, they could not, apart from some confirmation, be affirmed as OG. The agreement of L and 𝕃, however,
provides that confirmation.[137]

The following are examples of OG readings from the Judges
sixth column. The references are included in the total of 124
just given, but it seemed well to cite some of the evidence in
greater detail. In each case the MT reading is given first,
then what is apparently the OG, then any revisions that have
been made, and finally comment in selected instances.

3:1   יהוה; οι ⅄, A, L, K, 𝔤, 𝕃: Ιησους; B: Κυριος.

3:19c   הם; L: σιγα και ειπεν παντας εκ μεσου γενεσθαι
           (glnw, dptv: σιωπα...); 𝕃: *exire omnes de medio*;
           ϑ´, A, 𝔤: πασιν εκ μεσου; σ´: σιγα; K: σιωπα; B:
           προς αυτον σιωπα.

Either L or 𝕃 apparently preserves the OG. In any case,
the common elements in them and in ϑ´, A, 𝔤, the εκ μεσου and
a form of πας, are clearly OG. The καιγε text includes a
clarifying phrase, but is closer to MT. MT is reflected
exactly in σ´ and K, though σ´ apparently revises from a text

like L; whereas K brings καιγε into full conformity with MT.

4:21a בלאט; θ´, A, L, K, 𝔖, 𝓛: ησυχη; B: εν κρυφη.

The sixth column agrees with all other texts against
καιγε, which more literally renders MT, reflecting the preposition explicitly.

5:6 נתיבות; L, 𝔖: τριβους ουκ ευθειας (𝔖: ⊤ ο. ε.); θ´,
A, (K): τριβους; B: ατραπους.

The OG addition is dropped in the sixth column reading
and in B, but B also employs a different noun. 𝓛 has omitted,
apparently through haplography of the preceding and following
verbs.

5:14a אפרים שרשם בעמלק; θ´, A, L, K, 𝔖, 𝓛: (ο)λαος
Εφραιμ ετιμωρησατο αυτους εν κοιλαδι (𝔖: ⊤ λαος);
B: Εφραιμ εξεριζωσεν αυτους εν τω Αμαληκ.

The sixth column includes the OG addition and follows the
OG text throughout. The verb is translated literally in καιγε.

5:29 תשיב; θ´, A, K, 𝔖, 𝓛: απεκρινατο; B: απεστρεφεν.

The καιγε text is, characteristically, more literal, but
less idiomatic. L omits, probably through haplography.

6:26a המעוז הזה; A Fam., 𝔖: ορους Μαωζ τουτου (𝔖: ⊤
ορους ×); 𝓛 (Sab.): montis Macoth; θ´, K: Μανωζ
του ορους; L: ορους του εν τη καταδυσει; 𝓛 (Lug.):
Auch; B: του Μανουεκ τουτου; α´: κραταιωματος;
σ´ : κραταιου.

The widely attested OG addition (ορους) appears in θ´,
though in a different word order. Only καιγε exactly conforms
to MT. (It is not certain that τουτου did not appear in θ´,
though the agreement of θ´ with K may suggest that it did not.)

7:21a איש; θ´, A, L, K, 𝔖, 𝓛: εκαστος; B: ανηρ.

This is one example of the general agreement of θ´, where
readings are preserved, with the OG against an established
καιγε characteristic in the B family.

11:19   נעברה נא בארצך; ϑ´, A, L, ∮, 𝔏: παρελευσομαι δια
         της γης σου (∮: π. δη δ.); B, K: παρελθωμεν δη εν
         τη γη σου (K: παρελευσομαι).

Here καιγε revises the OG by making the verb plural (and
subjunctive), by adding δη for נא, and by rendering the ב more
literally as εν. On all three counts, ϑ´ retains the OG text.

11:39b   ויעש לה; ϑ´, A, L, ∮, 𝔏: και επετελεσεν Ιεφθαε
         (dptv: εποιησεν); B, K: και εποιησεν εν αυτη
         (K: om. εν).

13:8a   ויעתר מנוח אל יהוה; A, L, K, ∮, 𝔏: και εδεηθη
         Μανωε του Κυριου (abck, L: θεου); ϑ´: εδεηθη του
         Κυριου; B: και τροσηυξατο Μανωε προς Κυριον.

It seems clear that the OG used a form of δεω and did not
render the preposition explicitly. The same text appears in
ϑ´, but without Μανωε. The καιγε family employs a different
verb and translates the אל by προς.

18:21   וישימו את הטף ואת המקנה ואת הכבודה; ϑ´, A, L, K,
         ∮, 𝔏: και εταξαν (bcx, K, ∮: επαταξαν) την πανοι-
         κιαν (L: αποσκευην αυτου; 𝔏: actionem) και την
         κτησιν αυτου την ενδοξον (L: + και τα κτηνη
         αυτου); B: και εθηκαν τα τεκνα και την κτησιν και
         το βαρος.

What is clear in the OG text is its treatment of ואת הכבודה
as an adjective. This is followed by all Greek families except καιγε, including the sixth column.[138]

19:6b   הואל נא; ϑ´, K: αρξαμενος; bckx, ∮: αρξαμενος ※
         δη; L: επιεικως (varied sp.); 𝔏: —; B: αγε δη.

It appears that נא was not translated in the OG. It is
added in ∮, some of the A family, and B, but with a different
verb in B.

The second primary conclusion that can be drawn from a
study of the Judges sixth column is that the base text has
undergone extensive revision toward MT. Out of the total of

341 citations which are preserved, at least 70 show such revision, and 59 of these are best attributed to the hand that
produced the sixth column text.[139]

Most significant out of this total are those revisions
which are unique to the text of the sixth column, either in
whole or in part. These amount to a total of 32.[140]

Some examples which have been selected from the totals
given above will now be set forth.

> 2:5 ויקראו; A, L, K, 𝔖, 𝔏: δια τουτο εκληθη; ϑ΄: δια
> τουτο εκαλεσαν; B, σ΄: και επωνομασαν.

The sixth column shows unique revision of what is presumably a singular verb in the OG text to a plural, as in MT.

> 2:14b עוד לעמד; A Fam., L, K, 𝔖: αντιστηναι; B, 𝔏: ετι
> αντιστηναι; ϑ΄: ετι στηναι.

Whereas inner-Greek corruption (ετι/αντι) or haplography
due to the similarity of the Hebrew words could account for
the omission of עוד, it is restored in the καιγε text (and 𝔏).
The sixth column, however, conforms most literally to the Hebrew by rendering עמד with στηναι. Again the sixth column
revision is unique among the Greek families (appearing elsewhere only in minuscule a).

> 4:14 הלא יהוה יצא לפניך; A, L, 𝔖, 𝔏: ουκ ιδου Κυριος
> εξελευσεται (A: ελευσεται) εμπροσθεν σου; B, K:
> οτι Κυριος εξελευσεται (K: —) εμπροσθεν σου; ϑ΄:
> ουχι Κυριος εξελευσεται εμπροσθεν σου; α΄: μητι ου
> Κυριος εξελευσεται εις προσωπον σου; σ΄: ορα Κυριος
> προερχεται σου.

The likelihood of a different Hebrew *Vorlage* behind the
variants here is minimal; nevertheless recensional differences
are illustrated. The καιγε family in this case has not brought
the OG (presumably the text of A, L, 𝔖, 𝔏) perceptibly closer
to MT. The sixth column and Aquila, however, are precise in
rendering הלא; and Aquila alone revises εμπροσθεν to the more
literal εις προσωπον.[141] Symmachus, apparently with less
regard for a literal translation than either ϑ΄ or α΄, renders
the sense independently.

5:6 נתיבות; L, 𝕾: τριβους ουκ ευθειας (𝕾: ÷ 2-3); ϑ´,
A, K: τριβους; B: ατραπους; 𝕷: —.

The sixth column, A, and K revise the OG to MT by dropping
the addition; B drops the addition and employs a different
word.

5:12 קום ברק; A, L, 𝕾, 𝕷: ενισχυων (L, 𝕷: εν ισχυι)
εξανιστασο Βαρακ και ενισχυσον Δεββωρα τον Βαρακ
(𝕾: ÷ 1, 4-8); ϑ´: εξανιστασο; B: αναστα Βαρακ.

The sixth column seems to be dependent on the OG, but has
apparently omitted the additions vis-à-vis the MT. Whether it
contained Βαρακ is not clear. The καιγε text has also suppressed the addition and has employed a different word for קום.

6:5b ויבאו בארץ לשחתה; A, L, K, 𝕾: και παρεγινοντο (1n,
K: παρεγενοντο) εν τη γη Ισραηλ του διαφθειραι
(Aclwx: διαφθειρειν; n: om.) αυτην; B: και ηρχοντο
εις την γην Ισραηλ και διεφθειρον αυτην; ϑ´:
παρεγενοντο εν τη γη του διαφθειραι; 𝕷: et adu-
eniebant super terram corrumpere.

Whereas the καιγε text is actually the farthest from MT
as it stands in this case, one thing is clear, that is the early addition of Ισραηλ. The addition is suppressed in ϑ´ (which
otherwise follows the rendering divergent from that of the
καιγε text) and in 𝕷.

9:11b לנוע על העצים; A, L, K, B Fam.: (του) αρχειν (των)
ξυλων; 𝕾: (του) αρχειν ※ επι ⨯ (των) ξυλων; B
(only): κινεισθαι επι των ξυλων; ϑ´: ηγεισθαι επι
των ξυλων; 𝕷: regnare in lignis.

The OG rendering (which does not employ a preposition) is
filled out by Origen under the asterisk, in Vaticanus, and in
ϑ´. The most literal rendering of the verb is in Vaticanus
and probably represents καιγε revision (the same verb appearing in verses 9 and 13, in both cases also in Vaticanus alone).
Yet another translation is present uniquely in the sixth
column.

10:4 להם יקראו חות יאיר; A (only), L, Ɫ: και εκαλεσεν
αυτας Επαυλεις (Ɫ: *Aoth*) Ιαειρ; B: και εκαλουν
αυτας Επαυλεις Ιαειρ; A Fam. (Gabc): και αυτας
εκαλεσεν Επαυλεις Ιαειρ; ϑ: και αυτας εκαλεσαν
Επαυλεις Ιαειρ; ϑ´: και αυτας εκαλεσαν πολεις.

Two deviations from MT appear in the OG (presumably in
Alexandrinus, L, and Ɫ): reversed word order and a singular
verb. The second is revised by the καιγε text; the first by
the A family; and both by ϑ and ϑ´. The unique reading in ϑ´
may be due to inner-Greek corruption, or to confusion in the
verse between עָרִים and עֲיָרִים. The presence or absence of a
rendering of יאיר in ϑ´ is not clear from the citation.

11:35 הכרע הכרעתני; A, L, K, ϑ, Ɫ: εμπεποδοστατηκας με;
α´: καμψασα εκαμψας με; ϑ´: καταγχουσα κατηγξας
με; σ´: ωκλασας με (*vid.*); B: ταραχη εταραξας με.

The rendering in each of the Three and in καιγε is unique,
and all of these except Symmachus are more literal than the OG.

16:7 לא חרבו; L, Ɫ: μη εξηραμμεναις (gnow: οις); ϑ´, A,
K, ϑ: μη ηρημωμεναις; α´: αλιωτοις (*sic.*); σ´: μη
ξειρανθεισαις; B: μη διεφθαρμεναις.

The sixth column is presumably the source of the rendering
which appears also in A, K, and ϑ.

18:19c ולמשפחה בישראל; L, Ɫ: σκηπτρου (Ɫ: *cognationis*)
ενος εν Ισραηλ; ϑ´, A, K, ϑ: συγγενειας εν Ισραηλ; B: οικου εις δημον Ισραηλ.

The reading of ϑ´, A, K, ϑ omits the OG addition of ενος
and conforms fully to MT. The B family employs a form of
δημος, as it does in Judges 13:2; 17:7; 18:2 and 11 and as
appears generally in the OG throughout Numbers and Joshua.

19:4 ויילינו; L: υπνωσεν; Ɫ: *mansit*; ϑ´, A, K, ϑ: υπνω-
σαν; B: ηυλισθησαν.

The OG word choice (υπνοω) has been revised from the
singular to the plural in ϑ´, A, K, and ϑ. The B family alone,
however, employs the characteristic καιγε word for Hebrew לין.

19:22a בני בליעל; A, B, L, K: υιοι παρανομων; $\mathcal{S}$: gabrê bnayâ d'awlâ 'ābray 'al nāmôsâ; $\mathcal{L}$: filii iniquitatis; α´: αποστασιας; σ´: απαδευτοι; ϑ´: βελιαλ.

The OG seems clear in this case. The apparently conflate reading in $\mathcal{S}$ is curious. The rendering of each of the Three is unique, and ϑ alone transliterates.

A further significant observation about these 59 sixth column readings which show revision to MT is that in every case the revision is unrelated to the καιγε text and to specifically καιγε revision. The same disjunction between the sixth column and the B family exists for the 124 readings which are best classified as OG in the sixth column and also for the 128 readings which have been left unassigned in the present study due to a lack of adequate evidence.[142] In other words, for 311 of the 341 sixth column citations preserved in Judges, there is no common relationship with the καιγε family.

In his delineation of the καιγε recension, as has been noted, Barthélemy has included the sixth column in general throughout the Old Testament.[143] He did exclude from that generalization the sixth column of Thackeray's βγ in Samuel-Kings[144] and that of the Minor Prophets.[145] It seems clear from the present study that the sixth column of Judges must also be excepted. It is not a part of the καιγε recension. Neither does it have the καιγε text as its base, nor is the extensive revision which is present to be identified with the καιγε revision of Judges.[146]

This immediately raises the question of the source of these revisions, or, if the answer can be more precise, of the identity of the reviser whose work appears in the sixth column of Judges. In spite of recent opinions which might indicate otherwise,[147] it appears that the obvious answer is also the best answer in this case. Since the material comes to us under the label ϑ´, this is in itself *prima facie* evidence that the reviser is to be identified with the traditional Theodotion of the second century. What we have in Judges is quite different from the sixth column of βγ, which is labeled either with Barthélemy as the Old Greek,[148] with Tov as "either *the* OG translation or any OG translation" (italics his),[149] or with

Cross as "the Proto-Lucianic recension in relatively pure form,"[150] and also quite different from the Minor Prophets sixth column, which is, if Barthélemy's analysis is accurate, "late and eclectic."[151] In Judges we have a sixth column which has been extensively revised to MT or to a Hebrew so close to MT that it cannot be distinguished. In brief, we have systematic evidence of the work of a distinctive reviser.

Supporting evidence that this reviser is to be identified as Theodotion comes, first of all, from the tendency with which the name of Theodotion has traditionally been associated, i.e., transliteration.[152] Following Tov's categories, the sixth column contains 3 instances of transliteration of words probably unknown to the translator,[153] and 5 of words apparently transliterated as proper nouns, but translated by some of the major Greek families.[154] Of the last group, 1 is less significant because it is a collective reading of the Three;[155] and 1 most likely represents the OG reading.[156] Among the remaining 6, from the total of 8, 4 are transliterated uniquely in the sixth column[157] and 1 of these exclusively there.[158] Of the other 2, 1 is almost certainly the work of the sixth column reviser, which was taken up into the K family.[159] The other is in agreement with the B family and will be discussed further below.[160] The evidence is sufficient to affirm transliteration as a tendency of the reviser of the Judges sixth column. That the traditional attribution of this tendency to Theodotion is correct has been reaffirmed by Tov, although he did find it necessary to refine Field's treatment of the subject.[161]

Additional limited evidence comes from a rendering of the sixth column in Judges which is characteristic of the sixth column in general. It is the use of δυναστης or δυναστεια to render Hebrew גבור. In addition to Judges 5:23, where the rendering occurs uniquely in the sixth column, it appears in 2 Samuel 1:21; Isaiah 3:2 and 8:5; and Amos 2:16 (the only occurrence of δυναστεια). The only other rendering of this Hebrew word that occurs more than once in the sixth column appears to be the καιγε term, δυνατος, which occurs there 10 or 11 times.

It may be that more characteristic readings of the sixth column remain to be discovered in Judges; and, on the other

hand, it may also be that when the distinctive work of this
sixth column reviser has been fully analyzed, he will not be
seen to have consistently employed specific equivalents for
the Hebrew words he rendered to the same extent, for example,
as did the καιγε reviser(s).

To return to the characteristic just discussed, it is
especially suggestive to notice the renderings of גבור in the
sixth column of Isaiah. Of the 4 attested readings, 1 and
possibly 2 have the καιγε word, in both cases in common with
α´ and σ´ (5:22; 13:3 [?]). The other 2 have the distinctive
rendering of the sixth column (in the first against the καιγε
word in α´ and the distinctive rendering of σ´, a form of
ανδρειος, and in the second against the καιγε word in both α´
and σ´ [3:2; 9:5]). It appears that in Isaiah Theodotion employed a καιγε *Vorlage* and either left it as it was in the
former 1 or 2 cases, or changed it to his own distinctive word
in the latter 2.[162]

If this is correct, it may give a clue for understanding
the sixth column generally. Two tasks are paramount. The
first is that of identifying the *Vorlage* employed in each case
by the sixth column reviser. Perhaps the reason for the frequent tendency to identify Theodotion with καιγε is that often,
as in Isaiah, Theodotion may have employed a καιγε text as his
base. In some cases he may have felt it necessary to do very
little to further revise this base text. This would explain
why, for example, O'Connell saw "no decisive role" for the
second-century Theodotion of Ephesus in the formation of the
sixth column of Exodus.[163] In Judges, on the other hand, his
base was a form of the OG; and he perceived the need for revision to be extensive.[164]

The second task before the student of the sixth column is
that of isolating the work of the sixth column reviser, analyz-
ing his style and characteristics, and identifying him as
precisely as possible. It has been suggested above that the
traditional Theodotion be reinstated and given credit for the
work of the sixth column of Judges. This is not to rule out
the possibility of portions of that column elsewhere coming
from another source. Such a phenomenon is clearly possible,
being witnessed in the majority text itself which changes

between OG and καιγε more than once in Samuel-Kings.[165] The
apparent lack of the kind of revision expected from a καιγε
reviser or from Theodotion himself (if, as is being suggested
in this study, these may be distinguished) in the sixth column
of βγ may demand such an explanation there, however that text
be understood. Caution is nevertheless in order before that
conclusion be drawn in any given case. The first assumption,
on examining any portion of the sixth column, should be to
take the θ´ label seriously. The present investigation would
suggest that in Judges the label is correct. In any event, we
do have in the Judges sixth column an extensive work of revision which is distinct from the καιγε text.

The picture in Judges cannot be left simply at that,
however. The remaining 30 readings not yet classified must
also be discussed, for they represent a possible connection of
some sort between the sixth column and the καιγε text.[166]
Actually, upon closer examination, the number can be reduced
to 16, for 1 instance involves conflicting citations,[167] and
13 appear to be genetically unrelated to the καιγε text.[168]

The remaining 16 citations, however, do seem to suggest
at least the possibility of some sort of connection between
the sixth column and the B family.[169] Specifically καιγε
characteristics are not involved (with the exception of the
final instance). Some examples from this group of readings
will now be given with brief comment.

> 3:31   במלמד; A, L, K, 𝔖, 𝔏: εκτος; θ´, B: εν τω αροτροπο-
>   δι; σ´: εν τη εχετλη; α´: εν διδακτηρι.

It has been observed that A, etc. read the Hebrew as
מלבד.[170] Aquila's etymological rendering is characteristic.
The sixth column and the B text are apparently related, involving a rare lexical form.

> 5:4   נטפו; A Fam., K, 𝔖, 𝔏: εταραχθη; L: εξεστη; θ´,
>   Bir: εσταξε δροσους; (Br: εσταξεν; i: δροσον);
>   fsuza₂: εσταξεν.

There appears to be a relationship between the sixth
column and the B family. It seems, furthermore, that fsuza₂
of the latter has revised the common reading to precisely what

is in MT.

5:14b   משכים בשבט ספר; A, L, 𝔖: εκειθεν εν σκηπτρω
ενισχυοντος (𝔖: ⁻ εκειθεν, σκηπτροις ενισχυοντες);
𝔏: *inde in Syche*; B: ελκοντες εν ραβδω διηγησεως
γραμματεως; θ´: επισπωμενοι εν ραβδω διηγησεως;
K: ενισχυοντες εν σκηπτρω διηγησεως γραμματεως;
σ´: διδασκοντες μετα ραβδου γραμμα....

It seems likely that εκειθεν (= *inde* of 𝔏) is OG[171] and
that שבט was first rendered by a form of σκηπτρον. K conflates
OG and καιγε. Again a relationship can be seen between θ´ and
the B family. Here, however, the sixth column reading has
been revised both by the use of a different verb and by simp-
lifying the rendering of ספר.

5:28c   מדוע אחרו פעמי מרכבותיו; L: διοτι εχρονισαν διοσοι αναβαται αυτου ιχνη; 𝔏: *quia tardabant bini
ascensores eius*; A, (K), 𝔖: δια τι εχρονισαν ιχνη
αρματων αυτου; B: διοτι εχρονισαν ποδες αρματων
αυτου (irua₂: δια τι, efjsz: οτι); θ´: διοτι...
ποδες.

The L text appears to contain the OG with the addition of
ιχνη. The OG rendering of פעמי as διοσοι was revised to ιχνη
in A, K, 𝔖 (*vid*.) and to ποδες in B and θ´. Part of the B
family, irua₂, also has the more precise δια τι for מדוע.
(Presumably the notation in the margin of z stands for the full
reading which appears in B.)

6:8   אנכי העליתי; A, L, K, 𝔖 (*vid*.), 𝔏 (*vid*.): εγω ειμι
ο αναβιβασας; B: εγω ειμι ος ανηγαγον (iru: om. ος);
οι λ: ανηγαγον.

This citation leaves it ambiguous as to what preceded the
verb in the reading of the Three, although it was presumably
the longer reading, including the pronoun. It is clear that
the verb is that of the B family. Within that family, iru
revise to the exact καιγε equivalent of אנכי before a finite
verb.

14:18a לולא חרשתם בעגלתי; A, L, K, 𝔖, 𝕷, B Fam.: ει μη
κατεδαμασατε την δαμαλιν μου (L: 1, 4, 2 - 3);
ϑ´, B (only): ει μη ηροτριασατε εν τη δαμαλει μου.

Here only Vaticanus agrees with ϑ´ in a reading that more
literally renders MT.

18:23 נזעקה; A Fam., K, 𝔖 (*vid.*): εκραξας; ϑ´, B irua₂,
L: εβοησας; efjsz: ελαλησας.

In this final example, a rendering characteristic of the
καιγε family in Judges and possibly of the καιγε recension
more broadly appears also in ϑ´ and in L. This is the only
case in which the sixth column shares a καιγε characteristic
with the καιγε family in an apparently related reading. It
has been mentioned above that the sixth column on another
occasion sides with the OG against this same rendering in the
καιγε text,[172] and the agreement of L should also be noted in
this case. The example is somewhat ambiguous and, in any case,
does not alter the pattern already described.[173]

These final 16 references may indicate, however, that the
sixth column and the B family of Judges have something in
common in their background beyond the OG. A direct relationship of dependence between them is ruled out in either direction, most clearly by the 124 OG readings in the sixth column
which stand, in the great majority of cases, against a revision
in the B family[174] (showing that the sixth column was not
based directly on the B family) and by the 70 revisions in the
sixth column,[175] which stand, in at least 22 instances, against
the OG in the B family (showing that the B family was not based
directly on the sixth column).[176]

Perhaps the best explanation is to assume that the B family and the sixth column were both based on a form of the OG
which had already undergone some degree of revision toward a
Hebrew text like MT and that the 16 readings common to both
texts represent instances of that earlier revision which were
present in the *Vorlagen* of both. This would best account for
examples such as those cited above in which either the sixth
column or the B family seem to show a further revision carried
out beyond that which is common to both.[177]

Two further questions should be broached in light of the
foregoing. The first concerns the source of those readings in
which the text of ℊ seems to follow the καιγε family. Several
possibilities exist, including the work of Aquila himself, the
Vorlage of Aquila, and the *Vorlage* of Origen.

It has been shown above that Origen drew on both Aquila
and Theodotion for his revisions in Judges.[178] The work of
Theodotion is not included as a possible source, in keeping
with the preceding discussion; and his *Vorlage* should be excluded on the same basis. It is an open possibility that
Origen's *Vorlage* may have already undergone significant καιγε
revision, though it has been shown above that it is not identifiable with the καιγε text represented in the B family.[179]

Concerning Aquila, the evidence which would indicate his
Vorlage is much less extensive than that of Theodotion, but
would seem sufficient to exclude the καιγε text, as it appears
in the Judges B family at least. His readings stand with the
OG against a revision in the B family 11 times (with 2 of these
involving a recognized καιγε characteristic),[180] whereas his
dependence might be indicated only in 6 instances.[181] Further
indication against the B family as his base comes from the 9
references which might, rather, indicate that he employed
Theodotion's text as a *Vorlage*.[182] If anything can be said
about Aquila's *Vorlage* on the basis of the evidence that is
available, the possibility must be considered that he employed
the text of Theodotion.

Regardless of his *Vorlage*, however, it is known that
Aquila himself was a full-fledged member of the καιγε revisional movement and, in fact, that he represented perhaps the
consummation of that movement.[183] This being the case, and
given that Origen drew on Aquila as a major source of his
revisions, Aquila's text and, in particular, the revisions
which he carried out upon it appear to be the most likely
source of the καιγε readings in the fifth column.

The second question which should be addressed is that of
the source of the readings in Judges which are common to the
Three. It has been proposed that the καιγε text, or, as Tov
has it in the study in view, καιγε-Theodotion, represents the
source of these readings.[184] While this explanation would be

quite apt for those sections of text in which the καιγε recension constitutes the *Vorlage* of the Three, it cannot serve in Judges, since this possibility has already been ruled out for both Theodotion and Aquila.[185]

It appears, furthermore, that the same must be said of Symmachus. The evidence which is relevant to a search for his *Vorlage* is even more limited than that for Aquila; but it seems sufficient to exclude the καιγε text, in spite of his noteworthy agreement with καιγε in 2:4-5.[186] Against this are the 20 instances in which σ´ has, or is apparently derived from, the OG, often against a revised καιγε text and in 3 words against a known καιγε characteristic.[187] Nor is there any significant evidence that would point, in the case of Symmachus, to the sixth column as his base.[188] All that can be said is that he employed a form of the OG.[189]

The most likely proposal would seem to be that the common readings of the Three in Judges, when they are not simply a mutual preservation of the OG,[190] represent prior revision which was already present in their *Vorlagen*.[191]

The Nature of the Remaining Text Groups

The Alexandrinus Family. The following will offer a preliminary characterization of the two remaining text groups of Judges, the A family and K. While more study will be needed for a full analysis, the main lines of their agreement are clear.

The Alexandrinus family is primarily Hexaplaric in Judges. This is revealed perhaps most clearly by the asterisked references throughout the book. Of the total of 104, the A family is in agreement with the Origenic addition 59 times.[192] This total is surpassed only by the καιγε family with 64[193] (which agreements may represent καιγε type revision carried out later by Aquila and mediated through his text to Origen[194]). The next highest total is that of the K group with 30;[195] L has only 8.[196] Thus, the A family shows by far the greatest influence from Origen's revision in those readings which are as assuredly Origenic as any can be, the additions bearing his asterisk.

Billen has characterized the A family as having a full
text, both when the fullness faithfully represents the "LXX"
(in retaining passages with the obelus) and when it does not
(in including passages with the asterisk).[197] The evidence
for the latter observation has just been presented, and the
obelized references in the table given above bear out the former. Of the total of 19 obelized passages, the A family retains 13.[198] The only higher number is that of L with 17,[199]
which would add confirmation to the primary value of L in
identifying the OG of Judges. There are 11 of these additions
in Ⱡ,[200] 5 in K,[201] and 1 in the B family.[202]

Further confirmation of Hexaplaric influence on the A
family is found in its generally close agreement with 𝕊 in the
150 readings which are tabulated above in this chapter. The
total number of OG readings is 42 in 𝕊 and 32 in the A family.[203] The total number which conform to MT is 99 in 𝕊 and
106 in the A family.[204]

Therefore, the evidence of Judges would confirm the importance which has long been attached to Codex Alexandrinus in
the effort to reconstruct the text of Origen.[205] Margolis,
however, regarded it as a "crypto-hexaplaric," rather than a
pure hexaplaric, text.[206] The sources of this mixture in
Alexandrinus should be subjected to further study.

One strain in Alexandrinus in Judges is a preservation of
some OG readings which do not appear in the full A family. In
the asterisked references, in contrast to the general pattern,
there are a significant number of OG omissions.[207] These clear
preservations of the OG in Alexandrinus may suggest its value
in the pursuit of the OG in other, less clear instances as
well.

Cooper has written of the influence of the text of Theodotion on Alexandrinus.[208] He points out that the A text and
Theodotion have more readings in common than does the B text
with any of the Three or the A text itself with Aquila or
Symmachus.[209] While this is in keeping with what has been
concluded above, such a generalization must be tested in each
given instance. In many cases the agreement of Alexandrinus
with Theodotion will be found to represent, rather, the mutual

preservation of the OG. When revision is shown to be involved, it can plausibly be attributed to Theodotion.[210] In these cases, however, the revision was most likely mediated to Alexandrinus through the fifth column, for it is here that Alexandrinus, or better, the A family, finds its closest agreement. In this, the present study supports the conclusion of Soisalon-Soininen.[211]

The K Family. Concerning the character of the group MNh yb$_2$, the conclusion of the present study is essentially the same as that of Soisalon-Soininen as well.[212] The group designated here by K is a mixed text. The primary agreement is with the A family, L, $\cancel{S}$, and $\cancel{L}$ against the καιγε family. Nevertheless, καιγε influence on this text surpasses that which is evidenced by any of the other groups.

The basic alignment of K with the A family and others against the B family is seen in those readings from the table given above in which K is OG. The total number of potentially OG readings (49)[213] is more than that of any of the other groups or witnesses except L (115)[214] and $\cancel{L}$ (57).[215] The total number of readings which have early confirmation in K (32) stands between that of $\cancel{S}$ (40) and the A family (29).[216]

On the other hand, K shows the highest proportion of agreement with the καιγε text of all other groups. Of those readings which could be classified as καιγε revision in the B family with early confirmation elsewhere of the OG variant (69),[217] K has 34; the A family has 16; $\cancel{S}$ has 13; and L has none.[218]

Further evidence of the influence of the καιγε text on K is found in those specifically καιγε characteristics discussed in chapters one and two above. Of those which appear in the B family and only one other group or witness, K has the most (9 readings, each from a different characteristic); $\cancel{S}$ is next (5 readings from 4 characteristics); then L (2 readings from 2 characteristics); and the A family is last (with 1 reading).[219]

Both of these sets of data which indicate καιγε material in K also indicate that this material entered K independently of the revision of Origen, since in each case a large proportion of the readings are not present in $\cancel{S}$. Furthermore, the evidence that is available suggests that the καιγε readings also entered K independently of the Three.[220] The author of the K text appears to have drawn upon a form of the Judges καιγε text very close to that which is present in the B family.

Whereas the Three cannot be credited with the καιγε influence in K, the mark of Theodotion's text does seem to be present. In at least 5 cases of revision to MT, K agrees with the sixth column exclusively;[221] and in others the sixth column appears to be the most likely source of the revision, which K shares with others.[222] At least 4 references which are difficult to classify show exclusive agreement between Theodotion and K;[223] and others of this sort reveal agreement between Theodotion, A, and K.[224]

Concerning the fifth column, while it should not be seen as the source, as indicated above, of the καιγε readings in K, its influence is clearly present. Of the 10 readings from the chart given above which have been classified as Hexaplaric in K, 6 could potentially be due to the influence of the καιγε text; but the other 4 at least are to be traced to the fifth column.[225] More significant are the 41 out of 50 agreements with MT in K which are also present in Origen.[226]

Thus, the K family of Judges must be described as post-Origenic and as mixed. Its *Vorlage* is a form of the OG (and not the καιγε text), but it does show καιγε influence, as well as that of Theodotion and Origen.

Finally, Billen has characterized this family in Judges as a shorter text, both when the shortness is a valid indication of the earlier Greek and when it is not.[227] The present study bears this out. Of the 19 obelized references in the table above, K includes only 5, the smallest number next to the B family.[228] Of the total of 104 asterisked passages throughout the book, K includes 30, a number higher only than that of L, which has 8.[229]

NOTES

CHAPTER IV

1. The chapters are 1-2, 10-11, and 17-18. They were selected from the early, middle, and late portions of Judges in light of the possibility of a change of scribal hands or even of traditions in some of the text groups in the midst of the book. No such change has thus far been discerned by the writer, although such is not uncommon in other books of the Greek Old Testament (cf. H. St. John Thackeray, "The Greek Translators of Jeremiah," *JTS* 4 [1902-03], 245-66; "The Greek Translators of Ezekiel," ibid., 398-411; "The Bisection of Books in Primitive Septuagint Mss.," *JTS* 9 [1907-08], 88-98; and especially the situation in Samuel-Kings [Thackeray, "The Greek Translators of the Four Books of Kings," *JTS* 8 (1906-07), 262-78; DA; and CRDK]).

2. Recensional difference has been identified primarily through Greek renderings which appear to represent a different Hebrew *Vorlage*. Because of the lack of any significant Qumran discoveries for the book of Judges, a Hebrew basis cannot be proven for variant Greek readings. However, on the basis of this very evidence in other sections of the Old Testament, such can now be safely assumed for books like Judges where it is tangibly lacking. That a different Hebrew *Vorlage*, and not merely stylistic or theological tendencies on the part of a scribe, accounts for many of the variant readings in the Greek Old Testament now seems to be assured (cf., e.g., Cross, *The Ancient Library*, pp. 168-94; "The History of the Biblical Text"; "The Contribution of the Qumran Discoveries"; Patrick W. Skehan, "The Biblical Scrolls from Qumran and the Text of the Old Testament," *BA* 28 [1965], 87-100, etc.). The cave four remains have been briefly surveyed by Cross in Boling (*Judges*, p. 40).

3. Cf. the references given above in note 25 on page 60. Kahle's analysis of the Sahidic cannot be maintained for Judges, therefore, as will be seen from the discussion of the fifth column to follow. (Cf. Paul E. Kahle, *The Cairo Geniza* [New York, 1959], pp. 260-61.)

4. Cf. above p. 32, n.5, and the discussion of *Ƚ* to follow in this chapter.

5. Swete calls the Syro-hexapla "our chief authority for the text of Origen's revision" (Henry Barclay Sweete, *An Introduction to the Old Testament in Greek*, rev. by Richard Rusden Ottley [Cambridge, 1914], p. 114). Margolis implies the same judgment in his comment on Joshua (Max L. Margolis, "Hexapla and Hexaplaric," *AJSL* 32 [1915-16], 137). The translation by Paul of Tella has been employed in this study as the surest guide to the contents of Origen's revision.

The question of the Tetrapla and its relationship to the Hexapla will not be dealt with in the present study. Orlinsky has questioned the understanding of the Tetrapla as a separate work from the Hexapla; but, even if its existence were to be substantiated, the following conclusions would not be affected. What will be considered below is the revisional work of Origen. (Cf. H. M. Orlinsky, "Origen's Tetrapla - a Scholarly Fiction?" *Proceedings of the First World Congress of Jewish Studies*, 1947 [Jerusalem, 1952], pp. 173-82. In the same vein, cf. the observations of Swete [*Introduction*, pp. 500-02] and Jellicoe [Sidney Jellicoe, *The Septuagint and Modern Study* (Oxford, 1968), pp. 113-18, 135]. Studies which presume the distinct existence of the Tetrapla include those of Pretzl ["Septuaginta-Probleme im Buche der Richter," *Biblica* 7(1926), 353-83 and "Der hexaplarische und tetraplarische Septuagintatext des Origenes in den Büchern Josue und Richter," *ByZ* 30(1929-30), 262-68], and Procksch [O. Procksch, "Tetraplarische Studien," *ZAW* 53 (1935), 240-69 and 54 (1936), 61-90].)

6. The citations from Ⱬ given in B-M have been checked against the edition of Codex Lugdunensis by Robert (Ulysse Robert, *Heptateuchi partis posterioris versio latina antiquissima e codice Lugdunensi* [Lyons, 1900]). Any thorough analysis of the Ⱬ tradition of Judges would have to take account of all of the other sources that are available. (Cf. the comparison of Augustine's citations with the Lyons manuscript in Billen, "The Old Latin Version," and his full length treatment of the Ⱬ remains for the entire Heptateuch [*The Old Latin Texts of the Heptateuch* (Cambridge, 1927)]. Even the fragments collected by Sabatier, which must be used with caution, show Ⱬ variants from the Lyons text in the six chapters to be compared below [1:14; 2:13, 14a; 11:35c].)

7. For the text of Josephus, the more recent edition of Thackeray and Marcus has been employed (H. St. J. Thackeray and Ralph Marcus, *Jewish Antiquities*, Books V-VIII, vol. V of *Josephus*, The Loeb Classical Library, ed. T.E. Page, et al. [Cambridge, Massachusetts, 1934]), and this has been compared with the earlier edition by Niese (Benedictus Niese, ed., *Flavii Josephi Opera*, vol. I [Berlin, 1887).

Citations of the Vulgate will be drawn from the critical edition of the Benedictines (*Biblia Sacra iuxta latinam vulgatam versionem ...*, vol. IV [Rome, 1939]).

Targum Jonathan will be cited according to the edition of Sperber (Alexander Sperber, *The Bible in Aramaic*, vol. II [Leiden, 1959], and the Peshitta according to the Urmia edition (*Sacred Scriptures: Syriac Old Testament* [London, n.d.]).

8. Although these variants will not appear in continuous text and will, therefore, be difficult in some cases to evaluate fully, it was deemed best to present them in this way so that they could be consulted readily while reading the discussion to follow. The full context can be obtained from the edition of B-M. To have reproduced the context in each case would have made the length of the tables unmanageable.

9. For the discussion of Origen's revision, all of the asterisked readings throughout the book of Judges will be cited; and for the sixth column, all of the ϑ´ readings will likewise be presented.

10. This same procedure has been followed for readings in other text groups which have no confirming evidence that they are early.

11. These indications include corresponding variant readings in 𝕃, readings which bear the obelus or stand against the asterisk in the fifth column, and also variants in the fifth column which have no sign. Especially significant among the latter are Greek additions vis-à-vis the MT, since Origen is known to have retained the OG when it did not appear in his Hebrew. Such cases would involve only the loss of an obelus, a phenomenon known to have occurred (cf. Margolis, "Hexapla," p. 139). Greek minuses are more complicated, since Origen characteristically filled these in. They may represent the OG which escaped his revision, or they may have another explanation.

12. The asterisked readings in which the B family and 𝔊 agree are of primary importance in evaluating the nature of Origen's revision, as will be seen in the following discussion. Because of the asterisk, these readings have been classified as the work of Origen, which they are, at least in their incorporation. The question of the source upon which he draws for these additions will be considered in the discussion to follow.

13. Among the types of variation not included in this table are those that involve only a difference in number, the translation of a Hebrew preposition, a difference in which a proper name is involved, or the treatment of the conjunction *wāw*. It is possible that many of these instances, in the first three categories especially, do in fact indicate recensional differences and even variant *Vorlagen*; but they have been omitted from the present study in order to minimize the number of questionable examples to be used as evidence.
It should be said also that in the cases selected for analysis here in which a different Hebrew *Vorlage* is suspected, such was probably not present in some instances. Even so, these readings still constitute the best examples of recensional difference and are, therefore, the most reliable for use in the present study.

14. Since Origen customarily revised in cases like this by retaining OG additions under an obelus, this reading in 𝔊 cannot be classified as Hexaplaric. It must be regarded simply as being in accord with MT.
Such an agreement could represent a pre-Hexaplaric revision which stood in Origen's *Vorlage*, but in this case such an explanation has no basis. The only Greek text group agreeing is that of L, and it will be seen in the rest of the readings and in the discussion to follow that the L text shows no clear pattern of revision to MT.

15. *Judges*, p. 19.

16. "Septuagintaprobleme," p. 365.

17. *Septuaginta - Massora*, p. 90.

18. Ibid., p. 46.

19. G. F. Moore, *The Book of Judges*, vol. 7 of *The Sacred Books of the Old Testament* (Leipzig, 1900), p. 24.

20. Cf., for example, the reviews of Soisalon - Soininen by Lambert (p. 185) and J. R. Porter (*JTS* 4 [1953], p. 59), and Walters, *The Text of the Septuagint*, p. 272 (though his summary analysis of the B family must be emended).

21. Cf. Schreiner, *Septuaginta-Massora*, p. 90.

22. 10:15c; 11:17a, 19; 18:25.

23. 10:15c (where 𝔊 has ⸪) and 11:17a and 19 (where the omission is attested by 𝔏).

24. This is not to say that Origen himself made such changes on the direct basis of the Hebrew text he employed. The consensus of scholarship at present would seem to be, rather, that the changes which Origen introduced he drew from other Greek texts before him, notably the Three (cf. Jellicoe, *The Septuagint*, pp. 138-44 and the references there to Margolis [p. 143, n. 3] and Soisalon - Soininen [p. 142, n. 3]). Concerning Origen's knowledge of Hebrew, de Lange concludes that he could not speak or read Hebrew, but that he did have access to Jewish scholars of the time (N. R. M. de Lange, *Origen and the Jews* [Cambridge, 1976], p. 22).
This conclusion does not, however, indicate strict limits on the type of revision which Origen performed. Regarding the possibility of changes other than those of a purely quantitative nature, cf. J. W. Wevers, "Proto-Septuagint Studies," *The Seed of Wisdom*, ed. W. S. McCollough (Toronto, 1964), pp. 58-59.

25. A corruption of (ה)ברזל to הבדל may well account for the verb διεστειλατο in vs. 19 (so Moore, *Judges*, p. 39). The obelus in vs. 20 is apparently misleading and does not represent the OG (cf. Schreiner, *Septuaginta-Massora*, p. 96). Ordinarily readings of this sort, i.e., in which a variant *Vorlage* seems not to be represented, will be omitted without mention in the commentary henceforth.

26. Cf. Lagrange, who considers the shorter L and A text to be primitive on the basis of the motive of the one who later made the addition (Marie - Joseph Lagrange, *Le livre des Judges* [Paris, 1903], p. 15).

27. That this variant involves a shorter rendering in L suggests that it is early, since the work of historical Lucian is characterized, rather, by a filling in of the Greek text (cf. Metzger, pp. 24-27). A new study of the tendencies of late Lucian is needed, however, in light of Tov, "Lucian," pp. 107-08.

28. Cf. Moore, *Judges*, p. 42.

29. Ibid. This could be supported by the omission in the Vulgate.

30. Johannis Bern de Rossi, *Variae lectiones Veteris Testamenti* (Parma, 1784), I, 110. Cf., however, on the variation of בֵּיתֹה and בְּנֵי, Shemaryahu Talmon, "Synonymous Readings in the Textual Traditions of the Old Testament," *Scripta Hierosolymitana*, vol. VIII, ed. Chaim Rabin (Jerusalem, 1961), p. 346.

31. So Schreiner, *Septuaginta-Massora*, p. 91.

32. Cf. the discussion of the A family to follow in this chapter.

33. On the appearance of καιγε readings in non-καιγε texts in Judges, cf. note 4 of the first chapter and the discussion of 𝔖 to follow.

34. Cf. the similar passage in 6:8, which could have influenced the addition here.

35. The imperfect אעלה has occasioned much speculation, with many proposing a loss in the text after ויאמר. The Greek additions do not alleviate the difficulty, unless the change to third person should be accepted for all of the verbs in the angelic oracle. Rather than representing a different *Vorlage*, however, a tendentious explanation seems more likely (cf. Schreiner, *Septuaginta-Massora*, p. 68). The suppostion of Moore that the writer may have employed the same form as in Exod. 3:17 without changing the tense is attractive, though it is without other evidence than the coincidence of forms, since there is no other exact correspondence between the speeches (cf. Moore, *Judges*, p. 61).

36. Cf. the appendix regarding the suppression of OG additions in the καιγε text.

37. So Schreiner, *Septuaginta-Massora*, p. 58.

38. Ibid., p. 52. Cf. also Judg. 10:6.

39. So Rørdam, p. 70.

40. From the study of the B family in the preceding chapters, cf. Judg. 2:6; 9:40 (Bq); 11:35 and 37, where only B represents the καιγε recension.

41. Cf. above p. 44, n. 181 regarding irua₂ of the καιγε text.

42. So Lagrange, p. 37.

43. In light of the singular verb immediately preceding in the Greek tradition and 𝕃, one could regard the singular pronoun of ϑ´ and 𝕃 as OG. The *sou* of 𝕃 is a mistake (most likely a printer's error) for the dative *suo*, which would have its antecedent in the previous clause. The use of the singular *iudicio* with the singular pronoun continues the singular reference in the preceding verb *saluauit*, which agrees with the Greek εσωσεν. However, *iudicio* (with *suo*) is a free rendering

of the Hebrew שפטיהם and has no exact counterpart in the Greek
tradition. In addition, the αυτω of the sixth column is awk-
ward grammatically; and it is probably best to assume the loss
of a final *nun* (as Field) and read αυτων (with the A Fam., L,
and ₰).

44. The similarity to vs. 12 does not necessarily indicate that the addition is secondary here. Rather, the evidence
of ₺, the obelus of ₰, and the united witness of all groups
but καιγε make it most likely that the clause is a genuine OG
reading. This cannot be categorically proven for any reading
in the book, but the combination of these witnesses make it as
likely as possible.

45. It is possible in a case like this to regard the B
family reading as the OG and the added verb as a later phenomenon. However, the combined witness of ₺, ₰, and L and the
καιγε nature of the B family constitute objective data and seem
to give preference to the analysis suggested here. (Cf.
Schreiner, *Septuaginta-Massora*, pp. 65 and 80, regarding the
variants [without a proposal regarding the original Greek
translation].)

46. So C. F. Burney, *The Book of Judges* (New York, 1970
[first published 1903, 1918]), pp. 60-61.

47. Schreiner proposes a theological reason for the
addition, i.e., the view that all deliverance comes from God
(*Septuaginta-Massora*, p. 72).

48. Joh. Hollenberg, "Zur Textkritik des Buches Josua
und des Buches der Richter," *ZAW* 1 (1881), 104-5.

49. Cf. W. Nowack, *Richter, Ruth und Bücher Samuelis*,
Handkommentar zum Alten Testament, I:4, (Göttingen, 1902), pp.
96-97 for an extended discussion.

50. So Moore, *Judges*, p. 273.

51. Ibid.

52. Soisalon-Soininen proposes בשעה instead of בשנה (p.
78). It may be, however, that this reading was adopted in
order to avoid the difficulty of the following period of
eighteen years (So Moore, *Judges*, p. 278).

53. The Vulgate does omit the phrase.

54. The question of which text was original need not be
resolved. As in general, the present study does not attempt
to press back to a primitive Hebrew text, but only to the OG
in as far as it may be discerned and then to subsequent recensions.
    In this case, cf. Moore (*Judges*, pp. 281-82) against the
anacoluthon of MT being original; but in its favor, cf. Wilhelm
Rudolph ("Textkritische Anmerkungen zum Richterbuch," *Festschrift Otto Eissfeldt*, ed. Johann Fück [Halle, 1947], p. 204).

55. Whereas Φυλιστιειμ is standard in the OG throughout the Hexateuch, αλλοφυλοι becomes so in Judges and thereafter (cf. Swete, p. 317).

56. Cf. Moore, *The Book of Judges*, pp. 49-50 and Schreiner, *Septuaginta-Massora*, p. 95, both of whom refer to earlier sources for this explanation.

57. So explained by Rørdam, p. 128. It should be noted, however, that the Vulgate has the same omission.

58. So Moore, *Judges*, p. 289.

59. The Vulgate includes the latter two readings.

60. Pretzl has suggested the similar text of the preceding verse as the cause of the omission ("Septuatintaprobleme," p. 365).

61. Haplography of ועד likely accounts for this omission earlier in the history of the Greek (or Hebrew?) text (so Schreiner, *Septuaginta-Massora*, p. 87).

62. Schreiner sees it as an erring attempt to omit the asterisked reading in 22c above (ibid., p. 89).

63. Cf. Harrington, "Text and Biblical Text"; "The Biblical Text of Pseudo-Philo's *Liber Antiquitatum Biblicarum*," *CBQ* 33 (1971), 1-17; and "The Original Language of Pseudo-Philo's *Liber Antiquitatum Biblicarum*, *HTR* 63 (1970), 503-14. Hereafter this text will be cited as LAB, and all references to it will be drawn from Harrington's work. The present reference is LAB 39:10.

64. בעכרי may have stood (or been read) as בעיני. Moore suggests למכשול or למוקש for εις σκωλον (*The Book of Judges*, p. 51).

65. 40:2.

66. So Schreiner, *Septuaginta-Massora*, p. 97.

67. Ibid., p. 75. It is unusual to see an addition vis-à-vis the Hebrew as part of a καιγε revision; but this seems to be the best explanation, since the OG reading was clearly in the second person and the Hebrew is in the third.

68. 40:3.

69. So Schreiner, *Septuaginta-Massora*, p. 62.

70. Presuming δημου to render משפחת (as it does frequently; cf. Julius Bewer, "The Composition of Judges, Chaps. 17, 18," *AJSL* 29 [1912-13], 271-72). The nontextual problems raised by this verse are not of concern for the present study.

71. It may well be that this addition is ultimately a doublet of verse 7; but this is not so clear as to exclude it

from the present study, especially in light of the strong evidence that it was OG. Burney ambivalates between seeing it as original or as a doublet of verse 7 (p. 429).

72. Because of the apparent relation of the second L addition of this verse to verses 14 and 17 and the omission of the expression from verse 17 by L, these variants are not discussed here. They have no early support in either case (cf. Schreiner, *Septuaginta-Massora*, p. 54).

73. Ibid. p. 56.

74. This variation could have arisen, apart from a difference in *Vorlage*, due to the context (Schreiner, *Septuaginta-Massora*, p. 129), or due to inner-Greek corruption of επεταξαν to επαταξαν (first called to the writer's attention by Professor John Strugnell). Cf. verse 31 for the same rendering of this Hebrew verb as in the B family and L here.

75. For the conclusion of verse 22, κατοπισθεν/κατοπισω of 𝔊, the A family, L, and ㄥ should be seen as a rendering of וירדבקו, alternating with και κατελαβοντο/κατελαβον of the B family and K. This restores the reading of 𝔊 and the A family cited above to its proper place at the beginning of verse 23.

76. This is as precisely as this conclusion can be stated in the present study. The question of the earliest layer of the Lucianic text in general and its relation to the earliest translation of the Hebrew text into Greek constitutes at present a rigorous debate. It is primarily because of the Qumran evidence in Samuel that Cross is able to speak of a proto-Lucianic recension in that material. Cf. "The History of the Biblical Text in the Light of Discoveries in the Judaean Desert," *HTR* 57 (1964), esp. pp. 292-97; "The Evolution of a Theory of Local Texts," *1972 Proceedings IOSCS Pseudepigrapha*, Robert A. Kraft, ed., Septuagint and Cognate Studies, Number Two (Society of Biblical Literature, 1972), pp. 108-26; and the major study of this question by Eugene Charles Ulrich, *The Qumran Text of Samuel and Josephus*, Harvard Semitic Monographs 19 (Missoula, Montana, 1978). Since significant Qumran remains have not appeared for the book of Judges, this kind of evidence is lacking (cf. note 2 above).

77. 1:16a-b, 21, 27, 35a; 2:4, 11, 15; 10:1a-c, 2, 3, 4, 6a-b, 8a-b, 10a-b, 12, 15a, 16a, 16c; 11:11, 13a, 14, 15, 18, 19a-b, 22b-c, 24b-c, 26a-b, 27, 28, 31, 35b, 36, 38a-d, 39a; 17:4, 5b, 10; 18:3a-b, 6, 11a, 15a, 16, 19a-b, 24b.

78. Cf. note 27 above.

79. Whereas 19 of these 25 expansions found exclusively in the L text have no early confirmation and may be regarded as the work of Lucian himself, it is noteworthy that 3 of the 4 cases in which a reading is confirmed by the early witness of LAB are among these 25 readings (11:36, 38a-b).

80. Cf. note 11 above.

81. 1:16a-b, 35a; 2:4; 10:1b, 4, 6a, 12; 11:11, 13a, 14, 18, 19a-b, 22c, 31, 35b, 36, 38a-b; 17:4, 10; 18:11a, 16, 19b.

82. The totals shown by the other text groups and witnesses are as follows: 11 for B (1:24; 10:9a; 11:4; 17:7, 8, 9b, 12; 18:7c, 18a-b, 27a [of which none show early confirmation]), 5 for K (2:14a, 15, 17a; 11:22d; 18:30b [of which 2 show early confirmation (2:14a; 18:30b)]), 1 for ϑ´ (11:19b [which is confirmed by Ƚ as early]), none for ʃ or the A family.

83. The 47 cases in which L has early confirmation are as follows: 1:13a, 23, 35b, 36; 2:1e-f, 3b, 16b, 17b, 19, 22; 10:9b, 11a-c, 15b-c, 16c; 11:12b, 13b, 17a-c, 21, 23, 24a, 30, 35c, 37, 39b; 17:9a; 18:2b, 2d, 7a-b, 9, 10, 11b, 12, 13, 14, 15b, 21, 23, 24a, 24c, 30a.
The other 9 readings of this type in L are these: 1:13b, 30; 2:13, 14b, 16a; 11:16, 25; 18:25, 27b.

84. The totals for the other groups and witnesses are as follows: 44 for K, of which 30 have early confirmation (1:6, 13a, 14, 35b; 2:1e, 3b, 16b, 17b, 22; 10:8b, 9b, 11a-c, 16b; 11:30, 35c, 37; 18:2a-c, 7a-b, 10, 13, 14, 21, 23, 24a, 26). The other 14 are these: 1:7, 13b, 15, 30; 2:1a, 13, 14b, 21; 11:16, 22a, 25; 17:5a; 18:25, 27b.
42 for ʃ, of which 40 have confirmation that they stood in Origen's *Vorlage* and are, thus, earlier readings (1:14, 36; 2:1e-f, 3b, 16a-b, 17b, 19; 10:9b, 11a-c, 15b, 16c; 11:12a-b, 13b, 17a-c, 21, 23, 24a, 30, 35a, 35c, 37, 39b; 17:9a; 18:2c-d, 9, 12, 13, 15b, 21, 24a, 24c, 30a). This excepts 2:14b and 11:16, both of which constitute omissions vis-à-vis the MT. Although these could represent OG readings, their presence in ʃ does not add support to their being such. Instead of being OG, these omissions could also represent losses which occurred in the transmission of ʃ or in the actual copying done by Origen himself.
38 for Ƚ (1:6, 13a, 23, 35b, 36; 2:1e-f, 3b, 17b, 19, 22; 10:8b, 11a-c, 15b, 16b; 11:12b, 13b, 17a, 35a, 35c, 37, 39b; 18:2b-c, 7a-b, 9, 11b, 13, 14, 15b, 21, 23, 24a, 26, 30a).
32 for the A family, of which 29 have early confirmation (1:36; 2:1e-f, 3b, 16b, 17b; 10:9b, 11a-c, 15b-c, 16c; 11:13b, 17a, 23, 30, 35a, 35c, 37, 39b; 18:2c, 9, 11b, 13, 15b, 21, 24, 30a). The remaining 3 are these: 2:14b; 11:12a, 16.
21 for the B family, of which 12 have early confirmation (1:6, 13a, 14, 35b; 2:22; 10:8b, 16b; 18:2a-b, 10, 23, 26). The remaining 9 are these: 1:7, 13b, 15, 30; 2:1a, 13, 21; 11:22a; 17:5a.
4 for ϑ´, all of which stand in the text of Ƚ (11:37, 39b; 18:21, 24a).
1 for σ´, which also appears in Ƚ (11:35c).

85. Billen, "The Hexaplaric Element," p. 16.

86. DA, pp. 34-35, 49, 62, 66, 70.

87. Soisalon-Soininen, p. 111.

88. Billen, "The Old Latin Version," p. 144.

168

89. Ibid., p. 143. Cf. also note 5 of the first chapter above.

90. 1:16a-b, 35a; 2:4; 10:1b, 4, 12; 11:11, 13a, 14, 19a-b, 31, 35b; 17:4, 10; 18:11a, 16, 19b.

91. Cf. the references in notes 77, 81, and 82 above.

92. Cf. notes 83 (for L) and 84 for these references.

93. Cf. notes 83 and 84.

94. These totals are as follows: L-115, K - 49, 𝔾 - 42, the B family - 32, the A family - 32. Cf. notes 77, 82, 83, 84, and 90 above for the references.

95. These totals are as follows: L - 72, 𝔾 - 40, K - 32, the A family - 29, the B family - 12. Cf. notes 81-84 above for the references.

96. These instances would include omissions (e.g., 1:15, 22a-b [b with A]; 10:4; 11:23 [with A], 27, 33; 18:8, 19), variations (e.g., 10:14, 16; 18:29), and additions (e.g., 11:33).

97. Billen (notes 85, 88-89), Soisalon-Soininen (note 87), and Lambert (in his review of Soisalon-Soininen in *VT* 2 [1952], pp. 184-89 have made suggestions as to the alignment of 𝔏 with other text groups and manuscripts which produce the earliest recoverable form of the Greek of Judges; and all have recognized the importance of the agreement of 𝔏 and L in this connection. Their conclusion is confirmed by the present study. Whereas assured conclusions regarding individual readings must come from a detailed consideration of each variant in its own right, this much can be said. In general, the agreement of the L text and 𝔏 seems to provide the surest guide toward the identification of OG readings in the Judges text.

98. The lost section is 1:21b-32.

99. Cf. note 5 above.

100. These totals derive from the references given above in notes 82 and 84 (𝔾, K, A, B), 81 and 83 (L), and 84 and 90 (𝔏).

101. These are, in large part, those instances in which the text of L is the only witness to a variant. Since these readings are potentially OG, they were classified as such in the analysis of L, although the description of L did not depend on their total. In the case of the other Greek families in these instances, however, it seemed tenuous to define them as belonging to any certain recension. They were simply classified as being in agreement with MT. These references are as follows: 1:6, 7, 13b, 15, 21, 35b; 2:1a, 2, 3a, 11, 15, 17a, 21; 10:1a, 1c, 2, 3, 6b, 8a, 9a, 10a-b, 15a, 16a-b, 16d; 11:4, 15, 22a-b, 22d, 24b-c, 25, 26a-b, 27, 28, 38c-d, 39a; 17:5a-b, 7, 8, 9b, 12; 18:3a-b, 6, 7c, 15a, 18a-b, 19a-b, 24b, 25, 27a-b.

102. As was noted at the outset of this chapter's analysis, an agreement of 𝔊 with the MT in opposition to some early
variant best understood as OG has been classified as Origen's
own revision only if there has been some indication of this.
Such would be the presence of an asterisk, the lack of the
same reading in any text prior to Origen (this presumes the
conclusions yet to be presented about the nature of the A
family and of K; both will be described as post-Origenic), or
some variation in the text of 𝔊 from an earlier reading in the
καιγε text, which has itself been revised into conformity with
MT. Cf. above pp. 94-95 for a discussion of the principles
followed in classifying readings for the present analysis.
The references are as follows: 1:13a, 16a-b; 2:14a, 22;
10:4, 6a, 8b, 12, 15c; 11:11, 14, 18, 22c, 31; 18:2a-b, 7a-b,
10, 11a, 14, 16, 23, 26, 30b.

103. These references are as follows: 1:35a; 2:4; 10:1b;
11:13a, 19a-b, 35b, 36, 38a-b; 17:4, 10; 18:11b.
In 5 cases 𝔊 has a reading which seems to represent inner-
Greek (or Syriac) corruption (2:1b-d, 13; 10:18). The 4
readings which are missing from 𝔊 are these: 1:23, 24, 27, 30.

104. Billen's conclusion about the relationship of 𝓛 to
the Hexaplaric signs would add confirmation to this (cf. "The
Old Latin Version," p. 148).

105. Cf. DA, pp. 136-39.

106. Cf. note 103 above. It is significant that the variant of each of these 13 references appears in L and has the
early support either of 𝓛 or of LAB (the latter in 11:36, 38a-b).

107. The references will be listed according to the chapters above in which they are discussed, the characteristic
number, and the reference in the text of Judges. These 85
readings are as follows: chapter one: 1 - 2:3; 5:4b; 6:35; 7:
18; 8:9, 22a-c; 10:9; 19:9b; 20:48; 3 - 1:14; 3:19, 20; 8:3;
15:14; 16:12; 16:19; 4 - 3:22; 9:6; 20:2; 7 - 6:5; 11:34; 13:9;
14:6; 17:6; 18:1; 19:1, 28; 21:9, 25; 8 - 6:37; 7:17, 18; 11:9;
17:9b, 10; 10 - 2:14; 3:27; 4:14; 18:21; 11 - 6:22; 13 - 18:25;
18 - 2:11; 3:7, 12a-b; 4:1; 6:1; 10:6; 13:1; 19 - 16:23; 20 - 1:6;
3:28; 7:25; 28 - 3:16, 21, 22; 30 - 2:11, 13, 19; 3:6, 7, 24;
chapter two: 2 - 8:2; 5 - 10:15; 6 - 2:19; 3:19; 19:7; chapter
three: 3 - 1:7; 2:1; 5 - 3:9, 15; 4:13; 7 - 1:1, 8, 9; 5:19b; 8 -
3:1, 2, 10; 10 - 8:9; 11 - 3:3; 14 - 2:15; 20:34.

108. Chapter one: 1 - 2:10a-b, 21; 3:22, 31; 9:19; 17:2;
2 - 2:6; 4:20; 7:21; 9:49; 3 - 3:21; 4:15; 16:20; 6 - 1:7; 7 - 3:
25; 12:3; 18:7a-b; 8 - 5:3a; 8:5; 11:27, 35, 37; 10 - 9:39; 16:
25; 20:26a-b, 35, 39; 13 - 2:10; 3:13; 10:17; 18 - 10:15; 14:7;
19 - 2:5; 20 - 7:23; 8:4; 9:40; 20:43; 23 - 18:9; 25 - 5:27b;
26 - 18:7; 27 - 9:24; 28 - 7:22; 29 - 1:16; 30 - 10:6a, 10, 13, 16;
chapter two: 2 - 9:2, 16; 10:15; 15:2; 18:19; 3 - 14:3, 7; 4 -
18:2; 19:4, 9b, 15a-b, 20; 20:4; 5 - 6:9; 9:17; 11:26; 18:28;
6 - 7:3b; 11:8; 18:26; chapter three: 1 - 11:17; 19:10, 25;
20:13; 2 - 16:2; 19:26; 3 - 19:3; 5 - 4:10; 6:6; 10:10; 18:22, 23;
6 - 9:30; 10:7; 14:19; 7 - 1:3, 5; 5:19a, 20a-b, 8:1; 9:17, 38,
39, 45, 52; 10:9, 18; 11:5, 6, 8, 9, 12, 20, 25, 27, 32; 12:1,

3, 4; 8 - 8:13; 18:11, 16; 20:14, 17, 18, 20a, 22, 23, 28, 34, 39a-b, 42; 21:22; 11 - 16:5, 8, 18a-b, 23, 27, 30; 12 - 8:21; 15:12; 18:25; 13 - 11:6, 11; 14 - 9:56, 57; 15:3; 20:3, 12, 13, 41.

109. Cf. note 4 of chapter one above.

110. Chapter one: 1 - 1:3; 5:4a; 8:31; 9:49a; 11:17; 2 - 7:8; 8:24, 25; 9:55; 10:18; 17:6; 20:8b; 21:21, 22, 25; 5 - 7:8, 16, 18a-b, 19, 20a-b, 22; 7 - 18:28b; 8 - 5:3b, 15; 10 - 20:32; 15 - 2:20; 18 - 6:17; 19:24; 22 - 5:29; 28 - 7:22; 8:20; 9:54; 29 - 15:6; 19:5; 30 - 19:19; chapter two: 2 - 8:32, 35; 19:24; 3 - 17:6; 4 - 19:6, 13; chapter three: 5 - 6:34; 9 - 4:18, 22; 6:35; 11:31, 34; 14:5; 19:3; 20:25, 31; 10 - 2:2; 6:28, 30, 31, 32.
Concerning revisional work by Origen other than of a quantitative nature, cf. the article by Wevers cited above in note 24.

111. These references are as follows: chapter one: 1 - 2:17; 9:49b; 19:9a; 2 - 6:29; 7:7, 22; 16:5; 20:8a, 24a-b; 3 - 13:20; 5 - 3:27; 6:34; 8 - 6:8, 18; 17:9a; 19:18; 9 - 9:17; 20: 34; 10 - 4:15; 6:18; 8:28; 11:9, 11; 13:15; 20:23, 28, 42; 21:2; 11 - 15:19; 18:12; 12 - 2:1; 13 - 6:33; 9:6; 11:20; 16:23; 9:15, 18; 20:11, 14; 14 - 2:17, 23; 9:48, 54; 13:10; 18 - 14:3; 17:6; 21:25; 20 - 4:16, 22; 8:5, 12; 21 - 4:2, 7; 23 - 16:2; 18: 19; 24 - 13:5, 7; 25 - 4:5a-b, 17a-b; 5:11, 16, 27a; 9:23a-b; 11:10, 27a-b; 13:25a-b; 15:4; 16:25, 31a-b; 26 - 1:29, 30, 32, 33; 3:5; 18:20; 27 - 3:12; 16:28; 28 - 1:8; 4:15, 16; 7:14, 20; 8:10; 18:27; 20:2, 15, 17, 25, 35, 37, 46, 48; 21:10; 29 - 4:11; 19:4, 7, 9; 30 - 2:7, 8; 3:8, 14; 6:8, 27; 9:28a-c, 38; 10:6b; 15:18; chapter two: 2 - 9:11; 18:9; 3 - 21:25; 4 - 19:7, 10, 11; 5 - 8:34; 6 - 6:18; chapter three: 3 - 7:25; 6 - 2:14, 20; 3:8; 6:39; 9 - 7:24; 15:14; 10 - 9:45; 14 - 11:27.

112. In the case of 6 of these, questions have been raised in the first chapter about the validity or consistency of the characteristics they represent. They are the following: 4 - 18:16, 17; 7 - 7:12; 18:28a; 19:15; 24 - 13:3. The other 3 references are these (all from chapter one): 1 - 19:9c; 10 - 4:23; 17 - 13:8.
The explanation of these readings is likely the same as that of those asterisked readings in which 𝔊 is closer to MT than the καιγε text, for which see the following discussion.

113. This total omits those asterisked readings in which the asterisk is apparently a mistake for an obelus, i.e., in which the Greek text shows an addition vis-à-vis the MT (2:16; 3:8a; 4:9a-b, 20-21; 6:3, 27; 9:35, 52, 54; 11:23; 15:18; 16: 11 [with ※ in 𝔊, but ÷ in G], 13a-b, 21; 18:12; 19:4a-b, 10, 16, 17, 18, 21, 23; 20:13b; 21:7, 11); those in which there is no variant reading preserved among the Greek families or in which the situation is unclear (4:24; 5:26, 27; 7:4; 8:28b; 9:20a, 48, 49c; 12:11-12; 13:7; 14:2, 19; 16:17; 18:14b, 22; 20:10, 19, 30, 44, 45; 21:21b); and those in which only an article or a conjunction is involved (1:20; 7:1; 8:28a).

114. These references are as follows: 3:8b, 10, 27; 4:1; 5:3, 4, 8; 6:2, 14, 15, 25, 32; 7:13a-b; 8:10; 9:10, 11, 13, 20b, 38b, 49a, 49c; 10:6c, 15; 11:11, 14, 18 (✳ misplaced), 22, 31; 12:1, 4; 13:4, 6, 11, 14, 20, 23; 14:3, 12a-c, 16; 15:8, 10, 19; 16:9, 17; 17:3a; 18:7b-c, 11, 14, 15 (G ✳), 16; 19:3, 6, 8; 20:6, 24, 26a-b, 31, 38b; 21:21.

115. The references and characteristics are these: 5:3 (אנכי = εγω ειμι), 4; 9:49a, 49d (גם = και γε); 19:3 (✳ in 𝔊 cod., לקראת = εις συναντησιν, cf. note 91 of chapter three above for the 𝔊 rendering). The reading in 16:17 likely represents καιγε revision as well, although the Hebrew in this case is simple אני.
In 18:15 an additional instance of a καιγε reading under an asterisk in 𝔊 seems to occur. It involves the use of ειρηνη for שלום in a context of asking concerning one's welfare, in which OG would generally employ a form of ασπαζομαι or υγιαινω (the former of which appears here in L and 𝔏). The characteristic is alluded to in DA, p. 106.

116. Cooper, p. 67.

117. Those readings in which Origen has filled in a Greek omission, but in which the omission is retained in the B family, amount to a total of 16. The references are these: 1:13; 5:28; 6:13, 17 (𝔊 cod.), 22; 9:38a; 12:6, 9; 18:2a-b, 10; 19:9a-b; 20:22, 32, 39. (In 12 of these the omission is attested by the early witness of 𝔏 [1:13; 5:28; 6:13, 17 [?], 22; 9:38a; 12:6, 9; 18:2b, 10; 19:9a; 20:22]. The text of 𝔏 [Lug.] is not extant beyond 20:31.)
In the other 5 instances, the B text apparently shows καιγε revision, but the text of Origen is still closer to MT. The references are these: 1:16; 20:7, 16, 18, 23.
The remaining 6 instances show the following pattern. In 5 cases the difference is neutral, i.e., neither text can be said to be closer to MT (5:29; 6:28; 9:49b; 11:21; 20:38a [?]). In 1 case the text of Origen appears to be more distant from MT (18:30, though the signs in 𝔊 may be corrupt in this case, cf. Field).

118. Unfortunately no reading of Aquila is preserved in any case in which Origen employed the asterisk in Judges. Therefore, Origen's use of Aquila cannot be confirmed by the most direct evidence. However, that this characteristic is Aquila's has long been recognized by students of his Greek translation, e.g., Field, I, 22; F. Crawford Burkitt, *Fragments of the Book of Kings According to the Translation of Aquila* (Cambridge, 1898), p. 12; Swete, *Introduction*, p. 39; Joseph Reider, *Prolegomena to a Greek - Hebrew and Hebrew - Greek Index to Aquila* (Philadelphia, 1916), pp. 16-17; and DA, pp. 15-21. Cf. Kyösti Hyvärinen, *Die Übersetzung von Aquila* (Uppsala, 1977), pp. 26-29 for a recent discussion of the limits of Aquila's usage in this case. In the readings to be discussed below, all have an article following the את, except for 10:6b, which is in the construct state and definite, and 20:44, which has כל.

119. 4:21. The minuscule c also has συν in this case.

120. 6:26; 10:6a-b; 16:14a-b; 17:3b; 18:2c-d, 7a; 19:29; 20:5. (The final instance is 20:13.) *Lamad* was, of course, regularly employed in Syriac before the definite direct object.

121. It should also be noted that the reading συν appears in G consistently where it is extant and also in bc (6:26), ac (10:6a), cg (19:29), and c alone (16:14a-b; 17:3b; 18:2c-d; 20:5, 13). All of these manuscripts (except g) are members of the A family, which is Hexaplaric in Judges. (Cf. the discussion to follow in this chapter.)

122. Rørdam, pp. 23-27.

123. Barthélemy has affirmed the identification of the Greek Ecclesiastes with the version of Aquila (DA, pp. 21-30. Cf., however, the qualifications proposed by Hyvärinen (pp. 88-99).

124. Rørdam, p. 23.

125. Ibid. A progression may even be seen in Judges in the treatment of συν in this usage by Paul of Tella. He began by retaining the asterisk and rendering the συν literally (4:21); in the next reference, he retained the asterisk, but changed the literal rendering to *lamad* (6:26); and from then on he dropped the asterisk and continued to use *lamad* (with the exception of the final reference [20:13]).
Further confirmation that Origen was drawing on Aquila in this characteristic appears in 20:44 and 46. Although no asterisk appears in these references, ∅ renders the הא of MT by συν (followed by AGabcwx in vs. 44 and by AGabcglnowx in vs. 46). Cf. also 9:48, 49; 10:6a; and 19:17 (where α´ is cited with συν for הא).

126. DA, p. 85.

127. Cf. note 145 of chapter one.

128. The only other sixth column reading which is clearly coincident with an asterisk, 9:11, involves a preposition which also appears in Vaticanus. If the asterisk in 16:12 were correct, it would constitute further evidence. This reference, however, has been omitted from the present discussion due to the possibility of error in the transmission of the sign.

129. The only 2 readings of Symmachus which coincide with the asterisk (9:13 and 12:4) show no relationship between the texts, and no unambiguous evidence has appeared elsewhere in the writer's study thus far to indicate Origen's use of the fourth column in Judges. If present, it is apparently minimal.

130. DA, p. 47.

131. Ibid., pp. 128-36.

132. Ibid., pp. 253-60.

133. Ibid., pp. 144-57.

134. Schmitt does exclude from his data, in keeping with
Barthélemy, βγ and the Minor Prophets (cf. above p. 79, n.4).

135. TRE, especially pp. 274-93.

136. The following study of the Judges sixth column is
based on all readings labeled ϑ΄, γ΄, (οι) λ (unless ϑ΄ stands
in contrast), and παντ (cf. Field I, xcv-xcv̌i) which are recorded by B-M and Field. In some cases of doubt, a direct
photocopy of minuscule z (85), which contains in its margins
the greater part of these citations, has been consulted.
     It seems clear, for Judges at least, that Soisalon-Soininen
ᵕis right in correcting Moore regarding the significance of λ.
It does not stand for Lucian, but for λοιποι (Soisalon-Soininen, p. 106). Besides those 2 instances in which one manuscript reads λ and another γ΄ (1:35b; 15:9), there are 11
others in which λ cannot mean Lucian, since it stands before
a reading divergent from that of the L text (3:15, 19; 6:8;
7:1, 3, 16, 21, 22a; 10:6; 11:26; 18:28). The other 15 readings presumably represent cases in which λ and L are in
agreement (2:17; 3:1; 4:18; 5:20; 7:22b; 8:31, 32; 9:53; 11:17,
32; 12:3; 14:16; 15:6, 19; 16:29; the reading of L in 19:13 is
unclear). These latter instances are to be expected in light
of the following discussion.

137. Cf pp. 134-36 above for a discussion of the agreement
of the L and Ƶ texts as the surest guide in Judges to the OG.
The references are as follows: 1:5b; 3:1, 16, 19c, 19e;
4:6, 18a, 21a, 22; 5:2, 8b, 11, 14a, 15, 16b, 18, 20, 22, 27c,
28b, 29, 31a; 6:3, 9, 12, 13a-b, 15, 19, 21b, 25b, 26a, 29,
31, 36; 7:1b, 3, 5, 7, 15, 22b, 23; 8:5, 7, 13a-b, 27b; 9:16,
17, 30, 35, 44a-b, 52, 53, 55, 56, 57; 10:6b, 7, 9, 10, 16,
17; 11:13, 17, 19, 25, 32b, 37, 39b; 12:1b, 3b; 13:6, 7, 8a,
12, 20, 21, 23c-d; 14:3a-b, 7, 10, 19a-b; 15:1, 2, 3, 6a-b,
7, 14a-c, 19b; 16:2b, 3, 24, 28a; 17:7a, 10; 18:19b, 21, 25,
26, 28b, 29, 31; 19:3b, 5b-c, 6b, 7, 9, 10a, 12, 13a, 15, 18b,
20, 22b, 25a.
     Just as significant, although not included in the total of
124 just given, are those references in which the sixth
column shows a revision to MT from an OG base which can still
be discerned in each given sixth column citation. These would
include the following: 2:5; 5:12, 28a-b; 6:5a, 20; 7:11; 8:18;
10:4; 11:16, 21, 24a-b; 19:4.
     A small additional group exists in the instances in which
the sixth column and the B family agree and represent the OG.
In an effort to reckon with all possible connections between
the καιγε text and the sixth column, however, these will be
discussed later in that connection.

138. On επαταξαν, cf. note 74 above and Schreiner,
Septuaginta-Massora, p. 129.

139. These revisions include quantitative changes and
variations in word order, as well as vocabulary selections.
Readings which may be traceable to the καιγε text have not
been included and will be discussed separately below. Also

not included are all readings which show variation, but in
which revision could not be demonstrated by their closer conformity to the Hebrew text or by the uniqueness of the reading
to ϑ′ (cf. note 140 below for this latter category). Due to
these readings (which are shared with major Greek families
[except for the καιγε text] and are not demonstrably closer to
MT, and have, therefore, been classified as unclear for the
purposes of this study), the actual proportion of revision in
the sixth column can be assumed to be higher than what is
indicated above.

Cf. Cooper, "Theodotion's Influence" for a study of the
influence of the sixth column on the A text. The readings in
which the sixth column and the K text agree are also frequent.
Both of these texts will be described below as post-Hexaplaric.
Although the L text has already been discussed as the surest
guide among the Greek families to the OG, those revisions in
the L text which represent the hand of the martyr Lucian are
later in time than the work of revision which is represented
by the sixth column. Therefore, agreements between the sixth
column and any or all of these other families, when those
agreements represent revision, are potentially due to the
influence of the former.

The 70 references are as follows: 1:4b, 30, 31, 35b; 2:5,
12, 14a-b, 17a-b; 3:3, 18, 19d; 4:7, 14, 18c, 21c, 23a; 5:6,
9, 12, 17, 21b, 23b, 25, 26, 27a-b, 28a, 31b; 6:5a-b, 20, 22,
38; 7:4, 11, 12, 21b; 8:13c, 16, 18, 27a, 32b; 9:11b, 27; 10:4,
18; 11:16, 21, 24a-b, 26, 33, 35; 12:10; 14:14b, 18b; 15:9,
11; 16:7, 12, 19, 29b; 18:19c, 24; 19:4, 16, 22a, 25b.

The 11 readings which are to be omitted from this total
when referring to the specific revisional work of the translator of the sixth column are discussed below in note 191.
They are: 1:30, 31b, 35b; 2:17; 4:18; 6:38; 7:21; 8:27; 11:26;
15:9, 11.

140. 1:4b; 2:5, 14b; 3:3, 19d; 4:14, 18c, 23a; 5:12, 14b,
16a, 17, 21b, 23b, 25, 26, 27a; 6:22; 7:11, 12; 8:13c, 18;
9:11b, 27; 10:4; 11:35; 12:10; 14:14b; 16:29b; 19:16, 22a,
25b. Of this total, 2 show possible connections with the
καιγε text and, for that reason, will be discussed in this
regard below. However, they both have features which are
unique to the ϑ′ text and thus should be included in the
present total in any case. They are 5:14b and 16a.

141. Cf. concerning Aquila's rendering, DA, p. 84, n.1.

142. The unassigned references are as follows: 1:5a, 5c,
8, 14, 18, 21, 24, 26, 28, 31a, 33, 36; 2:7, 9, 13, 15; 3:7,
10, 25; 4:5, 8, 9, 18b, 20a-b, 21b, 23b; 5:8a, 10, 23a; 6:1,2,
25a, 26b, 28, 39; 7:1a, 25; 8:14, 15, 25, 28a-b, 31, 32a, 33;
9:1, 3, 4, 9a-b, 11a, 13, 14, 15, 20, 25, 34, 41, 46; 10:6a;
11:3, 29, 32a, 36, 39a; 12:3a, 14; 13:1, 2, 15, 16, 22, 23a-b;
14:14a, 14c, 16, 19a; 15:5, 19a; 16:2a, 9a-b, 15, 17a-b, 20,
21a-c, 26, 27, 28b, 29a; 17:7b, 8, 9; 18:6, 9, 10a-c, 14, 15,
16, 19a, 28c; 19:2, 3a, 5a, 6a, 10b, 17, 18a, 23, 26 (with
the additional 11 instances given at the close of note 139
above and discussed in note 191 below).

143. Cf. note 130 above .

144. Cf. note 131 above.

145. Cf. note 132 above.

146. It should be noted that the great majority of sixth column (and of all third, fourth, and fifth column) citations recorded by B-M and Field are preserved in the margins of minuscule z. It has been surmised that, if the scribe of z were recording only differences from his own text, the sixth column in its entirety may have in fact stood closer to the καιγε family than to the opposing texts (Soisalon-Soininen, pp. 106-09).
This assumption, however, is open to question. The recorded readings of the sixth column clearly stand with the other text groups against the B family. Furthermore, although the scribe of manuscript z did record readings which differed from his own text more often than not, this was not his exclusive principle, e.g., 2:4-5 (σ´); 2:7, 9 (both παντ); 2:12 (σ´); 3:15 (ϑ´ and λ). What that principle was, the extent to which he did engage in selection, and the completeness of the source from which he cited are all unknown. It could also be that the καιγε nature of the text of z is unrelated to the selection of his marginal citations and that, rather, he recorded all that he had before him of the Hexapla. While the uncertainty involved would caution against dogmatism, it does appear that the readings which are preserved are sufficient to indicate what the alignment of the sixth column as a whole would be, were it accessible.

147. Cf. DA, pp. 144-57, where Barthélemy identifies Theodotion with Jonathan ben ʿUzziel as well as with the καιγε recension. Tov inclines to recognize Theodotion as a distinct reviser, but as a member of a καιγε revisional school ("Transliterations," pp. 82, 85, 90).

148. DA, pp. 128-36.

149. "Lucian," p. 103.

150. "The History of the Biblical Text," p. 295.

151. DA, pp. 253-60.

152. For some of the early studies, cf. Field, I, xxxix-xlii; Swete, *Introduction*, p. 46; Thackeray, SJW, pp. 14, 24.

153. Tov, "Transliterations," p. 82. The 3 references are: 5:16a, 21b; 6:26a.

154. This listing does not include words transliterated as proper nouns by all of the major Greek families as well as ϑ´. The references are these: 1:35b; 3:3; 4:11a; 10:17; 19:22a.

155. 1:35b.

156. 10:17, in which ϑ´ = A, L, 𝕃.

157.   5:16a, 21b; 3:3; 19:22a.

158.   19:22a.

159.   6:26a.

160.   4:11a.   It should be noted that the divergent reading in the καιγε family in 7 of these 8 cases constitutes
further evidence of the distinction between the καιγε text and
the sixth column of Judges.   Cf. the appendix for instances of
transliteration in the B family.

161.   Tov, "Transliterations," *passim*.   The distinction
which Tov finds between the καιγε text and the sixth column
of γδ in the matter of transliteration is in accord with the
present argument (ibid., p. 90, n. 15; but also, however, p. 85).

162.   If the attribution to Theodotion of the OG reading
in Isa. 13:3 by Eusebius and Jerome is correct, as seems perhaps more likely, instead of that of the καιγε reading attested by Chrysostom, this would simply mean that, in this case,
the καιγε recension employed by Theodotion did not have the
revision, but that Aquila later made it himself and that it
also found its way into the text of Symmachus, or that the
καιγε text used by Aquila and Symmachus, in contrast to that
of Theodotion, did have it.

163.   TRE, pp. 292-93.

164.   If this proposal is correct, it would indicate the
need to dissociate, at least in part, the labels καιγε and
Theodotion, or better, *Ur-Theodotion*.   In those instances in
which Theodotion did employ a καιγε base, the latter (*Ur-Theodotion*) would be acceptable, if it were understood simply to
designate the καιγε text as the *Vorlage* later used by Theodotion.   In any case, the work of Theodotion himself and the
καιγε recension are to be distinguished.

165.   Cf.   Walters, *The Text of the Septuagint*, pp. 279-
80 for a discussion of one reason for such textual mixture.

166.   See p. 147 above for the totals in the other classifications.

167.   3:24 (z [mg]: θ´ = A, L, K, Ʂ, Ꝃ; g [txt]: θ´ = α´, B).

168.   These include readings in which the sixth column and
the B family mutually preserve the OG (3:19a; 5:1; 7:16; 8:2);
in which the sixth column contains the rendering generally
ascribed to the καιγε recension, but apparently through no
connection with the Judges καιγε text itself (7:22a; 11:34;
13:3, 8b; 18:28a; 19:13b); and in which there was apparently
independent revision to MT in the sixth column and the B family (1:4a, 35a [cf. 1:35b where γ´/λ̵ ≠ B]; 2:1).
The second group (which has specifically καιγε renderings)
and 18:23 (which will be discussed further below) could raise
the question of whether Theodotion should not be regarded as
a καιγε reviser after all.   Such a conclusion, however, does

not seem to be indicated. In the case of 2 of the renderings
which involve 3 references, qualifications have been noted in
chapter one regarding the characteristics (אין: 11:34; 18:28a
and הרה: 13:3). In the case of 2 of the other characteristics,
contrary readings occur elsewhere in the Judges sixth column
for the same Hebrew words (קעז: 18:23, but 10:10; לין: 19:13b,
but 19:4, 15, 20).

A quite different explanation is possible, especially for
those purportedly καιγε characteristics which are less consistent. It could be that some of these may be characteristics,
rather, of Theodotion himself and that their attribution to
the καιγε recension has been due to their presence in the
sixth column. Further study would be required before this explanation could be proposed for any specific reading by the
present writer. In the meantime, it must be reckoned with as
a possibility.

Most significant, however, against the notion of the reviser of the Judges sixth column doing specifically καιγε
revision is the evidence of the 34 instances in which his text
contains an OG reading against a recognized καιγε characteristic which appears in the same reference in the B family (1:5b;
4:18a; 5:20; 6:9; 7:21a, 22b, 23; 8:13a; 9:17, 30, 52, 56, 57;
10:7, 9, 10, 16; 11:17, 25, 32b; 12:1b, 3b; 14:3b, 7 [2];
15:2, 6a; 18:19b, 28b; 19:4, 5b, 15, 20, 25a). Of this total,
17 involve readings characteristic of the καιγε recension
generally (איש: 7:21a; בעיני: 14:7; חרב: 7:22b; חתן: 15:6a;
19:5b; טוב: 11:25; 15:2; 18:19b; ישר: 14:3b, 7; לין: 19:4, 15,
20; נצל: 6:9; 18:28b; עבד: 10:16; רדף: 7:23). The others are
characteristic only of the καιγε text of Judges.

In fairness it should be said that if the assumption discussed above in note 146 were to prove true, i.e., that the
recovery of more of the sixth column would show it to be more
closely related to the B family, it is this conclusion which
might be affected most directly. The base text would still be
a form of the OG, but simply one which had in fact undergone
some καιγε revision; and it would still not be identifiable
with the B family. The revisions of the sixth column discussed
above (cf. note 139) would still represent the work of a hand
distinct from that which produced the καιγε text in the B
family, and his identification as Theodotion would not be
impaired. It could be indicated in that case, however, that
Theodotion was himself a καιγε reviser. Nevertheless, it has
been shown in note 146, and the evidence presented earlier in
this note confirms that this assumption is improbable.

169. The references are as follows: 3:15, 19b, 31; 4:11a-
b; 5:4, 14b, 16a (for which see Field), 21a (assuming an error
in the plural of the z scribe), 28c; 6:8, 21a; 9:49; 12:1a;
14:18a; 18:23.

170. Burney, *The Book of Judges*, p. 77.

171. Reading משם for משכים?

172. 10:10.

173. Cf. especially note 168 above.

174. Cf. note 124 above for the references.

175. Cf. note 139 above for the references.

176. These references are as follows: 1:31b, 35b (B is conflate, but neither the OG nor the other member = ϑ'); 2:12, 14a, 17b (?); 3:3, 18; 4:7, 21c; 5:9; 7:21b; 8:13c, 16 (B Fam. less Bo), 27a; 9:11b, 27 (?); 10:18; 11:26; 14:18b; 16:19; 18:24; 19:25b.
The reason why this total is no larger is that in most of the other cases the B family also has revision, but a revision that is different from that of the sixth column.

177. Cf. 5:4, 14b, 28c; 6:8 (and 5:16a [in which either ϑ' or B could have carried out further revision]).
The alternative would be to assume that, since the total number of these examples is relatively small, they represent mere coincidence. Although the total is comparatively minor, it seems adequate to suggest the first explanation.
If anything were assumed on the basis of the argument discussed above in notes 146 and 168, i.e., that further readings from the sixth column beyond those preserved primarily in the margins of minuscule z would reveal a closer relationship to the B family, the soundest assumption would appear to be related to the question at hand. That is, the recovery of more of the sixth column of Judges could well elucidate an earlier stage(s) of revision which was present in the base texts of both B and ϑ'. This must remain, however, in the sphere of conjecture. The present study is an attempt to understand as well as possible the data that is available.

178. Cf. pp. 139-40.

179. Cf. p. 137 above.

180. 7:3 (B = επιστρεφω for שוב), 5; 11:29; 13:5c; 16:9b, 11, 13, 16a; 17:10; 18:19 (B = αγαθος for טוב); 19:17. In 4:21 and 8:26 Aquila also has what is apparently the OG, but in these cases B has it as well.

181. 3:24; 5:16b, 26; 9:27; 12:6 (?); 13:4.

182. 5:9, 27 (?); 7:1a, 4; 9:14, 20; 11:33; 16:9a, 15.
The larger part of the preserved readings of Aquila (49) involve a reading unique to him and cannot be aligned with any other witnesses. They are, therefore, irrelevant for the question of his *Vorlage*. These references are as follows: 1:15; 3:3, 16, 17, 23, 31; 4:7, 9b, 14; 5:2, 8, 11a-c, 13, 14, 15, 16a, 18, 21, 22; 6:12, 26; 7:1b, 13, 22; 8:7, 13,22, 27; 9:6, 15; 11:35; 12:2; 13:5a-b; 14:4, 19; 15:17; 16:2, 7, 16b; 17:5a-c; 18:7; 19:8, 22, 25. Due to uncertainty, 9:37 and 10:17 are unassigned.

183. Cf. DA *passim* and especially pp. 3-88.

184. Tov, "Transliterations," p. 80, n. 7.

185. Cf. above pp. 152-53.

186. To which 13:4 could be added. The lengthy citation in 2:4-5 could suggest that Symmachus was aware of the καιγε text and perhaps drew upon it at least in this instance (in which he agrees with B against A, L, K, 𝔖, 𝔏, and ϑ΄ [with revision, but clearly based on A, etc.]).

187. 2:12; 3:19 (?); 4:19 (?); 5:11a; 6:12 (?); 7:6, 15; 8:2, 7; 9:13a; 11:35; 14:3 (B = ευθυς for ישר), 7 (B = ευθυς for ישי and εν οφθαλμοις for בעיני), 9; 15:14, 19b; 16:13, 16; 17:10; 18:7c.

188. Whereas 2:14 and 6:38 could point in this direction, 2:12 would indicate otherwise. These few readings, of course, are insufficient for any conclusion.

189. Out of the total of 95 citations which are marked with σ΄, 69 appear to represent Symmachus' own revision (1:15; 2:18; 3:1, 16, 17, 22, 23, 31; 4:7, 9, 14, 18, 21-22; 5:2, 6, 9, 10a-b, 11b-c, 13, 14a-c, 15a-b, 16a-b, 18, 21, 26; 6:2, 26; 7:13, 25; 8:13, 21, 22, 26; 9:4, 6, 9, 13b; 10:8, 11, 17a-b; 11:3, 35, 37; 12:2, 4; 14:6; 15:17, 19a; 16:2, 9, 12; 17:2, 5a-c; 18:7a-b, 9; 19:8, 22; 20:38). In addition to the 20 cited above as OG (note 187), this leaves only 6, which are variously aligned (2:4-5, 14; 3:3; 6:38; 13:4,5).

190. There are 13 instances which seem best classified as OG: 5:20; 7:1, 3, 22b; 8:31; 9:53, 56, 57; 11:17, 32; 12:3; 15:6; 17:10. Note that 8 of these stand against a recognized καιγε characteristic in the B family (5:20; 7:22b; 9:56, 57; 11:17; 32; 12:3; 15:6).

191. Of the remainder of the 62 preserved readings which are specifically attributed to the Three, the 9 which seem to agree with the καιγε text have been discussed above (pp. 150-52; the references are: 1:35a; 2:1; 3:15, 19; 4:11; 6:8; 7:16, 22a; 12:1). The 11 which seem to represent revision to MT are the following: 1:30, 31b; 3:5b; 2:17; 4:18; 6:38; 7:21; 8:27; 11:26; 15:9, 11. Because, in light of the preceding discussion, these were probably already present in the *Vorlage* of Theodotion, they were excluded above from the number of revisions attributed to him (cf. p. 144 and n. 139). The remaining 29 have been left unassigned due to the uncertainty of their alignment (1:14a-b, 18, 21, 24, 26, 27a-b, 28, 31a, 33, 36; 2:5, 7, 9; 3:1, 10, 25; 4:9a; 5:26, 27; 7:22; 8:32; 10:6; 14:16; 15:19; 18:28; 19:8, 13).

192. 1:13, 16; 3:8b, 10, 27; 4:1; 5:8, 28, 29; 6:13, 14, 25, 28; 8:10; 9:20b, 38a, 49a-b; 10:6a; 11:11, 14, 18, 21, 22, 31; 12:1, 4; 13:6, 20, 23; 14:12a-c; 15:8, 10, 19; 16:9; 18:2a-b, 7b, 10 (?), 11, 14, 15, 16; 19:6, 8, 9b; 20:7, 22, 23, 24, 26a-b, 31, 38a-b, 39; 21:21.

193. Cf. above, note 114.

194. Cf. above, p. 153.

195. 5:8; 9:20b, 49a-c; 10:6c, 15; 11:11, 14 (?), 18, 21, 31; 12:1, 4; 13:11; 14:3, 12a; 15:8, 10; 16:9, 17; 18:11, 15,

16; 19:8; 20:18, 24, 26a, 31, 38a.

196. 6:13, 14, 28; 9:20b; 14:12c; 16:17; 17:3a (?); 18:30.

197. Billen, "The Hexaplaric Element," p. 16.

198. 1:36; 2:1e, 3b, 17b; 10:11b, 15b, 16c; 11:12a, 13b, 23; 18:9, 13, 30a. The alignment of the A family is uncertain in 2:16a and 11:12b; and the OG plus is missing in 11:17c, 24a; 18:2d, and 12.

199. 1:36; 2:1e, 3b, 16a (⁎ for ⸓), 17b; 10:11b, 15b, 16c; 11:12b, 13b, 17c, 23, 24a; 18:2d, 9, 12, 30a. L is divided in the other 2 references, but low have the addition in both cases.

200. 1:36; 2:1e, 3b, 17b; 10:11b, 15b; 11:12b, 13b; 18:9, 13, 30a.

201. 2:1e, 3b (conflate), 17b; 10:11b; 18:13.

202. 2:16a. In this case Vaticanus itself omits and may represent καιγε revision.

203. For the full list of references, cf. notes 82 and 84. The references that appear in 𝔊 but not in the A family are these: 1:14; 2:16a, 19; 11:12b, 17b-c, 21, 24a; 17:9a; 18:2d, 12, 24a. Those that appear in the A family but not in 𝔊 are 10:15c and 18:11b.

204. Of this total, 13 are in accord with καιγε in 𝔊 and 16 in the A family (cf. note 103 for the references in 𝔊). Those that appear in the A family but not in 𝔊 are these: 11:24a; 17:9a; 18:2d, 12, 30b. Those in 𝔊 but not the A family are 11:19b and 18:11b.
The readings classified as Hexaplaric total 26 in 𝔊, and 21 of these appear in the A family (cf. note 102 for the references in 𝔊). Those missing in A are: 2:14a; 10:4, 15c; 18:7b, 30b.
The readings simply classified as being in accord with MT total 60 in 𝔊 and 69 in the A family (cf. note 101 for the references in 𝔊). Those that appear in A but not in 𝔊 are these: 1:14, 23, 24, 27, 30; 2:13, 14a, 19; 10:4, 18; 11:17b-c. Those in 𝔊 but not in the A family are: 1:6, 7; 11:25.
In the A family, 4 readings seem to be due to inner-Greek change (2:1b-d), and 9 are unclear (1:6, 7; 2:16a; 11:12b, 19b, 21, 25; 18:7b, 24a). Cf. note 103 for these categories in 𝔊, where the totals are 5 and 4 respectively.
In all classifications, the A family is in closer conformity to 𝔊 than any of the other groups. The total number of OG readings in L is 115 (cf. notes 77 and 83), and those that conform to MT total only 28 (Hexaplaric: 2:14a; 18:26, 30b; MT: 1:6, 7, 14, 15, 24; 2:1a, 17a, 21; 10:9a, 16b, 18; 11:4, 22a, 22d; 17:5a, 7, 8, 9b, 12; 18:2a, 2c, 7c, 18a-b, 27a). Six seem to be due to inner-Greek change (2:1b-d, 2, 3a; 11:35), and 1 is unclear (11:12a).
The bare totals of the K group might seem to align it with

Ǥ even more closely than A is aligned, but this is not the actual case. Out of a total of 49 OG readings, only 18 conform to Ǥ (1:14; 2:1e, 3b, 14b, 16b, 17b; 10:9b, 11a-c; 11:16, 30, 35c, 37; 18:2c, 13, 21, 24a).

Although the total number of K readings that agree with MT is 94, 34 of these can be more precisely defined as καιγε; whereas only 10 appear also in Ǥ (cf. note 102 for Ǥ); 18:11b is unclear. The καιγε references in K are these: 1:16a (?)-b, 35a, 36; 2:4, 16a; 10:1b, 15b; 11:12a-b, 13a-b (?), 17a-c, 19a-b, 21, 23, 24a, 35b, 36, 38a-b, 39b; 17:4, 9a, 10; 18:2d, 9, 12, 15b, 24c, 30a.

Those K readings which agree with Ǥ and can be classified as Hexaplaric are 10 (10:4, 6a, 12, 15c; 11:11, 14, 18, 31; 18:11a, 16).

Those readings which must be classified simply as MT in K total 50 (1:21, 23, 24, 27; 2:2, 3a, 11; 10:1a, 1c, 2, 3, 6b, 8a, 9a, 10a-b, 15a, 16a, 16c-d; 11:4, 15, 22b-c, 24b-c, 26a-b, 27, 28, 35a, 38c-d, 39a; 17:5b, 7, 8, 9b; 18:3a-b, 6, 7c, 11b, 15a, 18a-b, 19a-b, 24b, 27a). Cf. note 101 for this category of reading in Ǥ. Of these totals, those appearing in Ǥ but not in K are these: 1:6, 7, 13b, 15, 35b; 2:1a, 15, 17a, 21; 11:22a, 22d, 25; 17:5a, 12; 18:25, 27b. Those appearing in K but not in Ǥ are these: 1:23, 24, 27; 11:22c, 35a; 18:11b.

The total number of MT readings shared by Ǥ and K is 44; the total shared by Ǥ and the A family is 57. Therefore, in all categories the A family stands closer to Ǥ than does K.

Inner-Greek corruption may be involved in 2:1f and 19; and uncertainty remains in 2:1b-d; 10:18; and 17:12 of K.

205.   Cf. Margolis, pp. 138-39.

206.   Ibid., p. 139.

207.   In the following references, A represents Alexandrinus alone, rather than the entire A family: 5:8 (A, L, Ƚ); 9:49a (Ak, L, Ƚ); 11:21 (A, Ƚ); 12:1 (Ak, Ƚ); 18:15 (A, L, Ƚ); 19:8 (Aa, L, Ƚ); 20:16 (Aab, L, Ƚ [*vid*.]), 18 (Ak, L, Ƚ), 23 (Aa, L, Ƚ), 24 (Aa, L, Ƚ), 30 (Ak).

208.   Cooper, pp. 63-68.

209.   Ibid., pp. 67-68.

210.   In some cases, of course, these revisions may have already been present in his *Vorlage* (cf. above pp. 152 and 154).

211.   Soisalon-Soininen, pp. 102-05, 110-15.

212.   Ibid., pp. 68-70, 102-05, 110-15.

213.   Cf. notes 82 and 84.

214.   Cf. notes 77 and 83.

215.   Cf. notes 84 and 90.   The other totals are 42 in Ǥ, 32 in B, and 32 in the A family.   Cf. notes 82-84 for all of

these references.

216. Cf. notes 82 and 84 above for the references.

217. These references are as follows: 1:16a-b, 35a, 36; 2:1e-f, 3b, 4, 14a, 16a-b, 17b, 19; 10:1b, 4, 6a, 9b, 11a-c, 12, 15b-c; 11:11, 12a-b, 13a-b (?), 14, 17a-c, 18, 19a-b, 21, 22c, 23, 24a, 30, 31, 35a-c, 36, 37, 38a-b, 39b; 17:4, 9a, 10; 18:2c-d, 7a-b, 9, 11a-b, 12, 13, 14, 15b, 16, 21, 24a, 24c, 30a-b.

The B family readings which have been classified simply as MT because of the lack of early confirmation of the OG else-where total 47. They are as follows: 1:21, 27; 2:1b-d, 2, 3a, 11, 14b, 15, 17a; 10:1a, 1c, 2, 3, 6b, 8a, 10a-b, 15a, 16a, 16c-d, 18; 11:15, 16, 22b, 22d, 24b-c, 25, 26a-b, 27, 28, 38c-d, 39a; 17:5b; 18:3a-b, 6, 15a, 19a, 24b, 25, 27b. Many of these readings probably represent καιγε revision as well.

Inner-Greek variation in the B family may be seen in 1:23 and 18:19b. No references were left unclassified in the case of B.

218. Cf. note 204 for all references except those of ϑ, which are given in note 103.

219. The characteristics and references are as follows: For K: chapter one: 1 - 2:10b, 6 - 1:29, 13 - 3:13, 20 - 20:43, 27 - 9:24, 30 - 10:13; chapter two: 4 - 19:9b, 5 - 9:17, 6 - 21:14.

For ϑ: chapter one: 1 - 5:4a; 8 - 5:3b; 28 - 7:22; 8:20; 29 - 15:6.

For L: chapter one: 1 - 9:19; chapter two: 2 - 9:16.

For the A family: chapter one: 1 - 3:22.

220. This question has not been pursued in detail through-out all of the preserved readings of the Three. However, in a brief scanning of the material, no agreement of K with the B family was detected which could be attributed to any of the Three. (Cf. also pp. 150-54 above.)

221. 5:28a, 31b; 6:20; 8:16, 32b (*vid.*). In this and the following notes the small letters serve to identify the cita-tion of Theodotion within each given verse.

222. E.g., 4:21c (which is especially significant, since γναθω appears to be Theodotion's rendering of רקה, as in 5:26); 5:27b; 6:22 (by conflation); 16:7; 18:19c; 19:4.

223. 6:25a; 8:15; 16:28b; 18:9.

224. E.g., 9:25; 11:29; 13:15 (ϑ, Ƚ [*vid.*]); 16:9b, 17b; 17:8; 19:2, 5a, 18a, 26.

It should also be mentioned that in 5 of the 7 instances discussed above in which the sixth column contains a character-istic καιγε word, but with no relation to the καιγε family, the reading is present also in K (11:34; 13:3, 8b; 18:28a; 19:13b).

225. Cf. note 204 for the references. Of these latter 4,

2 bear the asterisk (11:14; 18:16); the others are 10:4 (K divided) and 12.

226. 1:21; 2:2, 3a, 11; 10:1a, 1c, 2, 3, 6b, 8a, 9a, 10a-b, 15a, 16a, 16d; 11:4, 15, 22b, 24b-c, 26a-b, 27, 28, 38c-d, 39a; 17:5b, 7, 8, 9b; 18:3b, 6, 7c, 15a, 18a-b, 19a-b, 24b, 27a. Cf. note 204 for the complete list of references in K.

227. "The Hexaplaric Element," p. 16.

228. Cf. notes 198-202. One of the K references is conflate (2:3b), an example of the tendency referred to by Lambert in his review of Soisalon-Soininen (p. 184).

229. Cf. notes 114, 192, 195-96.

CONCLUSION

The foremost concern of this study has been with the Vaticanus family of the Greek text of Judges. In 1963 Barthélemy proposed that this family is a part of the καιγε recension, which he also described at that time in some detail. Since his writing, several other studies have been published which have further expanded the description of the recension, particularly in the area of lexical correspondents.

On the basis of this entire body of vocabulary equivalents thus far discovered, it has been demonstrated in chapter one that the B family of Judges is a genuine member of the καιγε recension. In chapter two, new characteristics discovered in the book of Judges and tested and found to be present generally in the καιγε recension have been presented. In chapter three, characteristics found in the B family of Judges, but not elsewhere in the καιγε recension, have been discussed.

In chapter four the other main Greek families and witnesses of Judges have been analyzed. It was concluded that the clearest preservation of the Old Greek in Judges is to be found first in the text of Lucian and then in the Old Latin, and especially in the two of these when they agree. The revision of Origen was found to be based on a form of the OG and to exhibit identifiable καιγε influence. The source of that influence was suggested to be the work of Aquila. The Judges sixth column was dissociated from a direct connection with the καιγε text, yet found to constitute a revision of an OG type of text toward MT. In light of this analysis and on the basis of the evidence discerned thus far, it was proposed that the Judges sixth column most likely represents the revisional work of the Theodotion of the second century. It was also suggested that the small ratio of revisions common to the sixth column and the B family may reflect earlier revision which was already present in the *Vorlagen* of both. The Alexandrinus family was found to be a full text primarily influenced by the Origenic revision. The family MNhyb₂ was described as a short, mixed text, based on a form of the OG and showing

several influences, including the καιγε text, the Origenic recension, and probably the sixth column.

In conclusion, this study indicates several areas of
Septuagintal research which are in need of pursuit. One of
these concerns the καιγε recension generally. The extent of
the recension needs to be reexamined in light of the increased
body of published characteristics in an effort to discover
other surviving parts and to test uncertain identifications.
On the other hand, those parts already indentified need to be
differentiated in their individual peculiarities; and stylistic features other than simple vocabulary correspondents need
to be defined, traced through the whole recension, and distinguished in its parts.

Another area of needed research is the entire text of the
sixth column of the Hexapla. The proposal of Barthélemy that
the ϑ´ text is equivalent to the καιγε recension except in βγ
and the Minor Prophets is in need of specific examination
throughout the remainder of the Old Testament, especially now
that this equivalence is also excluded for the book of Judges.
In particular, if the attribution of the greater part of the
revision in evidence in the Judges sixth column to second-
century Theodotion is valid, then his own work must be differentiated from prior revisional efforts and analyzed in its
distinctiveness.

More detailed work is also needed in other aspects of the
Greek text of Judges. However, it can now be said assuredly
that the peculiar problem presented by the extensive differences between the texts of the A and B families is resolved in
large measure. The latter constitutes a part of the revision
of a form of the Old Greek toward the developing Hebrew text
carried out near the turn of the era and known as the καιγε
recension, while the former represents a later form of text
which is influenced primarily by Origen's fifth column.

APPENDIX

OTHER FEATURES OF THE ΚΑΙΓΕ TEXT OF JUDGES

The following is intended as a preliminary discussion of
characteristics of the καιγε text of Judges other than specific
vocabulary correspondents. One of these was discussed above
in chapter one.[1] The others have been reserved for this appendix, since they have not yet been traced throughout the
book, but only through the six chapters which were tabulated
in chapter four.

The analysis of these six chapters has revealed several
features of the Judges B family which are in accord with its
nature as a member of the καιγε recension. Their discussion
here will add confirmation to the evidence in chapter one (and
in chapter two) that the B family of Judges is a καιγε text.

As an accommodation to the current Hebrew text, the καιγε
recension suppressed additions of the OG not found in the Hebrew.[2] This tendency is clearly present in Judges 1-2, 10-11,
and 17-18. One of the best ways to identify early Greek additions vis-à-vis the Hebrew text is by the presence of the
Origenic obelus. The B family is not entirely consistent in
eliminating these obelized references. There are 12 which are
included by all of the four main Greek families.[3] However, in
those cases in which one or more of the Greek families omit an
obelized reference, the καιγε nature of the B family is strikingly confirmed, for in 18 of these 19 cases the B family sup-
presses the addition.[4]

As might be expected, the καιγε nature of the B family is
evidenced also in the filling in of Greek minuses vis-à-vis
the MT,[5] although not quite so thoroughly as in the suppression of plusses. Just as the obelus has considerable value as a
guide to OG additions, so the asterisk must be given attention
in the search for OG omissions. Of the total of 104 of these
asterisked readings throughout the book, 64 had already been
filled in by the B family.[6] It is expected that Origen himself would have carried further the filling in of omissions of
the OG, and the high degree of Hexaplaric influence on the A

188

family accounts for the presence of 59 of these 104 readings
there.[7] The fact that 26 of the 30 additions which appear in
the K group are also in the B family would further confirm the
influence of the καιγε text on K.[8]

Another general type of Hebraizing revision which appears
to have characterized the καιγε movement was the effort to
secure closer conformity to the Hebrew text in matters of gram-
matical agreement. In the readings tabulated above, this
tendency can be observed specifically in the closer agreement
of the B family with MT in the person of its verb forms. Of
the 6 instances in these six chapters in which a difference of
this sort can be noted, the B family rendering corresponds to
that of MT in each case.[9]

Finally, in the matter of transliterating rather than
translating from the Hebrew, the B family displays a characteristic which has already been identified with the καιγε recension.[10] As was noted above, the tendencies discussed here
were reserved for this appendix because they have been traced
only through six chapters and not through the entire book.[11] In
this last trait, as in those already presented, however, the
data is sufficient to reveal a pattern. Of the 5 instances
in which transliteration can be observed in some, but not all,
of the Greek families, it appears in the B family alone 4
times.[12] Elsewhere in the B family, 3 examples have been
noted thus far.[13] It should be noted that in all but perhaps
the last reference the B family transliterates as a proper
name. At the same time, and again in every case except perhaps the last, the B family stands against what clearly seems
to be the OG reading elsewhere.

NOTES

APPENDIX

1. Cf. chapter one, page 14.

2. Cf. Ralph W. Klein, "New Evidence for an Old Recension of Reigns," *HTR* 60 (1967), pp. 99-100 and 102 concerning this type of καιγε revision.

3. These readings do not all appear in the table in chapter four. The references are as follows: 1:15a-b, 16, 17, 35, 36; 2:1, 2, 6, 19; 11:35; 18:8.

4. Cf. notes 198-202 of chapter four for the references.

5. Cf. Klein, "New Evidence," pp. 98-99 and 101-2.

6. Cf. note 114 in chapter four.

7. Cf. note 192 in chapter four.

8. Cf. note 195 in chapter four. The references not found in the B family are these: 9:49b; 11:21; 20:18, 38a.

9. 2:1b-d, 1f, 3a; 11:37. The other texts and groups vary as follows: 2:1b-d (A, L, ₰ [K is divided]), 1f (A, L, ₰), 3a (L); 11:37 (A, L, K, ₰, L, θ´).

10. Cf. Cross, "The History of the Biblical Text," p. 295, n. 44 for transliteration as a mark of the καιγε text of βγ and Tov, "Transliterations," for the tendency as a further trait of the καιγε recension as a whole.

11. With the exception of the second, which is full with regard to the asterisked additions.

12. These references are not included in the table. They are: 1:11; 10:6, 7; 11:16, 33. (Cf. also 1:15 in the text of Aquila [following Field].) In the final reference, irua₂ of the B family concur with all other groups in transliterating, while Bejsz translate (and may also read a different Hebrew text). In 1:11 B is conflate.

13. 5:14b (B alone); 7:1 (B, K); 9:27 (B, L).

189

BIBLIOGRAPHY OF WORKS CITED

Barthélemy, Dominique. *Les Devanciers d'Aquila.* Supplements
to *VT*, X. Leiden, 1963.

_____. "Redécouverte d'un chaînon manquant de l'histoire
de la Septante," *RB* 60 (1953), 18-29.

Bewer, Julius. "The Composition of Judges, Chaps. 17, 18,"
AJSL 29 (1912-13), 261-83.

*Biblia Sacra iuxta latinam vulgatam versionem ad codicum fidem
iussu Pii PP. XI cura et studio Monachorum Abbatiae Pon-
tificiae S. Hieronymi in urbe ordinis S. Benedicti edita.*
Vol. IV. Rome, 1939.

Billen, A. V. "The Hexaplaric Element in the LXX Version of
Judges," *JTS* 43 (1942), 12-19.

_____. *The Old Latin Texts of the Heptateuch.* Cambridge,
1927.

_____. "The Old Latin Version of Judges," *JTS* 43 (1942),
140-49.

Boling, Robert G. *Judges: Introduction, Translation and Commentary.* The Anchor Bible. Garden City, 1975.

Brock, S. P. "Lucian *redivivus*: Some Reflections on Barthélemy's *Les Devanciers d'Aquila*," *Studia Evangelica*, 5.
Texte und Untersuchungen, 103. Berlin, 1968, pp. 176-81.

Brooke, Alan England, and Norman McLean, with Henry St. John
Thackeray for vols. II and III, eds. *The Old Testament
in Greek According to the Text of Codex Vaticanus.* Vol.
I: *The Octateuch.* Vol II: *The Later Historical Books.*
Vol. III, part 1: *Esther, Judith, Tobit.* Cambridge,
1906-40.

Burkitt, F. Crawford. *The Book of Rules of Tychonius.* Texts
and Studies, III, ed. J. Armitage Robinson. Cambridge,
1895.

_____. *Fragments of the Book of Kings According to the
Translation of Aquila.* Cambridge, 1898.

Burney, C. F. *The Book of Judges.* New York, 1970 (first
published 1903, 1918).

Ceriani, Antonio Maria, ed. *Codex Syro-Hexaplaris Ambrosianus
photolithographica editus.* Monumenta sacra et profana.
Vol. VII. Milan, 1874.

Cooper, Charles M. "Theodotion's Influence on the Alexandrian
Text of Judges," *JBL* 67 (1948), 63-68.

191

192

Cross, Frank Moore, Jr. *The Ancient Library of Qumran and Modern Biblical Studies.* 2d ed. Garden City, New York, 1961.

_____. "The Contribution of the Qumran Discoveries to The Study of the Biblical Text," *IEJ* 16 (1966), 81-95.

_____. "The Evolution of a Theory of Local Texts," *1972 Proceedings: IOSCS and Pseudepigrapha.* Septuagint and Cognate Studies, Number Two, ed. Robert A. Kraft. Society of Biblical Literature, 1972, pp. 108-26.

_____. "The History of the Biblical Text in the Light of Discoveries in the Judaean Desert," *HTR* 57 (1964), 281-99.

Field, Frederick, ed. *Origenis Hexaplorum quae supersunt... Fragmenta.* 2 vols. Oxford, 1875.

Greenspoon, Leonard Jay. "Studies in the Textual Tradition of the Book of Joshua." Ph.D. dissertation, Harvard University, 1977.

Grindel, John A. "Another Characteristic of the καιγε Recension: נצח/νικος," *CBQ* 31 (1969), 499-513.

Harrington, Daniel Joseph. "The Biblical Text of Pseudo-Philo's *Liber Antiquitatum Biblicarum*," *CBQ* 33 (1971), 1-17.

_____. "The Original Language of Pseudo-Philo's *Liber Antiquitatum Biblicarum*," *HTR* 63 (1970), 503-14.

_____. "Text and Biblical Text in Pseudo-Philo's *Liber Antiquitatum Biblicarum*." Ph.D. dissertation, Harvard University, 1969.

Hatch, Edwin, and Henry A. Redpath. *A Concordance to the Septuagint and the Other Greek Versions of the Old Testament (Including the Apocryphal Books).* Photomechanical reprint of the 1897 Oxford ed. 3 vols. in 2. Graz, Austria, 1954.

Hollenberg, Joh. "Zur Textkritik des Buches Josua und des Buches der Richter," *ZAW* 1 (1881), 97-105.

Holmes, Robert, and James Parsons, eds. *Vetus Testamentum graecum cum variis lectionibus.* 5 vols. in 4. Oxford, 1798-1827.

Howard, G. "Frank Cross and Recensional Criticism," *VT* 21 (1971), 440-50.

_____. "Lucianic Readings in a Greek Twelve Prophets Scroll from the Judaean Desert," *JQR* 62 (1971-72), 51-60.

Hyvärinen, Kyösti. *Die Übersetzung von Aquila.* Coniectanea Biblica, Old Testament Series. Uppsala, 1977.

Jellicoe, Sidney. "The Hesychian Recension Reconsidered," *JBL* 82 (1963), 409-18.

_____. *The Septuagint and Modern Study.* Oxford, 1968.

Kahle, Paul E. *The Cairo Geniza.* New York, 1959.

Kittel, Rud., et al., eds. *Biblia Hebraica.* 11th ed., emended printing of 7th ed., a revised and expanded version of 3d ed. Stuttgart, n.d.

Klein, Ralph W. "New Evidence for an Old Recension of Reigns," *HTR* 60 (1967), 93-105.

_____. "Studies in the Greek Texts of the Chronicler." Th.D. dissertation, Harvard University, 1966.

_____. *Textual Criticism of the Old Testament.* Philadelphia, 1974.

Kraft, Robert A. "Review of Dominique Barthélemy, *Les Devanciers d'Aquila,*" *Gnomon* 37 (1965), 474-83.

de Lagarde, Paul Anton. *Bibliothecae Syriacae a Paulo de Lagarde collectae quae ad philologiam sacram pertinent.* Ed. Alfred Rahlfs. Göttingen, 1892.

_____. *Septuaginta Studien,* I. Göttingen, 1891.

Lagrange, Marie-Joseph. *Le livre des Judges.* Paris, 1903.

Lambert, W. G. "Review of I. Soisalon-Soininen, *Die Textformen der Septuaginta-Übersetzung des Richterbuches,*" *VT* 2 (1952), 184-89.

de Lange, N. M. R. *Origen and the Jews.* University of Cambridge Oriental Publications, 25. Cambridge, 1976.

Lisowsky, Gerhard. *Konkordanz zum Hebräischen Alten Testament.* Stuttgart, 1958.

Margolis, Max L. "Hexapla and Hexaplaric," *AJSL* 32 (1915-16), 126-40.

Metzger, Bruce M. *Chapters in the History of New Testament Textual Criticism.* New Testament Tools and Studies, IV, ed. Bruce M. Metzger. Grand Rapids, 1963.

Meyer. R., ed. *Josua et Judices. Biblia Hebraica Stuttgartensia,* IV, ed. K. Elliger et W. Rudolph. Stuttgart, 1972.

Moore, George F. "The Antiochian Recension of the Septuagint," *AJSL* 29 (1912-13), 37-62.

_____. *The Book of Judges. The Sacred Books of the Old Testament,* VII. Leipzig, 1900.

194

Moore, George F. *A Critical and Exegetical Commentary on Judges.* The International Critical Commentary. New York, 1895.

Niese, Benedictus, ed. *Flavii Josephi Opera.* Vol. I. Berlin, 1887.

Nowack, W. *Richter, Ruth, und Bücher Samuelis.* Handkommentar zum Alten Testament, I, 4. Göttingen, 1902.

O'Connell, Kevin G. *The Theodotionic Revision of the Book of Exodus.* Harvard Semitic Monographs, 3. Cambridge, Mass., 1972.

Orlinsky, Harry M. "Origen's Tetrapla - a Scholarly Fiction." *Proceedings of the First World Congress of Jewish Studies,* 1947. Jerusalem, 1952, pp. 173-82.

Porter, J. R. "Review of I. Soisalon-Soininen, *Die Textformen der Septuaginta-Übersetzung des Richterbuches,*" *JTS* 4 (1953), 57-59.

Pretzl, Otto. "Der hexaplarische und tetraplarische Septuagintatext des Origenes in den Büchern Josue und Richter," *ByZ* 30 (1929-30), 262-68.

_____. "Septuaginta Probleme im Buch der Richter," *Biblica* 7 (1926), 233-69, 353-83.

Procksch, D. O. "Tetraplarische Studien I," *ZAW* 53 (1935), 240-69; "Tetraplarische Studien II," *ZAW* 54 (1936), 61-90.

Rahlfs, Alfred. *Lucians Rezension der Königsbücher.* Septuaginta Studien, III. Göttingen, 1911.

_____. Septuaginta: *Id est vetus Testamentum graece iuxta LXX interpretes* I. Stuttgart, n.d.

_____, ed. *Septuaginta Vetus Testamentum Graecum Auctoritate Academiae Scientiarum Gottingensis editum.* Vol. X: *Psalmi.* Göttingen, 1931.

Redpath, H. A. "A Contribution towards Setting the Dates of the Translations of the Various Books of the Septuagint," *JTS* 7 (1905-06), 606-15.

Reider, Joseph. *An Index to Aquila.* Completed and revised by N. Turner. Supplements to *VT*, XII. Leiden, 1966.

_____. *Prolegomena to a Greek-Hebrew and Hebrew-Greek Index to Aquila.* Philadelphia, 1916.

Robert, Ulysse, ed. *Heptateuchi partis posterioris versio latina antiquissima e codice Lugdunensi.* Lyon, 1900.

Rørdam, T. Skat. *Libri Judicum et Ruth secundum versionem Syriaco-Hexaplarem.* Havniae, 1861.

195

de Rossi, Johannis Bern. *Variae lectiones Veteris Testamenti.* Vol. I. Paris, 1784.

Rudolph, Wilhelm. "Textkritische Anmerkungen zum Richterbuch," *Festschrift Otto Eissfeldt,* ed. Johann Fück. Halle, 1947.

Sabatier, Pierre, ed. *Bibliorum sacrorum latinae versiones antiquae.* Vol. I. Paris, 1751.

Sacred Scriptures: Syriac Old Testament. London, n.d.

Schmitt, A. *Stammt der sogenannte "ϑ´"-Text bei Daniel wirklich von Theodotion?* Göttingen, 1966.

Schreiner, Joseph. *Septuaginta-Massora des Buches der Richter.* Rome, 1957.

_____. "Zum B-Text des griechischen Canticum Deborae," *Biblica* 42 (1961), 333-58.

Shenkel, James Donald. *Chronology and Recensional Development in the Greek Text of Kings.* Harvard Semitic Monographs, 1. Cambridge, Mass., 1968.

Skehan, Patrick W. "The Biblical Scrolls from Qumran and the Text of the Old Testament," *BA* 28 (1965), 87-100.

Smith, Michael. "Another Criterion for the καιγε Recension," *Biblica* 48 (1967), 443-45.

Soisalon-Soininen, I. *Die Textformen der Septuaginta-Übersetzung des Richterbuches.* Helsinki, 1951.

Sperber, Alexander, ed. *The Former Prophets According to Targum Jonathan. The Bible in Aramaic,* II. Leiden, 1959.

Swete, Henry Barclay. *An Introduction to the Old Testament in Greek.* Rev. by Richard Rusden Ottley. Cambridge, 1914.

_____, ed. *The Old Testament in Greek.* 3 vols. Cambridge, 1889.

Talmon, Shemaryahu. "Synonymous Readings in the Textual Traditions of the Old Testament." *Scripta Hierosolymitana,* VIII, ed. Chaim Rabin. Jerusalem, 1961, pp. 335-83.

Thackeray, H. St. John. "The Bisection of Books in Primitive Septuagint Mss.," *JTS* 9 (1907-08), 88-98.

_____. "The Greek Translations of the Four Books of Kings," *JTS* 8 (1906-07), 262-78.

_____. "The Greek Translators of Ezekiel," *JTS* 4 (1902-03), 398-411.

_____. "The Greek Translators of Jeremiah," *JTS* 4 (1902-03), 245-66.

_____. *The Septuagint and Jewish Worship.* London, 1921.

196

Thackeray, H. St. John and Ralph Marcus. *Jewish Antiquities, Books V-VIII*, vol. V of *Josephus*. The Loeb Classical Library, ed. T. E. Page, et al. Cambridge, Mass., 1934.

Thornhill, Raymond. "Six or Seven Nations: A Pointer to the Lucianic Text in the Heptateuch, with Special Reference to the Old Latin Version," *JTS* 10 (1959), 233-46.

Tov, Emanuel. "Lucian and proto-Lucian: Toward a New Solution of the Problem," *RB* 79 (1972), 101-13.

_____. "The Textual History of the Song of Deborah in the A Text of the LXX," *VT* 28 (1978), 224-32.

_____. "Transliterations of Hebrew Words in the Greek Versions of the Old Testament: A Further Characteristic of the *kaige*-Th. Revision?" *Textus* 8 (1972), 78-92.

Ulrich, Eugene Charles. *The Qumran Text of Samuel and Josephus*. Harvard Semitic Monographs, 19. Missoula, 1978.

Vaccari, A. "The Hesychian Recension of the Septuagint," *Biblica* 46 (1965), 60-66.

Vercellone, Carolus, ed. *Variae Lectiones Vulgatae Latinae Bibliorum*. Vol. II. Rome, 1864.

Walters (formerly Katz), Peter. "Ein Aquila - Index in Vorbereitung: Prolegomena and Specimina I," *VT* 8 (1958), 264-85.

_____. "Review of I. Soisalon-Soininen, *Die Textformen der Septuaginta-Übersetzung des Richterbuches*," *ThLZ* 77 (1952), 154-58.

_____. *The Text of the Septuagint: Its Corruptions and Their Emendation*. Ed. D. W. Gooding. Cambridge, 1973.

Wevers, John William. "Proto-Septuagint Studies," *The Seed of Wisdom*, ed. W. S. McCollough. Toronto, 1964, pp. 58-77.

_____. *Text History of the Greek Genesis*. Mitteilungen des Septuaginta-Unternehmens XI. Göttingen, 1974.

_____, ed. *Septuaginta: Vetus Testamentum Graecum Auctoritate Academiae Scientiarum Gottingensis editum*. Vol. I: *Genesis*. Göttingen, 1974.

Ziegler, Joseph, ed. *Septuaginta: Vetus Testamentum Graecum Auctoritate Academiae Scientiarum Gottingensis editum*. Vol. XIII: *Duodecim Prophetae*. Vol. XIV: *Isaias*. Vol. XV: *Ieremias, Baruch, Threni, Epistula Ieremiae*. Vol. XVI, 1: *Ezechiel*. Vol. XVI, 2: *Susanna, Daniel, Bel et Draco*. Göttingen, 1939-1957.

INDEX OF MODERN AUTHORS

Barthélemy, Dominique, 2, 3-4, 7, 8, 11-18, 25, 34, 35, 41, 43, 44, 48, 57-58, 59, 60, 62, 74, 75, 79, 80, 82, 135, 137, 140, 147, 159, 172, 174, 175, 178, 185, 186

Benedictines, 160

Bewer, Julius, 165

Billen, A. V., 3, 8, 32, 135, 136, 155, 157, 160, 168, 169, 180

Boling, Robert G., 7, 159

Brock, S. P., 50-51, 61

Brooke, Alan England, 2, 7

Burkitt, F. C., 32, 171

Burney, C. F., 164, 166, 177

Ceriani, Antonio Maria, 8

Cooper, Charles M., 4, 7, 155, 171, 174, 181

Cross, Frank Moore, Jr., 9, 79, 80, 134, 148, 159, 166, 189

Field, Frederick, 2, 7, 8, 58, 59, 148, 171, 175

Greenspoon, Leonard Jay, 35, 38, 40

Grindel, John A., 25, 41, 64

Hanhart, Robert, 8

Harrington, Daniel Joseph, 59, 165

Hollenberg, Joh., 164

Holmes, R. H., 58

Howard, George, 80

Hyvärinen, Kyösti, 171 172

Jellicoe, Sidney, 44, 160, 162

Kahle, Paul E., 159

Kappler, Werner, 8

Kittel, R., 8

Klein, Ralph W., 9, 58, 189

Kraft, Robert A., 80

de Lagarde, Paul Anton, 7, 8

Lagrange, Marie-Joseph, 162, 163

Lambert, W. G., 40, 162, 168, 183

de Lange N. R. M., 162

Lisowsky, Gerhard, 58

198

McLean, Norman, 2, 7

Marcus, Ralph, 160

Margolis, Max L., 155, 159, 161, 181

Metzger, Bruce M., 34, 87, 162

Meyer, R., 8

Moore, George Foote, 2, 4, 7, 8, 60, 119, 121, 162, 163, 164, 165, 173

Niese, Benedictus, 160

Nowack, W., 164

O'Connell, Kevin G., 25-29, 35, 41-42, 58, 74, 80, 141, 149

Orlinsky, Harry M., 159-60

Parsons, J. 58

Pietersma, Albert, 34

Porter, J. R., 162

Pretzl, Otto, 2-3, 8, 31, 119, 160, 165

Procksch, O., 160

Rahlfs, Alfred, 7, 8, 39

Redpath, H. A., 9

Reider, Joseph, 42, 171

Robert, Ulysse, 160

Rørdam, T. Skat., 43, 139, 163, 165, 172

de Rossi, Johannis Bern, 163

Rudolph, Wilhelm, 164

Sabatier, Pierre, 160

Shenkel, James Donald, 18, 20-25, 34, 35, 39, 68, 159

Schmitt, Armin, 79, 140-41, 173

Schreiner, Joseph, 1-2, 4, 7, 9, 119, 162, 163, 164, 165, 166, 173

Skehan, Patrick W., 159

Smith, Michael, 19-20

Soisalon-Soininen, I., 1, 3, 4, 7, 8, 40, 41, 57, 60, 135, 156, 162, 164, 168, 173, 175, 181

Sperber, Alexander, 160

Swete, Henry Barclay, 8, 159, 160, 165, 171, 175

Talmon, Shemaryahu, 163

Thackeray, H. St. J., 3, 8, 9, 18-19, 38, 159, 160, 175

Thornhill, Raymond, 42

Tov, Emanuel, 9, 80, 147, 148, 162, 175, 176, 184, 189

Ulrich, Eugene Charles, 63, 166
Vaccari, Alberto, 44
Walters (Katz), Peter, 7, 42, 59, 162, 176
Wevers, John William, 8, 43, 162, 170
Ziegler, Joseph, 8, 59, 60, 66

INDEX OF GENERAL SUBJECTS
AND ANCIENT AUTHORS

A Family, 39, 154-56, 174, 185, 186, 187-88

Aquila, 28, 34, 42, 49, 64, 139-40, 144, 150, 153, 171, 185

Augustine, 160

B Family:

    identification as καιγε, 4-5, 11, 33, 39, 40, 41, 44, 47, 67, 74, 81, 84, 86, 90, 94, 185-86, 187-88

    later influence, 29, 44, 81, 86

    manuscript groupings, 2-3, 36, 40, 44, 163

Chronicles:

    text, 58

    the group be_2, 41, 63

Chrysostom, 176

Coptic, 60, 93

Daniel, 79, 141

Ecclesiastes, 62, 172

Eusebius, 176

Greek families: recensional differences, 94, 159, 161

Hesychius, 29, 44, 81

Jerome, 176

Jonathan ben 'Uzziel, 140, 175

Josephus, 59, 93-94

Judges:

    divergence of A and B texts, 1, 186

    groupings of manuscripts, 2-3, 36, 40, 44, 163

    history of study of, 1-2

K Group, 31, 156-57, 174, 185-86, 188

Καιγε Recension:

    characteristics:

        אין = ουκ εστιν (in a context of aorists), 14-15

        איש (each one) = ανηρ, 12

        אנכי = εγω ειμι, 15-16

        אסף = συναγω, 17-18

characteristics (continued):

בין = ανα μεσον, 25

בעיני = εν οφθαλμοις, 20-21

בקרב = εν μεσω, 25-26

גבור = δυνατος, 148

גלה (and cognates) = αποικιζω (and cognates), 48

וגם/גם = καιγε, 11-12

הורה = φωτιζω, 19-20

הרה = εν γαστρι εχω/λαμβανω, 23-25

זבח = θυσιαζω, 21-22

חזק (piel) = ενισχυω, 26

חכם = σοφ-, 22-23

חרב = ρομφαια, 26

חרש = κωφευω/חשה = σιωπαω, 23

חָתָן = νυμφιος/חֹתֵן = γαμβρος, 26-27

טוב (all forms of the root) = αγαθος (and cognates), 48-52

יען אשר = ανθ ων οσα, 18-19

נצב/יצב = στηλοω, 13-14

ישר (all forms of the root) = ευθυς (and cognates), 52

לין = αυλιζω, 52-53

לעולם = εις τον αιωνα, 17

לפני = ενωπιον, 16-17

מהר = ταχυνω, 18

מעל = επανωθεν (απανωθεν), 12-13

נגד = forms of εναντι, 16

נצל = ρυομαι, 53-54

עבד = δουλ-, 27-29

על כן = δια τουτο, 17

רדף = διωκω, 22

שר (ה)צבא = αρχων της δυναμεως, 22

שוב = επιστρεπω, 54-56

שופר = κερατινη, 14

The Elimination of the Historical Present, 14

Misc. = ηνικα, 19

Καιγε Recension (continued):

characteristics in Judges:

לא אבה = ευδοκεω, 68

אור = διαφαυσκω, 69

הביא = φερω/εισφερω, 69-70

בעיני = εν οφθαλμοις, 70

צעק/זעק = βοαω, 71

חרה אף = οργιζομαι θυμω, 71-72

נלחם = παρατασσομαι, 72-73

מלחמה = παραταξις, 73-74

לקראת = εις συναντησιν, 74-75

נתץ = καθαιρεω, 75

סרן = αρχων, 75-76

פגע = συνανταω, 76

קצין = αρχη, 76

רעה = πονηρια, 76-77

distinctiveness of individual members, 67-91

identification of, 3-5, 13, 18, 31-32, 33, 38,
41-42, 44, 47, 57, 67, 73, 74, 79, 80-81,
82, 84, 86, 137-38, 147-54, 156-57, 185,
186, 187-88

Lucian, 29, 32, 34, 42-43, 50-51, 63, 80, 87, 134-
35, 173, 174, 185

Masoretic Text, 8, 143-47

Minuscule z, 173, 175

Nehemiah, 53, 91

Old Greek, 24, 32, 35, 74, 81, 87-88, 94, 120,
134-36, 137, 141-43, 185, 187

Old Latin, 12, 32, 40, 42-43, 89, 94-95, 135-36,
160, 185

Origen, 32, 33, 39, 40, 43, 44, 63, 64, 65, 82, 83,
87, 88, 90, 94, 136-40, 155, 156, 157, 161,
162, 169, 170, 171, 185, 186, 187-88

Proto-Lucian, 80, 134, 166

Proto-MT, 36, 41, 128

Psalms, 64, 82

Pseudo-Philo, 59, 129-30

Quinta, 64

Revision prior to καιγε, 150-52, 153-54, 178

Sixth Column (cf. also Theodotion), 57, 62, 140-
54, 172, 185, 186

Symmachus, 27, 35, 43, 144, 149, 154, 172

Syriac Peshitta, 94
Syro-Hexapla, 139, 159-60
Targum Jonathan, 94
Tetrapla, 159-60
Texts cited, 7-8, 31, 93-94, 159-60
Theodotion (cf. also Sixth Column), 140, 141, 147-50, 153, 155-56, 157, 175, 185, 186
The Three, 173
Transliteration, 148, 188
Ur-Hebrew, 95, 164
Ur-Theodotion, 176
Vulgate, 94